National Farmers' Union of Scotland
17 Grosvenor Crescent
EDINBURGH EH12 5EN

Fit for Heroes?
Land Settlement in Scotland After World War I

AUP titles of related interest

PERSPECTIVES IN SCOTTISH SOCIAL HISTORY
essays in honour of Rosalind Mitchison
editor Leah Leneman

EMIGRATION FROM NORTH-EAST SCOTLAND
Marjory Harper
Vol One: Willing Exiles
Vol Two: Beyond the Broad Atlantic

THE CITY THAT REFUSED TO DIE
Glasgow: the Politics of Urban Regeneration
Michael Keating

THE SHAPING OF SCOTLAND
18th century patterns of land use and settlement
R J Brien

CROMARTIE: HIGHLAND LIFE 1650–1914
Eric Richards and Monica Clough

FIT FOR HEROES?

LAND SETTLEMENT IN SCOTLAND AFTER WORLD WAR I

Leah Leneman

ABERDEEN UNIVERSITY PRESS

First published 1989
Aberdeen University Press
A member of the Pergamon Group

British Library Cataloguing in Publication Data
Leneman, Leah
Fit for heroes: land settlement in Scotland after World War I.
1. Scotland. Rural regions. Settlement, history
I. Title
941.1′009′734

ISBN 0-08-037720-3

PRINTED IN GREAT BRITAIN
THE UNIVERSITY PRESS
ABERDEEN

CONTENTS

List of Maps and Illustrations

Key to Maps 2, 3, 5 and 7

Schemes on privately-owned land

Schemes on lands purchased by Board/Department of Agriculture

Schemes on lands purchased by Congested Districts Board

Abbreviations

B.O.A.S.	Board of Agriculture for Scotland
D.O.A.S.	Department of Agriculture for Scotland
H of C	House of Commons Debates
H of L	House of Lords Debates
SRO	Scottish Record Office

Acknowledgements

I would like to express my gratitude to those who helped to make this book:

The Economic & Social Research Council whose generous funding made the research possible.

Athol Murray, Keeper of the Records of Scotland, without whom I would never have discovered this neglected part of modern Scottish history.

T.C. Smout, whose backing enabled me to become a Research Fellow of St Andrews University, and who provided encouragement and assistance throughout.

Graham Sutton, R.H. Campbell, A.S. Mather, Donald Meek and Geoffrey Barrow, who read and commented on draft chapters.

The Department of Agriculture & Fisheries for Scotland, in particular the Estates Department who allowed me to work on the files and John Jamieson who made certain I obtained them.

The helpful staff at West Register House.

June Allan who handled the administrative side of the work so efficiently.

William Gillies who provided me with contacts in the islands.

Anona Lyons who drew the maps.

And all the smallholders, crofters and others who spent time sharing their experiences and knowledge with me.

Thank you.

The views expressed in this book are mine alone.

The scheme plans of Askernish and Grassmillees are reproduced courtesy of the Keeper of the Records of Scotland.

Has the Board of Agriculture ever estimated what the permanent loss to the country is going to be on these schemes, and are they satisfied that a very large number of discharged soldiers and sailors wish to be settled on the land on small holdings who *have qualifications* that will make the experiment a success? I have very grave doubts about the wisdom of the policy, but none as to the cost it is going to throw on the country.

King's & Lord Treasurer's Remembrancer to the Treasury, December 1919

During the Great War you had posters displayed everywhere throughout Scotland; posters which showed a beautiful Highland glen, and which showed just such a piece of country as these men would like to have, and underneath the picture were words like this: 'Is this worth fighting for?' They went from their glens. They went from their Highlands and islands and to-day they cannot get a small holding in their own country!

House of Commons Debate 30 May 1923

Introduction

Land settlement—the breaking up of large farms or estates into small holdings—has taken place in many parts of the world in various eras.[1] What made the post-World War One Scottish experience unique was the background of Highland land agitation and the intensity of demand emanating from that region, and also the attempts to impose legislation applicable to the crofting counties onto the rest of Scotland. The amount of time, attention, and money devoted to state-aided land settlement in Scotland was out of all proportion to the results. In Australia nearly 40,000 settlers were put on the land under Discharged Soldiers Settlement Acts passed in 1916 and 1918, 11,000 in Victoria state alone; in tiny Denmark more than 26,000 new holdings were created following legislation in 1899 and 1919.[2] Even within the British Isles, land settlement legislation for England and Wales after World War I led to the creation of nearly 17,000 smallholdings by county councils.[3] In Scotland fewer than 6,000 were formed, but the repercussions were great.

The impetus for Scottish land settlement in the early twentieth century came from two distinct sources. The first was the realisation that existing statutes were inadequate to deal with the situation in the Western Highlands and Islands, where too many people were crowded into congested townships at the edges of large empty sheep farms and deer forests. The second was dismay at the depopulation of rural areas in the Lowlands, which began to be manifested in the closing years of the nineteenth century.

The crofting system was introduced in the Western Highlands and Islands in the early nineteenth century. Until late in the eighteenth century, lands in those areas were runrig (individual plots intermixed and periodically reallocated), held by tacksmen (usually kin of the clan chief) with subtenants, or by groups of small tenants. It was only when landlords began to look south at more commercial uses of land that change occurred. Large-scale sheep farming and, later, deer forests, brought far greater profits to landowners than numerous tenants practising subsistence farming, and therefore many of those tenants were evicted. Some emigrated, but substantial numbers remained, crowded into coastal townships where, for a period, their labours contributed to landowners' profits in the lucrative kelp industry. When this collapsed after the Napoleonic wars, many more were evicted, but there was still the fishing industry to absorb those who preferred seasonal migration to permanent emigration.

It was a long time before any attempt was made to fight back for the land. However much romanticised clanship may later have been, the fact remains that in that kin-based society, 'economic inequalities were...transcended by an egalitarianism expressed in terms of blood relationship, however remote, and encapsulated in the right of every clansman to shake the hand of his chief.'[4] The advent of commercial landlordism was therefore exceptionally difficult for Highlanders to assimilate, especially as the landlord who was so ruthlessly evicting them was often still the titular chief of their clan. The emergence of a new breed with its own identity—the crofter in place of the clansman—is the theme of James Hunter's book, *The Making of the Crofting Community*. These men believed that occupation of the land gave men an inalienable right to that land.[5] While unique in Great Britain, such a belief has surfaced in many other cultures and times, and has been called the Agrarian Creed. As far as the crofters were concerned, the rightness of their belief was confirmed by the Bible.[6]

The struggle was bitter, for pitted against this belief was the inalienable right of any landowner in Britain to do as he wished with his land. Drawing on the example of Ireland, Highland crofters grew increasingly violent in their attempts to regain what they considered rightfully theirs. In 1884 the Napier Commission was set up, and as a result of that inquiry the Crofters Holdings (Scotland) Act was passed in 1886.[7]

This was radical legislation. Instead of the landowner setting the rent, a newly-formed Crofters Commission set a 'fair rent' for each croft. Landowners could no longer evict a tenant at will, for crofters were granted security of tenure and the right to bequeath the tenancy of their croft. And finally, a crofter who left his croft was entitled to compensation from the landlord for any permanent improvements he had made to it. Such inroads into the rights of landowners were only possible because of the scale of land agitation, because of fears engendered by the level of violence in Ireland at that time, and perhaps also because of the falling value of Highland estates, as the price of wool was undercut by imports from Australia.[8] The main shortcoming of the Act was that although the Crofters Commission could make orders for enlargements of existing crofts, it had no powers to create new ones.[9]

The demand for the opening up of deer forests and for the restoration to crofters of land on the large sheep farms from which they or their ancestors had been evicted, continued to be heard, and another Royal Commission was appointed in 1892. The report, issued in 1895, commented favourably on the improvement in the crofters' circumstances resulting from the 1886 Act and made further suggestions. The Congested Districts (Scotland) Act, 1897 set up the Congested Districts Board and provided a fund of £35,000 per annum which could be used to provide land for new holdings and enlargements.[10] The Board had no power of compulsory procedure, and its scope was confined to crofting parishes and to a restricted definition of what constituted available land.

Between 1897 and 1912 the Congested Districts Board created 640 new holdings and 1138 enlargements, so the effects of the 1897 Act were by no means negligible. However, given the scale of the demand, it was very clear that further legislation was necessary. And, while in some parishes in the crofting counties the population was higher than it had ever been,[11] elsewhere in Scotland (and England) it was a very different story, for the drift from rural areas into the towns was alarming many observers, who called for action to stop it. The Report of the Board of Agriculture[12] in 1906 began

> The reduction in the number of persons returned as engaged in Agriculture in Great Britain has been one of the most prominent features of the Census Returns for the past 50 years, and it has never been more apparent than in the figures for 1901, when a decline of about 20 per cent. in the number of agricultural labourers during the preceding decade was indicated.[13]

The Board were convinced that one way to halt the decline was to provide a 'ladder' whereby farm labourers could aspire to occupation of their own land. For this to occur smallholdings had to be readily available, and the Board therefore asked correspondents about the demand and availability of smallholdings in each county.[14] The replies were often inconclusive or indeed contradictory. For example, one Selkirk correspondent claimed there was no demand whatsoever for smallholdings while the other insisted there was a ready demand.[15] Nevertheless, the creation of smallholdings was concluded to be a means of halting rural depopulation.

The problem which the Board then encountered was one of definition: 'The term "Small Holding" receives a different interpretation in different districts. In some instances it is used almost as if it were synonymous with an allotment or with occupation of not more than half a dozen acres. In other cases it is extended so as to include what in many parts of the country would be considered large farms.' The definition which they felt was generally accepted was of 'an area of land as is sufficient to employ the whole labour of a man and his family and not enough to necessitate the employment of hired labour'.[16]

It would be very useful if that definition could be adopted for this book, but unfortunately it will not do, for the idea that a smallholding would utilise the whole labour of a man and his family was only realistic in larger holdings. In the crofting counties there was a permanent conflict between the creation of holdings large enough to be self-supporting, and the demands of many to be given land of their own of whatever size. The existing tradition of small crofts, with crofters engaging in ancillary occupations, combined with the clamorous demands for land, meant that the ideal of self-sufficiency usually had to be abandoned, and small crofts combined with ancillary occupations continued to be the norm. Some forms of work, such as the weaving of tweed in Harris and parts of Lewis, fitted in well with crofting; unfortunately, most forms necessitated prolonged absences from the croft, and—as will emerge in a later chapter—this could lead to neglect of the croft and evasion of township responsiblities.[17]

The question of ancillary occupations was by no means confined to the crofting counties, as tenants of smaller-sized holdings in many Lowland areas also carried on other occupations.[18] This remained a contentious issue as late as the mid-1940s when the Scottish Land Settlement Committee reported

> The view was expressed to us in evidence that holdings formed by the Department should be occupied by tenants prepared to work them as full-time subjects and that State holdings erected at the expense of the taxpayer should be planned on this basis. Some witnesses gave it as their experience that when a man is engaged partly in outside employment and partly on his holding, he neglects one or the other—generally the holding.[19]

Quite apart from the question of whether a holding provided full-time occupation, the land settlement programme encompassed many types and sizes of holdings. In the Highlands the largest holdings approximated to small family farms, comprising individually occupied hill and low ground. The middle-sized holdings had a share in a common grazing and low ground in individual occupation. The smallest unit simply provided a home with a share in a common grazing. In the Lowlands large holdings, suitable for mixed arable farming, dairying and stock raising, were created alongside holdings of only a few acres, suitable for intensive production, such as market gardening, poultry or pig keeping.

Before going on to a detailed study of land settlement legislation and schemes, it is worth noting the main aims and objectives of land settlement in the first half of the twentieth century as summarised by the Land Settlement Committee in the 1940s.

> (a) Increasing or at least retaining the rural population on the land and arresting the move to the towns.
> (b) Meeting the demand for land.
> (c) Providing an opening for farm workers as an avenue of promotion from ordinary employment.
> (d) Giving urban people an opportunity to enter the agricultural industry.
> (e) Settling special classes like ex-Service men or industrial unemployed.
> (f) Relieving congested areas in the Highlands and spreading out the population over the lands available.
> (g) Creating types of small holdings suitable for special agricultural and horticultural production.[20]

We will return to these aims at the conclusion of the book in an attempt to see how far the land settlement programme succeeded in achieving them.

CHAPTER 1

The Small Landholders (Scotland) Act 1911

The Liberals assumed power at the beginning of 1906 dedicated to the principles of land reform. Property, especially landed property, was seen within the context of securing the good of the community: 'As the land was the original primary resource of the nation, in and from which all natural resources were obtained, the state was justified in assuming an overall and positive responsibility for ensuring these resources were made available, upon utilitarian principles, to serve the greatest good of the greatest number.' The aim was to offer 'to as many men as possible the prospect of a secure, stable and independent livelihood in the country.'[1] In his opening speech, the new prime minister, Sir Henry Campbell-Bannerman—a Scot—proclaimed, 'We wish to make the land less of a pleasure ground for the rich and more of a treasure house for the nation.'

Legislation was drafted for both England and Scotland.[2] The English Bill provided county councils with powers to purchase farms suitable for breaking up into smallholdings. Landowners did not object to farms being purchased for land settlement, and the Bill was passed in August 1907. The progress of the Scottish bill, brainchild of the new Secretary for Scotland (the post did not become a Secretary of State until 1928), Sir John Sinclair, was very different. In the Small Landholders (Scotland) Bill the purchase of farms by the state was not a provision. It appears that this was chiefly because it was expected that most English smallholders would purchase their holdings from the county councils, whereas in Scotland it was known that few tenants wished to own their holdings.[3] It was clearly very difficult for anyone at that time to envisage the state becoming landlords on a large scale.

Basically, the proposed statute aimed to extend the system of creating holdings on privately-owned land, which prevailed in the crofting counties, to the rest of Scotland, and it was this system of dual tenure which caused the controversy. If a landowner objected to breaking a farm up into smallholdings, compulsory powers could be used to force him to do so. The need for compulsory powers had been made as early as 1903 when the Chairman of the Crofters Commission, Sheriff Brand, wrote in a memorandum to Sinclair that, although there were honourable exceptions, the majority of landowners would not of their own accord part with land for crofters 'no matter how serious the congestion on their estates, and no matter how poor and sterile the land presently is in occupation of the Crofting tenants.'[4]

The conditions which crofters enjoyed—security of tenure, the right to bequeath a holding, a fair rent set by an outside body, and compensation for permanent improvements on leaving—were to be extended to the Lowlands for all holders who paid a rent of £50 or less or had a holding not exceeding 50 acres. There was no question of delegating responsibility to county councils; a central body, the Board of Agriculture for Scotland (replacing the Congested Districts Board) would be created to prepare and carry out the schemes, and a Scottish Land Court would fix fair rents and determine the compensation due to landlords and tenants.

Such inroads into the rights of landowners might have been considered necessary in the crofting counties, but the proposal to extend them into the Lowlands provoked a tremendous outcry from the landed classes. The Scottish Land & Property Federation was formed in November 1906 to protect landowners' interests. The following extract from a memorandum of 1907 sums up their reactions to the bill.

> The Small Landholders Bill proposes to extend the Crofters Act, devised to meet the peculiar circumstances and special conditions of the well-known class of crofters in the Highlands, to the whole of Scotland...where the agricultural conditions, the character and habits of the population, and the relations between landlord and tenants are totally different from the Western Highlands. It treats as crofters persons who are not crofters at all in any sense of the word. ... It practically deprives every landowner of the management of his estate so far as let to tenants of £50 and under, or in holdings of 50 acres or less.[5]

The Bill passed through the Commons in 1907 but was rejected by the Lords. It was reintroduced—unchanged—in 1908, when Sir John Sinclair fiercely defended it in the Commons. He did not deny that landowners would lose some of their 'arbitrary rights' but, in true Liberal fashion, he went on: 'I say that the restraint of such arbitrary power and the giving to men of a sense of independence, is likely to increase their sense of justice and equality and fair play which is the salt and strength of the British nation.' The gist of the opposition's objections was that a form of tenure created for Highland conditions had no place in the Lowlands. Mr Younger, M.P. for Ayr Burghs, said his Lowland constituents did not approve of the 'crofterisation of their agriculture', while Mr H.J. Tennant, representing Berwickshire, 'contended that it was unsuitable to the needs of Scotland because there was no analogy between the Highlands and Lowlands.'[6]

The desirability of making county councils responsible for land settlement, as in England, was also debated. Sinclair insisted first of all that Scottish county councils were not truly representative because the geography of the country meant that there were remote and inaccessible regions in every county which made it difficult for members to attend all meetings. Another point made was that in England the financial liability for land settlement fell on the rates, whereas in Scotland it was directly on the Treasury, i.e. on taxes; local authorities were considered the proper persons to pronounce where rates were concerned, while government should do so where taxes were

1 Poster reproduced courtesy of People's Palace (Glasgow Museums).

concerned. Amongst the reasons put forward for centralisation, Sinclair mentioned that county councils were manned largely by landowners, and though he did not stress this point it seems likely that it was an important consideration for Scottish Liberals. Later in the debate the Lord Advocate (Mr Thomas Shaw, member for Hawick Burghs) pointed out that during the two years of discussion no county council had asked parliament to entrust the duty of creating smallholdings to them instead of to a central body. He also cited the example of Inverness county council who had appointed a committee to report on demand for holdings in the county; the committee had reported that there was a clamant demand and an abundance of land to meet it, but in the nine years which had since elapsed the county council had taken no action.[7]

The Bill once again passed through the Commons and was once again rejected by the Lords. In April 1908 Campbell-Bannerman died and was succeeded by Asquith who—publicly at least—was committed to the Land Bill. He retained Sinclair as Secretary for Scotland but persuaded him that his presence was needed in the Lords, at which time he assumed the title of Lord Pentland. The overwhelming Liberal majority in Scotland was actually increased in the two General Elections of 1910, and a newspaper remarked that, 'The steadiness of the Scottish county vote in the last two elections was unquestionably due above everything else to the enthusiasm aroused by the Pentland Bill and the determination to have it reach the Statute Book'.[8]

Clearly public pressure for the Bill was greater than ever, and in June 1911 it was passed in the Commons. The Lords veto had been abolished in May of that year, but the struggle to avoid making too many concessions and compromises was a fierce one, for Scottish landowners continued to fight the proposals.[9] One provision added to the Bill on the insistence of landowners was that in claims for compensation of over £300, the landlord was given the right to appeal to an arbiter in place of the Land Court. Lady Pentland commented in her memoir, 'Pentland's reluctance to agree to this proposal was amply justified by events.'[10]

By the new statute, the Small Landholders (Scotland) Act, 1911, crofting tenure was extended throughout Scotland (crofters along with their Lowland counterparts were termed landholders). This meant not only security of tenure but also the right to bequeath a holding to one's heirs and to receive compensation for permanent improvements on leaving. Tenants who had not provided or paid for permanent improvements on their holdings were not made landholders but were designated 'statutory small tenants'.

The Agriculture (Scotland) Fund, to be fed by sums not exceeding £200,000 annually, was placed under the administration of the new Board of Agriculture for Scotland (the Congested Districts Board having been disbanded), subject to sanction by the Secretary for Scotland.[11] The Board were authorised to make loans to new holders toward the costs of erecting buildings, and to assist them, by a loan or grant, to equip the lands. The only lands which the Board could not touch were farms of less than 150 acres, home farms, and lands under leases current at Whitsunday 1906.

The Board consisted of three persons: Robert (later Sir Robert) Greig, the

Chairman, Sir Robert Wright, and the Commissioner for Small Holdings, John D. Sutherland.[12] (There was also a Secretary, H.M. Conacher, sub-commissioners, a Chief Surveyor, a Poultry Superintendent, and a Superintendent of Statistics.) It was the duty of the Small Holdings Commissioner to ascertain the demand for holdings and enlargements in each district and what land was available to meet it. He was to attempt to negotiate an agreement with the landlord of suitable land; where he failed, the Board, after due notice and a full inquiry, could intimate to the landlord that it was in the public interest that one or more new holdings should be constituted and then apply to the Land Court for an order authorising the constitution of new holdings or enlargements. If the Court decided that the landlord's objections were not valid then a compulsory order would be issued, and applicants—chosen by the Board and approved by the landlord—were settled by the Board into their new holdings. These holders became the tenants of the landlord, the Board (in theory) playing no further part. If the compensation deemed payable to the landowner proved to be excessive, the Board were entitled to abandon the scheme. If a holding was not a success and the land was thrown back on the landlord's hands he had the right to claim further compensation.

It was already clear within a year of the passing of the Act that it would not have the hoped for success in settling large numbers of men on the land quickly. There were various reasons for this. The first was that the Land Division, which handled land settlement, was grossly understaffed at the start. In March 1912 when the Small Holdings Commissioner learned that the staff proposed for the Land Division was three clerks he expressed the view that the number was hopelessly inadequate but was told no change could be made in the arrangements concluded with the Treasury by Lord Pentland.[13] In April of that year the Secretary of the Board wrote to the Chairman

> We have issued nearly 4,000 forms of particulars to be filled in by applicants for new holdings and enlargements, and the filled in forms are coming in about 150 a day. To estimate the work involved in dealing with them, one may make a comparison with the case of England and Wales. Last year—according to the report of the Board of Agriculture and Fisheries just published—about 4,300 applications for land were received from individuals, besides others from 27 Societies. Even assuming the latter represented another 2,000 we have to deal with two-thirds of that demand with our restrictive Staff, whereas in England and Wales each of the 40 odd Counties has its own machinery, with the Board of Agriculture and Fisheries to supervise.[14]

Repeated requests led to increases of staff in the course of 1912, but in April 1913 the Small Holdings Commissioner desired to place on record his opinion 'that the requirements of the office as originally estimated were absolutely inadequate and that they are not now properly realised. Scarcely a day has passed without the necessity for drawing attention to undesirable delay in important cases or to mistakes made as a result of work under pressure, and notwithstanding these undesirable experiences, the staff are invariably labouring until 9 p.m. and later. My own work and the work of the Sub-Commissioners has to be conducted under equally impossible conditions.' Looking back in 1920 on the situation immediately following the passage of the Act, he reiterated 'The absence of a sufficient staff in the first fifteen to eighteen months not only delayed the work in hand at the moment, but gave rise to serious difficulties and loss of time later.'[15]

The second problem was the slow and cumbersome machinery of the Act. In an early Land Court hearing, the Small Holdings Commissioner described the various stages which had to be gone through.[16] First he had to enquire into the circumstances of the applicants for land and at the same time find out what land was available for land settlement purposes throughout Scotland. He then had to report to the Board 'both as to the demand and as to the possibility of meeting it.' It was also his duty to negotiate with landlords or their agents about the land and then to report the results of these (often protracted and sometimes fruitless) negotiations to the Board.

This was the end of the Small Holdings Commissioner's part in the proceedings—though to ask one man alone to do all that for the whole of Scotland and then to expect speedy land settlement seems sheer lunacy.[17] However it was by no means the end of the process. The Board next had to get the sanction of the Secretary for Scotland, and when that was secured they had to advise all the parties concerned that it was in the public interest that the scheme should proceed, and that it was their intention to apply to the Land Court for an order for the constitution of new holdings or enlargements. If objections were made by the landlord or tenant the Board had to consider them before deciding whether to proceed to the Land Court, and then a Land Court hearing could involve possible adjournments, inspection of the ground by the Court, and various other steps. 'It will therefore be seen', concluded Sutherland, 'that the Board is under the necessity of going through a long course of procedure which takes up a very considerable amount of time.'

J.P. Day, whose book on public administration in the Highlands and Islands was published in 1918, described the situation as it appeared to those who applied for a holding.

> The applicant, having filled up the form of application with the ages of his daughters and various other information, probably thinks that now they know all about it the matter ought to be settled. He waits and waits until at last a sub-commissioner comes along and presumably checks all this information and looks at the land, unless it happens to be under snow, when he goes away and has to return again later. The applicant now has his expectations raised again, but again a long period of waiting ensues without his having any knowledge of what is happening, and it is small wonder if he grows impatient. The delays are partly due to the complexity and multiplicity of the necessary arrangements and partly to the cumbrous machinery.[18]

One problem was that Section 17 (2) of the Act, which provided ultimate compensation to the landowner if a scheme proved a failure, only applied in cases where the holdings had been constituted otherwise than by agreement.

Therefore, many cases where the landlord had in fact been perfectly amenable to the Board's proposals, were submitted to the Land Court as *not* having reached agreement, in order to take advantage of the safeguards of the clause.[19] Congestion of work in the Land Court was later put forward by the Small Holdings Commissioner as one of the principal causes of slow progress under the Act.

All this would have been bad enough even if the majority of landowners had been in sympathy with the aims of the Act, but such was far from being the case; the opposition of the Scottish Land and Property Federation against land settlement policy continued. One important reason for this was the constitution of the Scottish Land Court, for the members were political appointees and were considered—with some reason—to be anti-landlord. In his book on administration in the Highlands and Islands before 1914, Day noted that 'owing to the peculiar structure of the Court, it never, generally speaking, commanded the confidence of the proprietors'.[20] That is borne out and amplified in a report submitted by the King's & Lord Treasurer's Remembrancer to the Treasury in 1920. The report advised the Treasury that many landowners outside of the crofting areas regarded the 1911 Act, which gave the Land Court jurisdiction over the whole of Scotland, 'as an attempt to despoil their property'. 'The impression was afoot that the decisions of the Land Court *at that time* did not err in favour of the proprietor, and whether this was correct or not, it increased the opposition to the way the Act was expected to be worked, and caused a number of land owners to decide that they would resist the carrying out of its provisions so far as they legally could.'[21]

In 1913 and 1914 the Scottish Land and Property Federation asked landowners about their experiences of the Land Court. One proprietor wrote, 'I have a tenant who has managed the place badly. We disagreed and I gave him warning to go last Martinmas. He applied to the Land Court to become a Statutory Small Tenant. We met Lord Kennedy and A. Dewar...and I am sure I proved to the full that the Holding was badly managed, but was cooly [sic] told that bad management was no disqualification of a Small Holder.' Witnesses bore this out, one writing that he had 'no hesitation in saying that Lord Kennedy was supporting the Small Holders on every hand and would scarcely listen to the Landlords or their Agents'.[22]

There were various delaying tactics which landowners opposed to land settlement could use, for example insisting that a scheme be submitted to them before they would give their consent and then arguing endlessly over whether the submission actually constituted a scheme or not. As the statute did not define what was meant by a scheme and set no limit on the length of time negotiations could take, there was little the Board could do. Another ploy that landowners used was to re-let a vacant farm in the course of negotiations. There was no power under the statute to prevent proprietors doing this, and the entry of a new tenant on lands which were the subject of negotiation obviously complicated the position and could add considerably to the expense since compensation would then be payable to the incoming tenant as well.[23]

There is admittedly another side to the story, for the Board of Agriculture at times really were every bit as inefficient and uncooperative as the Scottish Land and Property Federation claimed.[24] Even within the Board there were differing views on policy toward landowners, and the majority view, which prevailed, worsened an already difficult situation. The policy adopted by the Board—though opposed by John Sutherland, the Small Holdings Commissioner—was that no compensation was to be allowed for loss of selling value. The Board's view was that the claim that the value of an estate was diminished by the establishment of small holdings on it had neither competency nor validity.[25] Sutherland disagreed and later expressed the view that 'in the first year much could have been done by agreement if reasonable latitude was accorded to treat with owners equitably.'[26] The Board ended up in a quagmire of litigation—culminating in an appeal to the House of Lords—and was forced to pay out vast sums in compensation claims which had never been envisaged when the statute was drawn up. For the main weapon which landlords used, and the one which effectively ensured the failure of the Act, was their insistence on claiming compensation over £300 and being heard before an arbiter instead of the Land Court.[27]

The case which set the precedent for landlords' compensation claims involved Lindean, a farm in Selkirkshire.[28] The Small Holdings Commissioner submitted a scheme to the Board in 1912 which involved taking over the whole farm of 900 acres and creating 14 holdings ranging from six acres to 190 acres. The lease expired at Whitsunday 1913 and the farm was to let. The Small Holdings Commissioner at this stage estimated the cost of compensation to the owner at £500, with a total expenditure of £7690 (£4550 in loans and £3140 in grants). However, he advised the Board that the landlord, Charles Scott Plummer, was not prepared to negotiate for more than three holdings and would oppose an application to the Land Court for the taking of the whole farm.

In October 1912 the Board wrote to Scott Plummer asking him if he would refrain from coming to terms with any of the offerers for the farm. He replied that he thought the Board would see 'the unreasonableness of asking me at this period to throw over a good and certain offer for the farm and take my chance of a scheme which I have never seen...and which, for aught I know, may have serious consequences for myself and successor'. The Board responded that they would not withdraw their proposal and warned him of the problems which could arise between him and the offerer if the farm was leased while the Board was negotiating for it. In January 1913, after considerably more correspondence, he reiterated his chief objection to the scheme, which was that 'having a great mistrust of the form of tenure which is a necessary accompaniment of holdings formed by the Board, I object to so large a proportion of my estate being taken for small holdings.' He also renewed his protest at the Board's having commenced taking action so near the end of the lease of the farm when he had practically completed his arrangements for letting it.

The scheme went ahead and the holders were settled; meanwhile the proprietor intimated that he was claiming compensation in excess of £300 and desired the claim to be settled by arbitration. This was the first arbitration under Section 7 (11) of the Act and received press coverage as such. The hearing took place on 2 March 1914 (the transcript of the proceedings occupies 248 typewritten pages). Scott Plummer claimed £9000 in compensation. Much of his argument was concerned not with questions of financial loss but with the lack of control a landowner had over smallholders compared with tenants. His case was 'that residential estates are not purchased and not owned for purely pecuniary reasons and that by the interference, which I have suffered, with the rights of ownership in regard to these small holdings, the thing has been reduced to an investment basis. All the other attractions of landownership have been taken away.' He stated that he had been shown an agreement between the Board of Agriculture and one of the smallholders concerning the manner in which the holder was to cultivate the land. 'I don't think I ever before heard of the obligation to observe the laws of good husbandry being not to the landlord but to a third party outside. That is rather a novelty as far as landed estates in the south of Scotland are concerned.'

On the question of valuation he admitted that the south of Scotland had no experience of estates with smallholders on them being sold, but he had seen advertisements of sales of Highland estates in which the lack of crofters had been held out as an attraction. 'As far as the rights in the land are concerned, the people put down on Lindean are crofters. ... If the presence of crofters depreciates Highland estates, I have no reason to think the presence of crofters will appreciate my estate.'

The arbiter's proposed findings appeared on 18 March. His conclusion was that the estate had been damaged by the constitution of the smallholdings to the extent of £4600. Having reached that conclusion, he then had to consider whether the claim was a competent one under Section 7 (11) of the Act. The Solicitor General had argued for the Board that compensation would be due for loss of or injury to sporting rights, as well as loss of rental if proved, but not for 'the loss of personal attributes of ownership or for the effect which these had or might have upon the value of an estate.' However, the arbiter came to the view that the words of the section did provide for compensation under this head.

The Board disputed the award,[29] and their Counsel drafted a Representation to the arbiter. They rightly feared that if one claim for compensation for depreciation arising from the limitations of landowner's rights was made good, 'a similar claim will confront the Board of Agriculture every time that they seek to put in force a Land Court Order for the constitution of new holdings.' The arbiter considered the Board's Representations but maintained his original findings. The Board then decided to act on the Solicitor General's advice that the Claimant should have to sue them before the Court of Session for the contested sum of £3850 (the amount not covered by losses which the Board accepted as legitimate).

The Court of Session heard the case in October 1914.[30] The Lord Ordinary held that 'depreciation in the capital and saleable value of the Estate was not depreciation in the value of the Estate in consequence of and directly attributable to the constitution of new Holdings on the Farm of Lindean'. He therefore sustained the Board's Plea in Law. Scott Plummer promptly announced that he was reclaiming (appealing). This came before the Second Division of the Court of Session in July 1915, at which time the Lord Ordinary's decision was unanimously reversed. On the advice of the Solicitor General, and with the approval of the Secretary for Scotland, the Board appealed against the decision to the House of Lords. In January 1916 the Lords dismissed the appeal, and the Board had to pay not only the £3850 plus interest (and all of the outstanding claims which had been awaiting this decision), but also the full legal costs.[31]

The effects of this decision can be seen in a scheme for seven holdings on the farm of Harrietsfield, Roxburghshire. The estimated expenditure sanctioned by the Secretary for Scotland in August 1913 was £3625. As there was no loss of rent or sporting rights contemplated, no provision was made for landlord's compensation. The final expenditure was £9122.10*s*.4*d*., of which £2375 was compensation for loss in letting value, £2100 for depreciation in the value of the estate, and £892.17*s*.9*d*. for legal expenses.[32]

In another Roxburghshire scheme—Kinninghall—the landowner did not demand an arbiter, but the question of compensation still proved a very thorny one, and the correspondence in this case demonstrates the differing viewpoints that existed within the Board. There was no opposition from the proprietrix when a scheme was mooted in November 1912. The only possible bone of contention was the value of the buildings for which the Board would have to pay compensation, since the Board's estimates differed markedly from the estate's estimates. No other compensation claim was envisaged at that time.[33]

In the Order for the constitution of new holdings, the Land Court added the following note. 'We desire to record our appreciation of the friendly manner in which the Proprietrix has co-operated with the Board by suspending negotiations for the reletting of this farm, and in adjusting this Scheme for the constitution of nine new holdings.'[34] The holders obtained entry at Whitsunday 1913. In May 1914 the landlord lodged with the Land Court a claim for to £13,600, including £4500 for depreciation in the value of the estate.

The war held up proceedings for years, and in the spring of 1916 a fierce debate took place amongst members of the Board.[35] After further negotiations with the estate, the Small Holdings Commissioner recommended that the claim be settled out of court for the sum of £5650 plus expenses. One of the heads of the claim was for depreciation in the selling value of the estate which of course the Board (and the Secretary for Scotland) had always resisted, and it was this aspect which caused the controversy. Wright, the Chairman, opposed the idea of an out of court settlement and wrote at length to Sutherland, the Small Holdings Commissioner, explaining his reasons. One point he made certainly had validity. 'We have constantly complained that landlords would not allow their cases to go to the Land Court, but would insist on the appeal to unknown arbiters. We want just such cases as this to go to the Land Court in order to have determined authoritatively for our guidance and the public guidance just such questions as are raised in this claim'. He expected the award to be considerably less than the agreed sum, even with expenses, and did not believe there was any danger of an award like that of Lindean being made against the Board. Sutherland insisted that in spite of the differences between the cases, the fact remained that after the Lindean decision claims for selling value had to be treated in the same manner as other competent claims. He believed depreciation was likely to be proved and reiterated his conviction that a settlement would be preferable to a contested case in court. Wright disagreed with Sutherland's view that depreciation was likely to be proved and added that 'even if the result were as you say, I hold it so important to have a Land Court decision on the point, that I think the risk ought to be run.' Eventually it was decided to submit the case to the Secretary for Scotland for a decision, and the latter decided it should go to the Land Court.

The Land Court hearing was held in November 1917.[36] The two main points contended were the value of the buildings—the Board thought them worth £2100 while the agents claimed £4000—and depreciation of the value of the estate. The Court's Order was issued in May 1918. The sum payable for the buildings was £2950; for damage to letting value £1452.18*s*.4*d*.; for depreciation of the value of the estate £847.3*s*., making a total of £5250.1*s*.4*d*. plus interest and expenses. The Court explained that they could not uphold the contention of the Board that the conversion of the farm into small holdings had caused no depreciation in the capital value of the estate but neither could they admit the justice of the whole claim put forward by the proprietor.

> It seems indisputable that Kinninghall itself, if now put up for sale, would not attract the same competition as it would have done prior to 1913. The ordinary landowner will prefer a property where he has control of his tenants, their rents, and their leases. The outsider who wants a small holding for his own occupation knows that after he buys he must undertake the disagreeable task of turning out the present tenant, and must pay some yet to be ascertained sum for his farm buildings. The tenants themselves, if they purchase, at once cease to be under the protection of the Land Acts, and may find themselves called upon by the Board for immediate repayment of the money lent them for erection of buildings. These three classes constitute the most likely buyers of land in ordinary circumstances, and from none of them could keen competition be expected.

Therefore they found that the value of the estate had been depreciated in one of its parts by the constitution of the new holdings. However, regarding depreciation of the whole of the estate, they agreed with the Board's view. The estate had a gross rental of £8000 and many characteristics that made it a highly desirable property; apart from Kinninghall none of these attractions had been interfered with, and the estate was as saleable as before. The Board recorded this decision in their Annual Report, noting that it would have to be taken into account 'in considering the probable outlay on any settlements that may be carried out in future under the Act, so long as depreciation in capital value constitutes a competent claim.'[37]

Although landowners in the crofting counties had not been able to claim compensation under the 1886 and 1897 statutes, that did not mean that such landowners failed to take advantage of the clause which allowed them to do so under the 1911 Act. In fact, some of the strongest resistance to land settlement came from the crofting counties, and therefore the clause allowing independent arbitration on claims over £300 was frequently invoked there. The proprietor of Borrowston Mains in Caithness was one example. After the hearing (in April 1915), the arbiter noted

> There was, as usual, a considerable conflict of evidence as to whether the farm divided up as proposed would be of the same marketable value as it is in its present condition. On that point, I am clearly of opinion that the Claimant is right, and that the farm as split up, if put into the market for sale or as a security subject, either in whole or in separate lots would not fetch the same price or have the same value attached to it as it would as an individual property. ... Until it can be clearly demonstrated, by actual transactions, that Small Holdings such as these, and situated where they are, will sell at the same price as a large farm, I consider the justice of the case demands that an adequate award of compensation be made to a Landlord whose property is interfered with for what admittedly is a public purpose.[38]

Consideration of most of the geographically Highland areas will be deferred to later chapters, as the situation pre and post-war formed a continuum and will be looked at as such. However, there was one Highland landowner who did not oppose the Small Landholders Act, and on whose lands various schemes went forward under this statute, and that was the Duke of Argyll. It is unlikely that altruism played much part in the Duke's willingness to cooperate with the Board; rather, he appears to have been a tired old man who realised he could not buck the tide and who wanted everything sorted out with a minimum of inconvenience to himself. In fact, in January 1914 the Duke handed over his island estates to his nephew, Niall Diarmid Campbell (who promptly dispensed with the services of the chamberlain with whom the Board had built up a good working relationship). Not long after that the Duke died, and Niall Diarmid Campbell inherited the title.

Before this happened, a representative of the Duke called at the Board's office in connection with Hynish, Tiree. The proposal was that if the Board could arrange matters with the outgoing tenant without bringing the Duke into the negotiations at all, 'the Duke, on his part, would leave other questions, both in Tiree and elsewhere, which might arise between himself and the Board, to the settlement of the Land Court, no matter what sum might be involved.'[39] The Board were, of course, delighted to oblige, though their readiness to fall in with the Duke's wishes whenever possible caused more than a little resentment amongst the crofters. For example, the first Tiree scheme, at Baugh, was for only two new holdings and four enlargements, and there was a good deal of grumbling by islanders at the way the Board had taken only a portion of the farm and not the whole of it.[40] A scheme at Greenhill created thirteen new holdings and four enlargements, but here too there was dissatisfaction, because the holdings were no larger than allotments.[41]

Apart from Balephetrish, which was not settled until after the war, and which is discussed in Chapter 5, the only Tiree scheme which appears to have involved any controversy with the landlord was Heylipol. This was a farm of 990 acres which the Board considered suitable for ten holdings. The farm was occupied by the factor, whose lease expired Whitsunday 1914. Agreement was reached with him at that time, and the estate did not object to having smallholders on the farm. However, they did object to the scheme which the Board submitted, because it did not leave sufficient land around the mansion house which, it was felt, would have to form the residence of any island factor. The estate wanted only four new holdings to be created. 'Seeing that so much is being taken by the Board in Tiree, and that his Grace has given, and is giving, every facility for its acquisition subject to his rights under the Act being reserved', wrote the Duke's chamberlain in September 1913, 'you will I feel sure agree with me that little enough is being asked for.' The Small Holdings Commissioner did *not* agree and in November suggested the best course would be to lodge an application in the Land Court 'so that the Duke could then have an opportunity of stating his opposition.'[42]

The applicants for holdings wrote to the Secretary for Scotland, expressing their approval of the Board's scheme and their objections to the landlord retaining a large portion of the farm for the use of the factor. However, the Land Court considered the landlord's arguments valid (which indicates that, contrary to the Scottish Land and Property Federation's view, the Court did not invariably take the side of crofters against landlords), and the final order was for seven new holdings.

The Board's negotiations with the Duke of Argyll regarding farms on the island of Mull also caused some controversy, for a deal was struck whereby the Duke allowed the Board to take two complete farms—Ardfenaig and Eorabus—on the understanding that all the remaining farms on the island be left untouched. Word of this got out, and the islanders protested strongly, but to no avail.[43] Although the Board's arrangements with the Duke of Argyll may have left many crofters unsatisfied, the fact remains that they were much better off on those estates (from the point of view of getting land) than were crofters in the Outer Hebrides where—as will be seen in later chapters—most landowners fought tooth and nail against having any one of their farms broken up into holdings.

To turn back from the particular to the general, what can be concluded about the operation of the Land Settlement (Scotland) Act, 1911? In the course of an Enquiry carried out in 1912 and 1913 by a small committee appointed by the Chancellor of the Exchequer, a strong unsatisfied demand for smallholdings was found throughout Scotland.[44] The committee highlighted various limitations in the statute which handicapped action and which they believed required amendment,[45] the first and foremost of these being the amount of money being diverted to litigation and compensation claims (and this was *before* the result of the Lindean case was known). The committee commented: 'The trend of legislation has continuously modified the relations of landlord and tenant without compensating the landlord for the loss of unfair privileges and advantages sustained in the process.'[46]

The provision for the Board to abandon a scheme if the sum payable for compensation was too high did not prove to be of much use, because arbitration proceedings were often delayed for so long after the issuing of the Land Court Order authorising the scheme that the Board had little choice but to go ahead with it or else disappoint all the applicants who had been promised holdings. However, by 1915 the Board was forced to abandon some promising schemes for fear of excessive compensation awards.[47]

In 1914 the Liberal M.P. for Edinburgh East, James Hogge, had brought an amending Bill before parliament which would have removed the offending clause; this Bill was hotly debated in the House of Commons on 13 March. *The Scotsman* on 14 March represented the views of the landowning class in an editorial condemning the attempt to remove the right of proprietors to appeal to an independent arbiter for compensation, as a distinct breach of the 'understanding' that allowed the 1911 Act to pass. Landowners were certainly girding themselves up for a fight, and what the outcome would have been is impossible to say, but the war put an end to the Bill.[48]

Naturally the outbreak of war considerably slowed down the already slow process of land settlement. The Board had to concentrate mainly on schemes already projected rather than try to initiate new ones; many landlords, agents, and applicants were away, and the Small Holdings Commissioner himself was on active service in France for some of the period. An important consideration in the war years was the rapid rise in costs of building materials and fencing. The Board's grant was first curtailed and then cut.

However the 1911 Act, apart from forming the basis for future legislation, had an effect in many parts of the country. Under it a total of 502 new holdings and 536 enlargements were created in the Highlands, and 238 new holdings and 11 enlargements in the Lowlands, encompassing 142,460 acres. In 1919 a detailed investigation was carried out into the financial position of smallholders. The authors expressed cautious optimism.

> On the whole, considering the position during the last generation, the small holder who has an adequate amount of land, and is prepared to lead the hard-working and thrifty life which his occupation demands, has a reasonable chance of bringing up a family in frugal comfort, and of making a moderate addition to his capital. If he is fortunate he may be sufficiently successful to move to a larger farm.[49]

Although the operation of the Small Landholders Act involved a great deal of dispute, there were in fact many farms settled with no difficulty at all. One such case was the farm of Backaskaill in Orkney.[50] When the scheme was first suggested to the proprietor, Lord Zetland, in August 1914, he was not very keen, but in February 1915 he handed the property over to his eldest son, Lord Ronaldsay, who was perfectly amenable to the Board's scheme for two new holdings and four enlargements. At the hearing in March 1916, the Land Court complained about 'the inconsistency of the procedure adopted, viz:—Application for a compulsory Order when details of the scheme have been agreed to, rents fixed and holders in occupation.'

There was clearly much that needed to be done to the 1911 Act to make it more generally effective, and doubtless change would have come in any case, but the Great War was to have a profound effect on land settlement policy.

CHAPTER 2

Land Settlement Immediately After the War

Recruitment propaganda for the Great War promised men who enlisted voluntarily that they would get land on their return.[1] Those who fought and survived and wanted holdings were widely considered to deserve them. Many landowners or their relatives had served as officers, and they too had softened up toward the idea of land settlement.[2]

Contrary to what one might think from reading James Hunter on the subject,[3] the initial impetus for land settlement during the war years did not emanate from the Highlands of Scotland but from England. In 1915 the Board of Agriculture and Fisheries set up a committee to consider what steps could be taken to promote the settlement or employment of sailors and soldiers on the land after the war. As with land settlement in Lowland Scotland, there was no question of having to satisfy any kind of land hunger, but a desire to encourage a large rural population. The report pointed out that a much greater proportion of recruits rejected for active service came from towns than from country districts. 'If, therefore, we desire a strong and healthy race, we must encourage as large a proportion of our people as possible to live on the land.'[4] Also, the war had shown clearly how necessary it was for the nation to produce as much of its own food as possible, and this was considered another reason for promoting land settlement.[5]

The legislation resulting from the committee's report was the Small Holdings Colonies Act, 1916, which empowered the acquisition by agreement of up to 2000 acres for the purpose of providing 'experimental small holding colonies'; no special funds were provided for this purpose. The Sailors and Soldiers (Gifts for Land Settlement) Act was also passed in 1916, and in 1918 the Small Holding Colonies (Amendment) Act authorised the acquisition of 20,000 instead of 2000 acres but still did not provide extra funds. These Acts were applicable to Scotland as well as England and, as will be seen in later chapters, some farms were acquired under the 1918 Act. However, the provision that three-fourths of the land acquired must be arable ruled out geographically Highland estates.[6]

In the House of Commons debate in August 1916 there was a good deal of criticism of the Scottish Board of Agriculture for their failure to consider the question of land settlement of demobilised servicemen.[7] At that debate the Secretary for Scotland announced that the Duke of Sutherland had gifted the Board with the 12,000-acre farm of Borgie, the terms being that it was to be used 'for the settlement of sailors and soldiers who have been on foreign service and who had volunteered without compulsion and have a good record of foreign service.'[8] The gift was, in fact, a contentious one, because many people believed that the Duke was simply offloading a particularly undesirable part of his estate (in the long run, however, a viable settlement was created there).[9]

In May 1917 the Duke of Sutherland approached the Board with the offer of another farm, Shinness, not as a gift this time, but by negotiation under the terms of the 1911 Act (though with the promise not to claim compensation for depreciation of selling value). This too was aimed at the settlement of ex-soldiers and sailors, on lands which actually encompassed four separate farms, with a total area of 16,000 acres. The main problem was the cost of the exercise. The estimated expenditure was £18,862, at a time when the Lords of the Treasury had written that they assumed 'the Board does not ...contemplate any considerable measure of new expenditure upon the provision of small holdings...during the continuance of the War.' In spite of this the Secretary for Scotland sanctioned the scheme, which, it was said, promised 'to be an exceptionally successful one in that it provides for the settlement of 21 [ultimately 31] men on Small Holdings of good size and quality where with the exercise of industry and skill and with the aid of co-operative methods their success is assured.'[10] (The question of how far this optimism was justified is dealt with in Chapter 4). Apart from those schemes, very little in the way of land settlement was done during this period, and in 1917 there was renewed agitation for Highland land reform.[11]

There was, however, a certain amount of political activity going on behind the scenes. In July 1916 Scottish Liberal M.P.s appointed a committee; their remit was 'to formulate proposals for a non-controversial settlement of the outstanding difficulties existing on the land question in Scotland with a view to advancing a wide and comprehensive system of Land Colonisation, having special regard to the new conditions created by the war.' The Scottish Land and Property Federation were fairly scathing about the report which resulted in February 1917.[12] They would doubtless have reacted similarly to *any* report produced by a committee composed solely of Liberal M.P.s, especially since five members of the committee had been supporters of the 1914 Amendment Bill which the landowners had so strongly opposed; nevertheless, to the non-partisan reader the report does appear to be nothing more than pious waffle (in view of their remit, that was probably all that could have been expected).

The Liberals presumably came to realise that they could achieve nothing without the cooperation of the Unionist opposition, for in the summer of 1917 Scottish M.P.s of all political parties got together to prepare a memorandum on land settlement; a deputation of Liberal and Unionist M.P.s presented this to the Secretary for Scotland in December 1917, and it was agreed that a meeting would be held between Scottish landowners and the Secretary for Scotland to discuss the whole question. The Secretary for Scotland at that time, Robert Munro, was a Highlander and known to be wholeheartedly on the side of crofters in any dispute over land. Lord Lovat's comments to the leader of the Unionist party, Sir George Younger (in a letter of 2 January 1918), are revealing.

> I think you will agree that it is of first rate importance that there should be a preliminary meeting of landowners before the meeting with the Secretary for Scotland. ... We must face the fact at once that Lowland and Highland Landowners do not see eye to eye on all the big land problems. ... It is imperative that both groups of proprietors should consult together so that the astute Mr. Munro should not be able to play one party against the other in order to circumvent both.[13]

There followed various meetings, memoranda etc. between landowners; the objective of the meeting, they decided, must be to pin Munro down on specifics regarding government plans, but when the conference was held on 22 February 1918 they did not succeed in doing so. The main result of that conference was the adoption of the Secretary for Scotland's suggestion that a small committee of proprietors be formed to act as a channel of communication with him. The committee was formed, but in the year that followed Munro made no attempt to communicate with it.

Meanwhile, *The Glasgow Herald* (20 July 1918) noted the resolve of a meeting to take steps 'that every discharged Scottish soldier received full information as to where small holdings or rural employment were obtainable.' Information on this subject was certainly made available at the end of the war, but it was by no means exclusively Scottish. The booklet, *Land Settlement in the Mother Country*, which provided the details as well as the application form was issued jointly by the English and Scottish Boards of Agriculture with the approval of the Admiralty and the War Office.[14]

When the war was over the Coalition Government presented their election manifesto.

> The care of the soldiers and sailors, officers and men, whose heroism has won for us this great deliverance, and who return to civil life, is a primary obligation of patriotism. ... Plans have been prepared, and will be put into execution as soon as the new Parliament assembles, whereby it will be the duty of public authorities and, if necessary, of the State itself to acquire land on simple economical bases for men who have served in the war, either for...allotments, or small holdings, as the applicants may desire and be suited for, with grants provided to assist in training and in initial equipment.[15]

New legislation was being framed by the English as the Land Settlement (Facilities) Bill. Initially it was believed this statute could have covered Scotland as well by means of special clauses.[16] The members of the Board of Agriculture for Scotland each submitted a memorandum, commenting on various clauses of the Bill. In February 1919 the Chairman of the Board sent these to the Secretary for Scotland, along with his own comments. He stated that although he and the other members of the Board had felt that a separate Bill for Scotland would be preferable, he now thought 'it may be better to attempt to adapt the English Bill to suit Scottish requirements, in view especially of the postponement of legislation for Scotland that would most likely take place if a separate Bill were introduced, and of the greater dangers that would attend such a Bill in its passage through Parliament.'

No further correspondence on the subject has been uncovered, but reading the Board's memoranda must have convinced the Secretary for Scotland that separate legislation was necessary, for the English localised system of land settlement administered by county councils, let alone the very different forms of land tenure in the two countries, would have made the drafting of a single Act for both countries a nightmare.

During this period Scottish landowners were frantically trying to get access to the Secretary for Scotland, and complaining bitterly at Munro's failing to keep his promise to consult with them about the new legislation.[17] Even after a meeting was held the proprietors were not happy, and it was left to the Scottish Unionist leader, Sir George Younger, to soothe ruffled feathers; in May 1919 he wrote to the secretary of the The Scottish Land and Property Federation that he did not think Munro had meant to treat Scottish landowners 'in a supercilious way'. The reason a further meeting had not been arranged, he advised, was because Munro had been appointed to the cabinet committee considering land settlement legislation. He added, 'I do not personally see what good would have been served in these circumstances by any further communication with Munro, who was fully acquainted with the views of our friends on the subject.'

In the summer of 1919 the contents of the Bill were known. Part I made provision for purchase of estates, which was something landowners had been pressing for all along. However, Part II of the Bill continued to allow the constitution of holdings on privately-owned land, and removed the clauses which had caused so much trouble in applying the 1911 Act. Compensation for any reduction in the selling value (as distinct from the letting value) was no longer to be allowed, and the Land Court was to be the sole assessor. Sir George Younger commented to the The Scottish Land and Property Federation, 'Fortunately the constitution of the Land Court is very different from what it was in the past and there is, I should think, greater confidence in its fairness and its decisions.'[18] The Unionist leader was well aware that the proposed restriction in compensation would be very unpopular with Scottish landowners, but, he wrote in a private letter to the secretary of the The Scottish Land and Property Federation: 'There seems to be an impression, not confined to Liberal quarters, that the awards in certain cases for loss of capital value have been somewhat excessive, more particularly in cases where there is no intention whatever of realising the estate.'[19]

The Land Settlement (Scotland) Act came into operation in December 1919, four months after the Land Settlement (Facilities) Act.[20] It seems clear from the Board's memoranda and notes—and from a comparison of the two Acts—that the Scottish Act gained muscle from the English one. Part I of the Scottish Act paralleled the English statute in allowing, for the first time, the purchase by the Board, either by agreement or compulsorily, of lands anywhere in Scotland, subject to the approval of the Secretary for Scotland

and Treasury. This power was at first operative for only two years, but it was continued in succeeding years by Expiring Laws Continuance Acts.

Part II of the Act modified the Small Landholders Act, 1911 quite radically. The office of Small Holdings Commissioner was abolished, and the Board became responsible for ascertaining demand and for preparing schemes. The Board authorised their own schemes without recourse to the Land Court, and any objections by tenants or landlords were heard before the Board, who would then decide whether to go ahead with the scheme, amended or not. However, before it was put into operation an order had to be confirmed by the Secretary for Scotland, who, if a landlord objected, could refer the case for inquiry by the Land Court before coming to a decision. As indicated above, two other key changes were the abolition of the right to submit cases to arbitration where compensation over £300 was claimed and the right to claim compensation for depreciation of selling value. And, under the new Act, landlords could not re-let a farm under negotiation for a period of time fixed by the Land Court.

Part IV of the Act provided a new method of financing land settlement: for two years the Board were empowered to borrow a sum of £2,750,000 from the Public Works Loan Commissioners out of the Consolidated Fund, the annual loss, approved by the Treasury, to be made good by parliamentary vote. Part V directed the Board to give a preference for two years after the passing of the Act to applicants who had served in the armed forces. (In fact, as will be seen, this preference continued for much longer than two years.) This part of the Act also conferred power on the Board (initially for two years but extended more than once and ceasing only in 1926) to make advances to holders to enable them to purchase livestock, seeds, fertilisers and implements.[21]

In view of the strong hostility of the landed classes to so many of the provisions of the new Bill, and considering the way in which their influence had affected the framing of the 1911 Act, it may be asked how this statute passed into law with all those provisions intact. The answer is that the social and political climate of the post-war era was a very different one from that of the pre-war period; rank and privilege no longer held the same power and mystique, and men who had survived brutal warfare would not forget the promises of land that had been made to them. Also, Labour M.P.s were pressing for much more radical land reforms—public ownership in effect—so that between those proposals and the extreme right-wing demands of the Scottish Land and Property Federation, the Liberals were seen as steering a middle course.[22]

With radical new powers to purchase farms, the removal of the aspects of the 1911 Act which had rendered it ineffective, the seemingly realistic funding, and the supposed willingness on the part of all sections of society to ensure that men returning from the war were provided with small holdings, the stage seemed set for the rapid settlement of large numbers of these men. But it did not work out that way. Partly, as indicated above, it was lack of preparedness. Then, too, many of the procedures which had been necessary under the 1911 Act remained so under the new Act: interviewing and assessing the suitability of applicants, inspecting potential farms, and then providing those acquired with buildings, fences, roads and water supplies, all of which took time.[23] Financial constraints also operated. Prices after the war rose so rapidly that within five months of the passing of the Act the funds allocated for land settlement were already used up.[24]

Furthermore, one element of the new legislation actually served to retard land settlement. Under the 1911 Act the only financial sanction required was that of the Secretary for Scotland, while under the 1919 Act Treasury sanction was also necessary. This applied to all expenditure, from the purchase of a complete estate to material for fencing. As will be seen in later chapters, the Treasury almost invariably considered any expenditure proposed by the Board to be excessive, though perversely, after causing delays by endless quibbling, in almost every case (in the immediate post-war years at least) the Treasury ended up sanctioning the expenditure originally proposed by the Board.

Mediating between the Treasury and Board was the King's & Lord Treasurer's Remembrancer. The Barons of the Exchequer and their principal officers, the Queen's Remembrancer and the Lord Treasurer's Remembrancer, were created by The Exchequer Court (Scotland) Act, 1707. The offices were united in 1837 (by which time the Barons of the Exchequer had been abolished), and the holder of the office exercised a number of important powers.[25] He was, in effect, the Treasury's man in Scotland. Although his advice was not always heeded, the K & LTR was a key figure as he had the inside knowledge of Scottish affairs. Of course, the influence of the office depended to some extent on the holder of it at any particular time. Until 1922 it was Sir Kenneth Mackenzie of Gairloch, a landed proprietor with strong views and an acerbic tongue.

The reaction of ex-service men to the endless delays might not have been so violent had the propaganda prior to and immediately after the war not been so eloquent. As one bitter Highlander put it, 'At the last general election Sir R.L. Harmsworth and his agents flooded Sutherland with literature containing rosy promises to all of land &c, not even [sic] were they to break up farms and pay compensation for the same, but they were also to find capital for soldiers and others who they said could not be expected to have capital with only a shilling a day of pay.'[26] W.R. Scott wrote in the early twenties that men who had survived two to nearly four years of active service expected the promises made to them would be fulfilled: 'And this disposition was encouraged by the gorgeous, and even poetic expectations that had been scattered broadcast in aid of recruiting and by other forms of propaganda.'[27]

Not surprisingly, it was in the Highlands and Islands where real trouble erupted, as demobilised and land hungry men used the only weapon that had proved efficacious since the late nineteenth century: raiding. As early as the spring of 1918 forcible seizures of land took place in the Hebrides, and matters worsened in 1919. In the Board's report for that year, published in 1920, they noted that there had been extensive land raiding and 'feared that seizures in the North and West will increase in number, and will tend to spread to other parts of the country unless a more rapid rate of progress is secured than has hitherto been possible.'[28] (These and later raids are fully dealt with in the appropriate chapters.)

The Times encapsulated the press's views in their comments on the Board's report concerning forcible seizures.

> Having made these disclosures, the Board calmly turn to the discussion of cattle breeding and heather burning and kindred topics. They show no recognition of their own share of responsibility, nor do they give any indication of the way in which they or their superiors propose to deal with a situation which now contains elements of danger. The report is framed in such a spirit of aloofness that it might well have been drafted by philosophers in Saturn.[29]

The journalist went on to say that 'since the period dealt with the outlook has become worse', which was true.[30]

In an attempt to take some positive action to improve the situation, the Secretary for Scotland (with Treasury approval) created a new temporary post, Director of Land Settlement, and appointed to it an esteemed public figure, Sir Arthur Rose.[31] It is a measure of the respect he inspired that in the period he held the post, whilst the Board was criticised continually for not doing enough, none of this criticism was aimed at Sir Arthur.[32]

As the funding provided by the 1919 Act was proving altogether inadequate for Scottish land settlement under the existing system, a conference of government ministers was held on 5 July 1920. The Secretary for Scotland had prepared a memorandum for the Cabinet on the current position. It stated that if operations under the Act were closed down less than a year after its passing into law nearly 9000 applicants would be left unsatisfied and the situation would be intolerable. 'The Cabinet were reminded of the election pledges which had been given and were impressed with the social and political discontent which would be aroused by any sudden or substantial decline in land settlement policy.' However, to meet fully the demand at current prices might have involved the Treasury in an additional expenditure (including England) of £100,000,000, which was inconceivable given the state of the country's finances. The conclusion, therefore, was that the machinery of settlement would have to be overhauled 'with a view to the most rigorous economies'. It was estimated that whereas in England 40% of the expenditure on each holding was irrecoverable (i.e. given as grants rather than loans), in Scotland it was as high as 60-70%, so naturally Scotland received much greater attention. A Committee was appointed to consider the best way to overhaul the policy and machinery of land settlement.[33]

Subsequently letters and memoranda flowed between the Treasury and the K & LTR. In an August memorandum the Treasury noted, 'The broad question which is suggested for consideration is whether the better results might not be obtained in Scotland at less expense by acceptance of the less ambitious standards adopted in England and by a similar decentralisation of the work.' Sir Kenneth Mackenzie replied at length; he was highly critical of many aspects of the Board's policies and practices but thought it right 'to point out that the conditions in England and Scotland differ considerably. The bulk of the rural population in England live in villages, and the demands for land there can frequently be met by the provision of allotments. ... Generally speaking the land in England is more fertile than that in Scotland, and the latter country has a much longer winter. On a 10-15 acre holding in many parts of England, beasts can graze for nine months in the year, in Scotland there is little grass till May. Probably, therefore, there may be fair reason to have rather larger holdings in Scotland from which winter keep can be procured.'

As far as decentralisation was concerned, Sir Kenneth had no doubt that 'had the system been the same in both countries from the outset, much better results at far less expense would have been obtained in Scotland.' However, he doubted if the existing system could now be altered. He advised the Treasury that he had written privately to the chairmen of county councils where the Board owned considerable estates to ask if they would be willing and able to undertake the work, and they had all agreed they could have done it at the outset, but several did not think it would be desirable to transfer the work to them at this stage.

The Treasury also commissioned an outside report, by George Fraser F.S.I., hoping that he would suggest increasing smallholders' rents, but this he did not do. Though very critical of some of the Board's schemes, his only suggestions for economies concerned buildings and equipment.[34] The K & LTR did not think much of Fraser's report and doubted if the man could be considered an agricultural expert. He added, 'I rather think he was a good deal employed by the Board at one time and it seems dubious taste for him now to turn round and rend them.'

The Cabinet Committee report was produced at the end of 1920 and its main recommendations made public at the beginning of January 1921.[35] The Committee recognised that there were significant differences between Scotland and England (for example, the great demand for allotments in England hardly existed in Scotland), and that the situation in the crofting counties was unique. The reasons for the higher cost per holding in Scotland than in England were seen as (1) the fact that virtually all Scottish holdings had to be equipped with buildings, which was not the case in England; (2) the average Scottish holding was 36 acres compared with 15 acres in England; and (3) in Scotland most holders were given loans for stock acquisition out of land settlement funds, whereas in England the bank loaned this money with a State guarantee.

The Committee estimated the total ex-service demand at 7220 applicants, of whom 1284 had been, or could be, satisfied out of available funds. There were also approximately 500 disabled ex-service applicants, 3000 civilian applicants for new holdings, and 3500 civilian applicants for enlargements. The Committee realised that it would be quite impossible for the Treasury to provide the scale of expenditure which these figures suggested, but they felt that 'it would be difficult to maintain that the pledge to the ex-service man in Scotland was satisfied by the provision of holdings for only 1500 Scottish applicants—approximately the number which it will be possible to settle on present lines if Scotland is accorded financial treatment on the lines recommended in the case of England and Wales'.

The meat of the report was, of course, the question of ways of economising. After careful consideration the Committee came to the conclusion that 'the objections to transferring the control and management of Land Settlement in Scotland to the county councils or other representative bodies are insuperable'. Not did they did think it a good idea to give such bodies advisory or consultative functions while the entire financial responsibility lay with the Exchequer. The Committee suggested five ways in which economies could be effected.

(1) By reducing the number of applicants.
(2) By acquiring land in future otherwise than for cash, and by adopting the practice of acquiring individual farms already equipped rather than large estates.
(3) By reducing the size of holdings and endeavouring to extend 'bare' land settlement.
(4) By instituting a most rigid control over capital and other expenditure per holding.
(5) By limiting the amounts lent to applicants for purchase of stock, &c.

However, after a full discussion of the above, the Committee returned to the differences between Scotland and England, and recommended that additional funds be made available in order to satisfy more of the pressing demand. As a result of this, an amending Act was passed in 1921.[36] The Board's borrowing power was enlarged up to £3,500,000, and the period for borrowing was extended for a further two years, or a later date as the Treasury, after consultation with the Secretary for Scotland, should fix.[37]

As an attempt to reduce the number of applicants, it was announced that no applicant would be eligible for the preference given to ex-service men unless his application was received on or before 1st March 1921. Also, the names of men not prepared to accept holdings which the Board thought suitable were to be removed from the lists of ex-service applicants. The public announcement also stressed the importance of reducing the average expenditure per holding and advised that it would be necessary to limit the size of individual holdings, and provide only the minimum equipment.[38] Inevitably, the Treasury's views and the Board's views on what constituted minimum expenditure differed markedly.[39]

Meanwhile, the barrage of criticism against the Board continued, reaching its peak in the early months of 1921. On 26 March George W. Constable, Traquair Estate Office, used the Letters page of *The Scottish Farmer* to attack the Board for their high expenditure on salaries (he reckoned that the Board and its staff were costing the taxpayer £700 a day). Letters agreeing with him appeared the following week. On 9 April the journal responded with a leading article entitled 'The Board and its Critics'. 'The Small Holdings and Land Settlement work of the Board is anathema to Mr Constable and his friends', it noted, 'and the Board has been handicapped in its purely agricultural duties by that fact.' But—it went on—as 'the section of the statutory duties of the Board, which they do not like, does not represent the policy of the Board, but of the Government, and is a phase of a deliberate national policy which the Board was created primarily to carry out, their attacks will not affect that policy one iota.' Constable returned to the attack in the next two issues and again on 13 August; it was clear that he had landowner support.[40]

Indeed, it is one of the ironies of the situation that criticism of the inefficiency of the Board's land settlement activities should have come not only from politicians representing the landless but also from Unionist politicians representing the landowners. As *The Scottish Farmer* had so astutely pointed out, it was the policy of land settlement more than the Board's carrying out of that policy that proprietors were objecting to; nevertheless, a Board of Agriculture so utterly distasteful to the owners of the farms on which it was hoped to settle thousands of ex-servicemen was unlikely to make much progress. The Scottish Land and Property Federation spent a good deal of time and effort in 1921 attempting to gather evidence of maladministration by the Board for use in the House of Commons debate that summer. However, the secretary of the Federation found himself frustrated by the wealth of second-hand stories and dearth of concrete cases. He thought this was because people were 'so timid about attacking a body that may be able some day to retaliate with unpleasant consequences',[41] which is hardly credible.

When it came to the actual House of Commons debate in July, the Secretary for Scotland, Robert Munro, was able to deflect some of the criticism against the Board by announcing that the Chairman would be retiring and the Board be reconstituted.[42] The Unionist leader, Sir George Younger, wrote to the secretary of the Scottish Land and Property Federation after the debate

> Just before going to the House, Munro got hold of me and told me in confidence that he had got Wright to resign his office as at 31st August. This was the result of a conversation I had with Munro and the Prime Minister on the previous day, when I said perfectly plainly that we were not going to stand the present state of affairs any longer, and that I proposed to demand an immediate enquiry into the present position. The P.M. promised me that they would take immediate action. Knowing that Wright's resignation was in Munro's pocket and that he meant immediately to follow me and to announce the fact, I felt it would be rather inhuman on my part to say all that I had intended to say on the subject of the mess they had created for their successors.[43]

The Scotsman commented, 'There is ample justification for the criticism to which the Scottish Board of Agriculture was subjected in the debate on the Scottish Estimates. It is the expression of well-defined opinion in every part of Scotland. The Board is costly, ill-directed, and to a large extent ineffective. Its reconstitution is a step in the right direction.'[44] Criticism of the Board continued to be heard in the months following the debate. In response to remarks made by the Lord Advocate, on 19 October the Director of Land Settlement wrote to the Scottish Office

> I am making enquiry about the alleged waste of time and money by officials; but as you know this is a charge repeatedly made, usually by irresponsible people,

> who have no knowledge of the facts. Unnecessary expense is incurred by calls for immediate enquiry into cases, like Raasay for example, where although nothing effective can be done at the moment, a visit is required for policy's sake. It is rather curious that a short time ago I had a note from a man in the Orbest district of Skye whose complaint was that the Board's official never visited his district. It is pretty much like 'Mortons Fork'. If we visit we are wasting money, if we don't visit we are neglecting our duties.[45]

The question of who would become Chairman and new member of the reconstituted Board of Agriculture occupied the minds of landowners during this period. The crucial thing, opined *The Scottish Farmer*, was that the two new appointments be made on the basis of ability and not political affiliation. 'Efficiency, and efficiency alone, should be the determining factor. The Act, 1911, has to a large extent been rendered abortive because of the political "deals" which lay behind its passing into law.'[46] The Scottish Land and Property Federation were particularly anxious that Sir Robert Greig did not get promoted to the chairmanship,[47] but this was indeed what happened. Fortunately for relations between the Board and landowners, the man newly put in charge of land settlement, James Mather, was highly thought of by everyone.

All this was taking place against a background of constant land raids in the Highlands and Islands. At the end of 1921, in an effort to be seen to be taking a firm line, the Scottish Office used the case of the Raasay land raid (see Chapter 8) to prepare a press release in which the Secretary for Scotland announced: 'I have issued instructions to the Board of Agriculture that in future land raiding is to operate as an absolute bar to land settlement, and that persons taking part in such raiding shall be removed from the Board's list of approved applicants for small holdings.'[48] As will be seen in subsequent chapters, the statement turned out to be meaningless, as public pressure ensured that the Raasay (and other) raiders got the land they wanted.

Attempts by the reconstituted Board to improve matters in the first few months of 1922 took various forms. In January a meeting was held between James Mather and representatives of the Scottish Land and Property Federation. The secretary of the Federation advised members, 'The main object of his visit was to ascertain if a better atmosphere could be created, which would enable the Board to carry out its statutory duties with a minimum of friction and a maximum of consideration of the interests of the Landowners concerned.'[49] As a result of this meeting, a conference was held in June between the Board of Agriculture, the Scottish Land and Property Federation, the National Farmers' Union, and the Northern Agricultural Committees, on the subject of land settlement in the northern counties of Scotland. Although nothing concrete emerged from the conference, the absence of virulent campaigns against the Board in the years following it may indicate a better relationship. However, this might in part have been because, in spite of Treasury opposition, the Board made every effort to purchase Lowland properties outright instead of creating holdings on land remaining in private hands, which was what the Federation had been campaigning for all along.[50]

The conference certainly did nothing to improve relations between the Board and the NFU. At first glance landowners and the Farmers' Union may seem unlikely bedfellows, but the latter represented the men who were being pushed off large farms to make room for smallholders, and there really was no way of sweetening that pill. In December 1924 the Board wrote to the Under Secretary for Scotland in response to a letter from the NFU to the Scottish Office.

> It may be fairly stated that the attitude of the National Farmers' Union as disclosed by their actions in relation to schemes formulated by the Board during the last few years is essentially one of direct hostility to the whole policy of land settlement in Scotland in so far as such policy involves, as it necessarily must involve in the long run, the displacement of tenant farmers by small holders.[51]

Apart from attempting to dispel hostility, the reconstituted Board in 1922 also worked for improvements in its own workings. In February of that year the new Chairman wrote to the Secretary suggesting that a small committee be formed to gather information to enable the Board to review the situation and plan future policy. The information required was about the number and distribution of applicants and of the intensity of the demand; the allocation of funds already made to various districts and the apparent unsatisfied demand in each district; and the estimated funds available for the year ahead. At a preliminary meeting on 1 March it was decided to interview the senior sub-commissioner for each of the six geographical districts in order to ascertain the 'atmosphere' and relative urgency of the demand, and to ask Land Division to supply a statement showing by parishes the number of applicants already settled, those to be settled on 'committed' schemes, pre-1st March and post-1st March (1921) ex-service applicants, and civilian applicants. Meetings were held throughout March, with a different area covered each time, resulting in a very thorough review of all the areas.[52]

The committee presented the minutes of each meeting, the figures for effective demand, suggested allocation of funds for each district, overall financial position, and general conclusions, to the Chairman on 7 July. One point which came up in several of the senior sub-commissioners' reports, and which the committee endorsed, was the difficulty in enforcing the preference for ex-service applicants. The reasons given were as follows.

1. That the number of ex-service men who are willing and able to accept holdings on a particular scheme is often insufficient to take up the whole of the farm, although there are more than sufficient civilian applicants in the vicinity, and that schemes which would be for the mutual benefit of ex-service men and civilians have in consequence to be deferred or abandoned.
2. That in many parts of the Highlands the farms available and suitable for settlement are limited in number and that permanent injury may be done by establishing new ex-service holders on the whole of a farm which offers the only natural outlet for enlargement of holdings of existing landholders who are mostly older men and have not themselves seen service.
3. That many of the civilian applicants are farm servants on farms which it is

proposed to sub-divide or resident thereon under temporary tenure; that numbers of these men have had some or other relatives killed in the war; and that to displace them in favour of men who, though they may technically possess the ex-service qualification may have less claim to consideration, gives rise to criticisms to which it is difficult to find a satisfactory answer.

4. That in the interest of the Board, as well as of the holders, it is desirable that a proportion of civilian applicants of lifelong experience in agricultural work and possessing probably a large amount of capital, should be selected for holdings.

The committee asked that the Board be given a wide discretion in the application of the ex-service preference rule.

The Board wrote to the Treasury requesting that the instruction be withdrawn and the Board be allowed to exercise their own discretion, affirming that they would continue to give preference to ex-service applicants over civilian applicants whenever possible. The Treasury wrote to the Ministry of Agriculture & Fisheries to ascertain how a relaxation of the rule would affect England and received the following reply on 31 July.

> The demand from civilians in most parts of England and Wales is very great indeed, and in certain counties the civilians, if they could be settled, would undoubtedly be a better type of applicant, and the County Councils would in many cases prefer these men as their tenants. We here are unanimously of opinion that if there were any sign that the Government were prepared to provide land for civilians with or without annual loss, the prospect of settling the outstanding ex-service applicants would be reduced almost to disappearing point. Many County Councillors in England and Wales have estates in Scotland, or visit that country for pleasure or other reasons, and if they became aware of the fact that in Scotland land was being acquired for civilians, I cannot possibly see how we could keep the 'brake' on Local Authorities any longer in England and Wales.

The Treasury forwarded this letter on to the K & LTR (Sir James Adam), asking his views. The Exchequer had no objection to allowing the Board a certain discretion to include a small proportion of civilians in Highland schemes but considered that 'any extension of this practice must be strenuously opposed for financial reasons. The Government pledge was given to ex-service men. It does not appear possible to satisfy ex-service demand from the funds available; and though civilians may make better settlers I think they must clearly stand by till the ex-service claim is met.'

The K & LTR replied on 9 August, advising the Treasury that a certain discretion had to be allowed. 'I entirely agree', he wrote, 'that the practice of settling civilians except for the sole purpose of making a settlement of ex-service men possible should cease at present, but you cannot get away from the fact that the land settlement question in Scotland, particularly in the Highlands, is a very different one to that in England.' The Treasury informed the Board on 20 September that the Lords Commissioners were unable to agree to the withdrawal of the instruction by which only ex-service men whose applications had been received on or before 1st March 1921 would be given preference. However, they were prepared to 'concede a certain discretion to the Board in the selection of applicants on the understanding that the Board will act on the instruction as framed except where in their opinion it would retard the settlement of men entitled to the ex-service preference.' The Treasury insisted on being given a full explanation whenever someone other than a first preference applicant was proposed for a holding and reserved the right to withhold their sanction from any scheme where a large proportion of the holdings were not for the benefit of men entitled to the ex-service preference.[53]

The other controversial matter which came to the fore in the summer of 1922 was the annual burden which the smallholders had to meet. Immediately after the war prices for building materials continued very high, but by 1922 they had fallen sharply. Smallholders settled when prices were at their peak now found themselves crippled by their rents and annuities. On 18 April Mather suggested that the Treasury be approached on the matter.[54] On 14 August the Board wrote to the Treasury, enclosing Mather's memorandum, which concluded: 'Let us admit that some of the holdings are over-burdened financially owing to the high cost of equipment, and that they are not an economic proposition even at the very low interest of $1\frac{1}{4}$% for building loans. In some form or other and sooner or later it is inevitable that the Treasury will suffer loss in respect of these holdings.' The following proposals were made by the Board:

> (1) That in cases where the sum of the fair rent of a holding and the building loan annuity is more than the holding can carry by way of annual charge, the total annual payment should be lessened by a reduction in the interest on the building loan to the extent (if necessary) of making the loan free of interest, leaving only the capital repayments to replace the loan. This proposal should apply to schemes both on the Board's estates and on the estates of private owners.
>
> (2) That, although it does not fall within their statutory duties, the Scottish Land Court might be asked to undertake the responsibility of fixing the maximum amount of the annual burden which the holding should be called upon to bear in respect of the building loan, keeping in view the whole circumstances of each individual case.[55]

The Treasury consulted the K & LTR on this matter. Sir James Adam replied on 14 September that he agreed with Mather's conclusion and that he was inclined to agree with the suggestion to call in the aid of the Land Court.[56]

There followed a good many internal memoranda. One Treasury official (E.F.S. Bamford) travelled to Scotland and recorded his impressions on 16 November. He visited a number of Lowland settlements and found that 'in practically all the early settlements there seemed to be considerable dissatisfaction at the burden of rents and still more at the uncertainty of the position. On these holdings settlers were placed at "equipped rents" temporarily pending the working out of the cost of the buildings. ... In some cases even yet the holders have not been informed of the annuity to be charged to them: in most cases they know but refuse to sign the bonds: in a few they have signed the bonds but find the burden too large for them to bear.' His impression was that the problem was confined to these older Lowland settlements, and that the main thing needed was a definite and final decision. 'As long as the holders feel they can get something by grumbling and obstructing a Govt. Dept. they will naturally continue to fall in arrears with rents and refuse to accept the loan burden by signing the bonds.'

In spite of such strictures, Bamford admitted the necessity of reducing the annuities and went on to consider who should decide the revisions. The Treasury might have more say if the Board did so, but the Board 'would be largely in the hands of their local Commissioners who are I think more in favour of the small holders than the small holders are themselves! The revision is bound to cause heart-burning and jealousies between holder and holder and the position would be especially difficult on the Board's own estates.' Therefore the idea of using the Land Court seemed a good one. Bamford concluded by suggesting two modifications to the Board's proposals. First, that cases should only be considered for holders who made application and, second, that the position be reviewed again after a period of perhaps seven years, when either fair rents or annuities might be revised upwards if agriculture were less depressed.

The Treasury wrote to the Board on 21 December, with such typical remarks as, 'It is with great reluctance that My Lords contemplate this further concession to Scottish smallholders especially in view of the heavy loss already involved by the system of settlement which has recently been the subject of comment by the Public Accounts Committee.' However, they agreed in principle to the reduction of annuity payments along the general lines suggested by the Board, to be administered by the Land Court, but put forward the two suggestions which Bamford had made to modify the Board's proposals. A meeting was to be held between the Land Court, K & LTR, and a representative of the Board.

The Board replied to the Treasury on 22 January 1923.[57] In their opinion it was necessary that *all* holders who entered under the exceptional conditions that existed in the building trade as a result of the war be given the option of having their buildings valued by the Land Court, though they might not all avail themselves of the offer. The idea of a septennial review by the Land Court did not appear practicable to them. An important change was proposed to the original idea, which had been that the Land Court would fix the maximum annual burden which the holdings should bear in respect of building loans with the adjustment to be made by reducing the interest rate and leaving the capital value untouched. The new proposal was that after the present value of the buildings to an incoming holder was assessed the annuity rate would be *increased* from $1\frac{1}{4}\%$ over 80 years to $3\frac{1}{8}\%$ over 50 years. After further internal Treasury memoranda (in which Bamford welcomed the upward revision of interest rates as a 'return to financial sanity'), the proposals were agreed to.[58] A press notice was sent to all the Scottish newspapers and the major London ones on 14 March 1923 advising that the Board were setting in motion the Land Court's revaluation of payments by holders settled at the time of post-war high prices.[59]

The move to ease the lot of smallholders was welcomed, but 1923 saw a heightening of Highland agitation at the slowness of land settlement. The depression made it much harder for men to wait for the chance of a holding and led to a wave of emigration from the Highlands and Islands,[60] which, in turn, increased the pressure to expedite land settlement. In May a deputation from the Highlands and Islands Committee of the Free Church of Scotland called on the Secretary for Scotland (Viscount Novar) to plead for the government to do more.[61] In June the Highlands Reconstruction Association presented a Memorial to the Secretary for Scotland with many of the same pleas. 'Whatever difficulties the Board of Agriculture have had to contend with', it stated, 'the rate of settlement has been painfully slow.' The reply which the Board provided for the Secretary for Scotland was that 'the scope and progress of Land Settlement, like every other administrative problem, is governed finally by considerations of finance.'[62]

It is highly unlikely (to put it mildly) that deputations and memorials alone would have persuaded the government to expedite land settlement in those areas, but land raiding was continuing apace and causing growing concern.[63] The Skye land raids (discussed in Chapter 8) occupied a significant amount of parliamentary time in that year, and the House of Commons debate in the summer was one of the lengthiest ever.[64] The one thing on which all parties were agreed was that some kind of action would have to be taken.

In June 1923 the Secretary for Scotland presented the following Instructions to the Board of Agriculture.

1. Lowland Settlement to be confined to present commitments, subject to such exceptions as may be unavoidable.
2. Settlement in the seven Crofting Counties to receive prior consideration. All Skye ex-service men to be settled by the end of 1924 if possible.
3. Staff to be increased. Estimated increased cost of Staff £3,200 per annum.
4. Land to be acquired by compulsion if necessary.
5. Schemes sanctioned by the Secretary for Scotland to be proceeded with, without waiting for settlement of compensation claims if the Secretary for Scotland approves.
6. Treasury controls to be removed as long as £3,000,000 not exceeded. Board to consult with Treasury before adopting a Scheme the cost of which is likely to exceed the present Treasury limitations.
7. Board to proceed at once on these lines.

In order to carry out these instructions a statutory order was necessary, and discussions had to take place between the Board and the Treasury.[65] On 4 August the former sent detailed proposals to the latter. The Treasury asked for the K & LTR's views on these, along with their own suggestions, e.g. that specific Treasury sanction should still be sought for new Lowland settlements. Sir James Adam agreed with this and with most of the other Treasury suggestions. He worried about a section of the Board's letter which had not been commented on by the Treasury. This was the proposal that in cases where the Secretary for Scotland so approved, schemes should be proceeded with before the amount of compensation payable to a landlord or tenant had been determined. 'It is all right from the point of view of avoiding delay', wrote the K & LTR, 'but the Board's position for negotiating such a very troublesome matter as compensation would be very weak. Could not a limit of compensation be fixed in any case before a scheme is proceeded with?'

On 5 October the Treasury sent a detailed reply to the Board's proposals. A long letter from the Board followed on 25 October. Concerning the restriction on Lowland schemes, they pointed out that schemes of a Lowland character were sometimes made in nominally Highland areas, and asked that they be authorised to apply the new procedures to all schemes formulated in the crofting counties, irrespective of their character. On the question of compensation, they believed that if the Board followed the Treasury's suggestion and agreed beforehand the limit of compensation to be paid, 'this would mean either that the maximum would always be paid or that the Board in coming before the Land Court or an arbiter would be prejudiced by having offered so much.' In any case they anticipated that most lands would be acquired under Part I rather than Part II of the Act, and it was in the latter cases where the more serious questions of compensation were raised.

The K & LTR advised the Treasury, 'You should not agree to the Board's proposal for a free hand in connection with all schemes in the crofting counties. The schemes in that district where it could be said that they partake of a Lowland character will be few in number and need not be subject to unreasonable delay. Besides they will almost certainly be in parts of the country where raiding or anything of that kind is hardly to be thought of.' He still felt the Treasury should 'insist on the Board laying before them the best estimate available of compensation required in the exceptional or doubtful cases.' He granted that 'if the plan of purchase is largely adopted questions of compensation will decrease in importance.' The Treasury wrote to the Board along those lines on 7 December. On 24 January 1924 the Board sent the Secretary for Scotland a summary of their own proposals and the Treasury's concessions, extracted from the correspondence between 4 August and 7 December.[66] The letter concluded by stating that a further communication had been addressed to the Treasury asking '(1) that prior examination of schemes by the Treasury be waived in the case of all schemes of whatever type initiated in the Hebrides, and (2) that general Treasury Authority to proceed in advance of the settlement of compensation in the case of Highland schemes be deemed to include all schemes of whatever type in the Hebrides in additional to pastoral schemes in the seven crofting counties.' A final Treasury letter of 5 April 1924 sanctioned both these modifications.

In the course of 1924 land raiding died down. A report of that year entitled 'Economic Conditions in the Crofting Counties' noted that a great deal had been achieved by the remedial legislation of the past generation, and that in some districts nearly all the farms had been taken. 'The difference made by such wholesale action is very great in such islands as Tiree and Barra, and can be appreciated by those, who remember the discontented state of the inhabitants of those two islands not so many years ago.' It was estimated that on the more thinly populated island of Skye so much land had been taken that by the end of the year 'probably one half of the population will have had their position improved thereby.'[67]

In their report for 1925, the Board noted that the demand for land settlement showed no signs of abating; they continued to receive more applications than they could hope to satisfy under prevailing conditions. They recorded their conviction that the time had come to relax the strict preference accorded to ex-service men.[68] In 1926 all of the Board's senior sub-commissioners, chief factors and the chief surveyor submitted reports containing their views on land settlement; once again the need to remove the ex-service qualification was emphasised. 'Any restriction in point of fact operates against ex-service men, in many cases, besides impeding the projection of land settlement generally.'[69] At the end of that year the Board were finally given authority to modify the preference given to ex-service men and to choose applicants on the basis of merit alone (though, other things being equal, ex-service men would still be chosen). An era had come to an end.

What had been accomplished during that era? In answer to a question in parliament in March 1926 the following information as to numbers of new holdings constituted since the end of the war was provided:

1919...........282
1920...........227
1921...........415
1922...........433
1923...........322
1924...........269
1925...........102

The outstanding applications at that time numbered 6838.[70] In answer to a further question—in May 1928—a breakdown of holdings created between 1919 and 1927 was given by counties (see Table 1).[71]

The number of holdings created is only one measure of the success of land settlement policy, and it is significant that in a review of 1938, the Department of Agriculture noted that most of the failures which had occurred were 'ex-service applicants settled under Government pledge in the post-war period, who being for the most part hurriedly trained in agriculture and subsidised for stock and equipment, could not stand up against the heavy fall in agricultural prices that occurred before they were properly established.' About three-quarters of the unsuccessful holders on the Department's estates had been settled between 1919 and 1924.[72] That is, perhaps, the saddest fact about the frantic push for land settlement immediately after the war.

TABLE 1
Holdings and Enlargements Created 1919-1927

County	*New Holdings*	*Enlargements*
Aberdeen	42	—
Argyll	153	42
Ayr	95	2
Banff	2	—
Berwick	95	—
Bute	23	4
Caithness	147	59
Clackmannan	—	—
Dumfries	144	—
Dunbarton	81	—
East Lothian	45	—
Fife	73	—
Forfar	57	—
Inverness—Mainland	97	23
Inverness—Skye	313	147
Inverness—Harris	58	27
Inverness—North Uist	84	87
Inverness—South Uist	84	47
Inverness—Barra	66	33
Kincardine	27	—
Kinross	—	—
Kirkcudbright	74	—
Lanark	—	—
Midlothian	41	—
Moray	—	—
Nairn	—	—
Orkney	6	20
Peebles	19	—
Perth	23	—
Renfrew	19	—
Ross—Mainland	87	83
Ross—Lewis	251	276
Roxburgh	—	—
Selkirk	—	—
Shetland	74	149
Stirling	—	—
Sutherland	70	207
West Lothian	12	—
Wigtown	11	—
Total	2331	1206

CHAPTER 3

Land Settlement in the Later 1920s and 1930s

From the mid 1920s onward most land settlement schemes were settled peacefully and amicably; the conflicts and difficulties which beset so many early schemes became rare. There were, inevitably, some exceptions, which are discussed in the appropriate chapters, but for the most part land settlement was accepted and the procedures had become routine. Prices were more stable than in the volatile period just after the war, and by the mid 1920s the Board had gained much valuable experience in settling smallholders, so the bitter complaints of inefficiency and delays were no longer so prevalent. The only continuing conflict was between the Board and the Treasury over the cost of many of the new schemes proposed, but even this had become routine.

However, there was still concern about some aspects of land settlement. Every year there were questions in parliament, usually about the gross disparity between the thousands of applications outstanding and the small numbers (as seen at the end of Chapter 2) actually settled each year.

In 1927 the Secretary of State for Scotland appointed a Committee (under the chairmanship of Lord Nairne) to investigate land settlement in Scotland; the report was published in 1928. The Committee's remit was

> To inquire into the settlement of small holders in Scotland under the Small Landholders and Land Settlement (Scotland) Acts, with a view to reporting upon the cost incurred by the State in carrying out such settlement; the value of the results achieved both economic and social; the defects, if any, in the procedure under the said Acts with suggestions for such amendments as the Committee may deem expedient; the desirability of devolving upon local authorities any of the powers and duties under the said Acts; and whether any amendment of the law is desirable as regards the valuation of rating of small holdings within the meaning of the said Acts.[1]

The report's review of the history of the legislation was admirably lucid. Their statement of the cost of land settlement was also very clear. In preparing this statement, the Committee divided the work of the Board into three periods: the 'pre-armistice' period of schemes under the 1911 Act, from about April 1912 to Martinmas 1918, the 'ex-service' period, from Martinmas 1918 to Martinmas 1922, and the 'current' period, from Martinmas 1922 to 31 March 1927. The average net cost to the State of each holding or enlargement formed by the Board since 1912 was estimated actuarially to amount in the crofting counties to £263, in the other counties to £841, and for the whole country to £399. Those figures included expensive schemes which had been set up during the first two periods; the respective figures for the current period were £285, £596, and £360.

The Nairne Committee produced no such clear-cut statement about the economic and social results of land settlement. Their remarks about the western Highlands and Islands (classified simply as 'the Highlands') once again emphasised the unique nature of this area within Great Britain.

> The problem in the Highlands involves historical, racial, economic, and social considerations entirely different from those in other parts of Great Britain. We are dealing with a community which has never been industrialised, and resists any attempt at industrialisation. Land is the basis of its existence and determines the form of its social life. It has refused to acquiesce in any of the attempts to change the method of holding or using land which have been made in the last 150 years, and the legislature has been compelled to meet the claims it has made to be allowed to live its life in its own way. The Highlander not only insists on living in the Highlands, but insists on living in his own strath or on his own island. What seems an obvious fact to an observer accustomed to other modes of life, that there is not sufficient land to provide for the population in an island or a strath, is not accepted as a fact by the Highlander. He insists on being given land in his own district, and would rather have a hopeless patch of his own native heath than a fair holding in a strange glen.[2]

'To apply the ordinary economic test to land settlement under such conditions would be absurd', concluded the Committee. As for the criticisms that too many holdings had been created, that most of them were too small to be economic, and that it would have been better to have created fewer but larger ones, they considered the points valid but added, 'the demand has to be kept in mind, and the demand is still unsatisfied.'

The Committee did make some attempt to apply economic criteria to Lowland land settlement, although having been unable to gather convincing statistical evidence they contented themselves with indicating 'tendencies'. In their visits to arable farms which had been broken up into holdings giving full-time employment to a man and a pair of horses, where the system of cropping and stock-raising usual in the district was carried on, the Committee found no indication of any greater economic returns resulting from such settlements. Where a holding of this nature was too small to provide full work for a pair of horses, they did not think the holder had much chance of making a success of his holding. On the other hand, where holders had been innovative—turning to milk production in corn-growing districts or to pig and poultry keeping alongside ordinary cropping and stock-raising—there was more likelihood of increased production. The best chances of increased production, they felt, lay with the smaller holdings where holders concentrated on the intensive cultivation of fruit and vegetables, or to pig or poultry keeping, or small dairying.

Overall, the Committee thought that 'the time has not arrived when any definite conclusion can be reached as to the economic result of the policy of land settlement, because of the absence of data on which such a conclusion can be based, and the fact that most of the settlers have not yet found their feet.'[3] The Committee found it even more difficult to pronounce on the social effects of land settlement but summed these up as having been 'to increase the number of people living on the land, to provide something over 1000 new dwellings of a higher standard than previously existed, and to give to a large number of the people who have been settled the satisfaction of an independent status.'[4]

The Committee made a number of recommendations for improving the legislation, but none of them were of any real import. Their first recommendation was that no more holdings should be created on privately-owned estates in Lowland areas, which was in fact already the Board's unofficial policy. The second recommendation was that landholders' tenure, which had been extended by the 1911 Act from the crofting counties to the rest of Scotland ('where it was entirely alien') should be discontinued in the Lowlands; they pointed out that nothing in the existing legislation precluded the Board from settling holders on their estates under ordinary agricultural holdings tenure. Their third recommendation was that the present limit of 50 acres or £50 rent be enlarged to 100 acres or £100.[5]

Although landowners at least were happy with the first two recommendations, it is difficult to see how the pace of land settlement would have been accelerated by such measures. In any event, there is no indication that the government took any notice whatsoever of the report, toothless though it was. In fact the Board of Agriculture's budget for land settlement was reduced from £175,000 in 1927 to £75,000 in 1928.[6] As the government clearly was not going to legislate, the stage was set for a Private Member's Bill, the Small Landholders (Scotland) Acts (1886 to 1919) Amendment Bill, presented to parliament by the Liberal M.P. for Kincardine, James Scott.[7] How sensitive the land settlement issue still was is clear from the controversy following the introduction of this Bill. The view of the Department[8] was that it was 'a somewhat ambitious attempt to remove defects real (or other) in the Small Landholders Acts, and is one that would more appropriately form the subject of a Government Bill.' They welcomed some of the proposed changes, found others unnecessary or undesirable, and thought there were important points not covered in the Bill.[9]

The Bill was in no way the result of the Nairne report; far from abolishing landholders' tenure it actually proposed its *extension*, which set Scottish landowners up in arms.[10] As one of them put it, 'I consider the Bill a most unfair attempt to confiscate further valuable interests from the landlord and pass them gratuitously to the tenant.'[11] Three clauses were particularly contentious.[12]

The first of these abolished the class of 'statutory small tenants', a category created by the 1911 Act. Landholders' tenure, previously known as crofters' tenure, had been granted to tenants who (themselves or predecessors in the same family) had provided or paid for permanent improvements on their holdings. Holders whose improvements had been provided by the landlord became statutory small tenants, with the right to a renewal of their tenancy at an equitable rent (unless the landlord objected and the Land Court upheld his objection) but without the rights granted to landholders of 'fair rents', fixity of tenure, and payment of compensation for improvements. The category of statutory small tenant had been set up in 1911 because of the enormous resistance of Lowland landowners to the extension of crofting tenure on to their lands.[13] The idea of now abolishing that category and making all those on government-created holdings—whether on private or state-owned estates—into landholders was therefore anathema to Lowland landowners. They argued that tenants had not asked for this change and did not require it.

A second contentious clause concerned resumption of holdings. Under the 1919 Act a tenant could be removed from a holding on privately-owned land if the owner could prove that he had no other landed estate and that he intended to occupy the holding in question. When farms were sold piecemeal (as occurred frequently in the early 1920s), the buyer of an individual section of a farm containing one or more holdings could justifiably claim that this was his only landed property. He therefore had the right to take possession, and any holders would have to go. In 1924 the Secretary for Scotland had drafted a Bill to stop this happening[14] but nothing came of it because of landowner opposition.

This opposition was launched anew in 1929. If the clause disallowing resumption of holdings for personal possession went through, argued one landowner, then all landholders' holdings would become unsaleable.[15] The importance of encouraging owner occupation was stressed by the Scottish Land and Property Federation.

The only contentious clause which echoed a recommendation made by the Nairne Committee was one extending the 50 acre/£50 limit to 100 acres/£100. The Scottish Chamber of Agriculture wrote to the Scottish Land and Property Federation

> as regards the formation of new holdings, above the present limits in size or rent, by the Department of Agriculture, the Chamber does not consider this necessary or advisable. The really urgent demand is for holdings within the present statutory limits, and the dissipation of the funds of the Department in the provision of larger holdings or farms, for the benefit presumably of better-off smallholders will simply mean that less will be available for the smaller and more needy and possibly also more deserving applicants. Further, if larger holdings are to be formed, this will mean more displacement of present tenants, with no economic advantage, and, in all probability, greatly increased national expense.[16]

The Bill was hotly debated in parliament at the end of 1929.[17] Even its supporters admitted it had defects, but they called for a second reading so that the Bill could go to committee stage. During the eleven days of debate in the Standing Committee on Scottish Bills, one important concession was made: the clause relating to statutory small tenants became optional, so that instead of all statutory small tenants automatically becoming landholders, it would now be up to the individual tenant to apply for a change in tenure.

The Bill came before the House again in the spring of 1930.[18] After that it was up to the government to give the time necessary for the completion of the further stages before the House adjourned in August, and this they did not do.

Instead, at the commencement of the next session the government produced a completely new Bill, the Small Landholders and Agricultural Holdings (Scotland) Bill. Part I amended the Small Landholders Acts while Part II amended the Agricultural Holdings Acts. This Bill was debated in the autumn of 1930.[19] Two clauses which had appeared in the Private Member's Bill were absent from the government's Bill: the clause on statutory small tenants and the extension from £50/50 acres to £100/100 acres. The government argued that it had been the irreconcilable divergence of opinion over statutory small tenants which had caused Scott's Bill to be lost. ('It is because the Bill was fought so bitterly and so strenuously that, although it contained other beneficent Clauses...we could not carry it into law.') From 26 November 1930 until 25 February 1931 the Bill was debated by the Standing Committee on Scottish Bills.[20] It came before the House of Commons again on 20 March 1931 and, after many more hours of debate, was passed.[21] Further discussion followed in the House of Lords before the Small Landholders and Agricultural Holdings (Scotland) Act, 1931 became law.[22]

The right of resumption by a landlord of a holding for the purpose of residing there was removed by Clause 8 of the new Act. And the option for a statutory small tenant to became a landholder was replaced as Clause 14. But the size and value of smallholdings was not extended beyond the £50/50 acre limit. Perusing the Act, one does rather agree with those M.P.s who had argued that completely new legislation would have been preferable to such a piecemeal Act, since nearly every clause in it is an amendment of either the 1886 Act, the 1911 Act, or the 1919 Act, and has to be read in conjunction with all three statutes.

There was yet another important piece of legislation to come in this period. During the early 1930s the focus of Scottish land settlement shifted from the Highlands to the Lowlands, especially to the central industrial belt where unemployment was high. In England by the mid 1920s the emphasis had already changed from the settlement of ex-servicemen on the land to the relief of unemployment.[23] However, in Scotland the unfulfilled promise to ex-servicemen still dominated thinking. One reason was doubtless the continuing intensity of Highland land hunger. However, there were other reasons why, when the Scottish Office were thinking of measures to alleviate unemployment, land settlement did not figure amongst them.

The Liberal Party manifesto of 1920 suggested various remedies for unemployment, one of which (for both England and Scotland) was accelerated land settlement. The Department commented that the idea that this offered a substantial and inexpensive solution was not true for Scotland.

> Land Settlement in Scotland must be carried out gradually because the land which is suitable is limited in amount and unless the suitable farms are to be taken and broken up during the currency of leases, regardless of the cost of

compensation, the suitable land in a given district only becomes available gradually as long leases expire. After the land is acquired its division and equipment with roads, buildings, etc. may take a considerable period. In short Land Settlement desirable as it is on other grounds has little bearing on the problem of unemployment. As a proposed remedy for unemployment it is neither substantial, quick nor inexpensive.[24]

In the early 1930s the Department began to experiment with small intensive holdings of about 8-10 acres and found a ready demand for them. Unfortunately, this was a period of financial stringency for the Department, forcing them to abandon negotiations for the acquisition of several estates.[25] With this in mind the Secretary of State for Scotland presented a memorandum to the Cabinet in July 1935. He proposed a policy of encouraging the formation of small sized holdings to the extent of 5000 new holdings at a cost of about £4,000,000 to be financed by government borrowing. A simple Bill was drafted, as it was only the finance side of the proposal which required new legislation. However, the Chancellor of the Exchequer was not prepared to accede to the proposal as he considered borrowing for 'uneconomic purposes' inadmissible. As an alternative he was prepared to increase the revenue allocation to £250,000 for three years, and the Secretary of State agreed to this on 14 November.[26]

On 20 November the Department supplied the Scottish Office with notes for a press conference in which the Secretary of State for Scotland was to announce the intention of creating some 800 small holdings in the industrial area of Scotland, devoted to the intensive production of pigs, poultry, eggs, vegetables and fruit.

> This type of holding will, I think, serve the applicant with some acquaintance with the working of land—and there are many such—who is ready to abandon employment in an urban occupation and so leave a gap to be filled by some unemployed man. It will also serve some unemployed men directly, take them back to the land, and relieving them of the distresses of unemployment will give them a new life. This is in present times the most important aspect of the land settlement programme we envisage, and it should not be forgotten that the equipment of the holdings with buildings, roads, fences and water supplies will make a not inconsiderable call for work and materials, so enlarging the amount of work available in the country.[27]

On 3 July 1934 the Department sent the Secretary of State notes for the second reading of the Land Settlement (Scotland) Bill in the House of Lords. The emphasis on the creation of small sized units for intensive production was reiterated (though it is interesting to note that the reason given was the need for a better distribution of the population between town and country, and that relief of unemployment was not mentioned). The Land Settlement (Scotland) Act, 1934—providing the extra funds for three years for this purpose—became law on 12 July 1934.

One change which occurred in the wake of the new Act was that henceforth Lowland tenants were no longer settled under landholders' tenure; holdings were let as equipped subjects on seven-year leases under the Agricultural Holdings Acts.[28] Some 22 years after the experiment began, Lowland landowners' belief that a form of tenure suitable for Highland conditions was inappropriate to the Lowlands was finally vindicated.

In 1933 the Department initiated a new scheme of providing allotments for unemployed miners and others; by 1937 over 2000 allotments were under cultivation.[29] From 1935 unemployed men who had proved successful as allotment holders were helped by the Scottish Commissioner for Special Areas (Sir Arthur Rose) to obtain small holdings.[30] In that year of 506 holdings were formed and settled, the largest number for a single year.[31]

In the mid 1930s the first serious attempts were made to evaluate the economic effects of land settlement policy (although these attempts focused almost entirely on the Lowlands). The first such investigation was carried out in the late summer and early autumn of 1934, with a view to obtaining some measure of the economic position of occupiers of various types of small holdings.[32] The investigation concentrated on holdings which occupied the whole time of the occupier and on which he and his family were dependent for their living. Such holdings, it must be pointed out, were the exception rather than the rule. Indeed, with reference to a table showing the distribution by counties in southern Scotland of various types of holdings between one and fifty acres in 1927 (produced in order to demonstrate that the distribution of holdings investigated in 1934 was representative), it was noted that only 25% of these holdings were full-time small holdings. The information sought for each holding included

> (a) general particulars as to aims, acreage of crops, etc., and details of the labour, both family and other, employed on the holdings;
> (b) a financial account comprising a record of receipts and expenditure over a recent twelve-months' period, with, wherever possible, quantitative as well as financial information;
> (c) a record of the number and values of the different classes of live- and deadstock on hand at the beginning and end of the accounting period;
> (d) such information regarding markets, other sources of income, etc., as seemed to bear upon the holders' returns.

Some 300 smallholdings were visited, and financial records were obtained for 201 holdings (49 of these were for holdings not visited). The report began by noting that relatively few holders kept 'anything approaching an accurate or detailed account of their transactions' (poultry keepers were said to be the only exception). Therefore, although very possible assistance was given to holders, 'the novelty of the request for financial records resulted in a comparatively small number of thoroughly considered statements.' In fact, the quantitative results of this investigation were hedged about with so many qualifications that they are not even worth discussing.

The interest of the report really lies in its qualitative findings, as was implied in a statement that some holders 'were perfectly satisfied with the results of their effort and others were emphatically dissatisfied, and not all of the latter were working their farms unprofitably—a point which emphasises the importance of factors which cannot be reduced to figures.' There was fairly general agreement among holders that their position had deteriorated over the past few years and a tendency to invoke government aid to secure higher prices.

Two points which cropped up most frequently were the long hours involved in working a holding and the importance of the contribution of the holder's wife. The report summed up the first point in this way.

> It cannot be denied that, as compared with the hired farm worker, the small holder is frequently called upon to work hours far in excess of those which would receive a Trade Union sanction. There are times of the year when the phrase 'daylight to dark' can certainly be applied without exaggeration, and the responsibility which rests on the holder as manager in addition to being a labourer necessitates a degree of liberality with his time which puts him in a different category to the farm worker and implies that his returns should be commensurately greater. On the other hand, as many holders agreed, the degree of independence which the owner of a small holding possesses—the absence of someone else 'looking for work for him' enables him to take advantage of those relatively slack periods which do occur on all agricultural holdings. This consideration would undoubtedly go some way in counterbalancing the long hours worked at other periods, and the independence which makes it possible must be counted as in some degree a return for these.

Concerning the second point it was noted that 'many successful holders attributed the degree of success they had attained to the assistance received from their wives. It was obvious that in such cases there was no part of the work of the holding in which the wife was not competent to assist'.

One of the more interesting conclusions of the report emerged from a supplementary question which asked whether the holding was a suitable size; frequent complaints were made that holdings were too small for economical working. The report broke holdings down by type (Dairy, Mixed, Market Gardening, Pig, and Poultry) and then looked at the number of double holdings (i.e. two adjoining holdings being worked as one), the number renting extra land, the number sub-letting, and the number who stated their holding was too small. From this breakdown it was found that the inadequacy of the normal size of holding was felt most keenly by holders following dairying or mixed farming.[33] Indeed, the authors noted that their evidence of the report suggested that small holdings were not so well adapted to general practices as to more intensive forms of production.

The report concluded that the holders were utilising their land as fully as possible and that efficiency was relatively high. (A point made at the beginning of the report—that holders willing to cooperate with the Department in such a study were likely to be of a higher calibre than the average—was not reiterated here.) The authors noted that the opinion had frequently been expressed by holders that small holdings were only suitable for people brought up on the land. It was found that most mixed, dairy and market garden holders had previous agricultural or horticultural experience; however, some of the most successful poultry keepers interviewed were city bred and had only recently taken to the land for their livelihood.

The question of experience surfaced again in a study carried out in 1935-6 on 110 new intensive-type smallholdings in the east of Scotland.[34] The study was done by the Farm Economics Branch of the Department, who enlisted the cooperation of new holders on entry; after a year 77 accounts were completed and analysed (55 holdings were in the Lothians, four in Fife, five in Perthshire, and 13 in Angus). The majority (53) were between five and eight acres in extent; 17 were larger than eight acres and seven were less than five acres. Poultry predominated on 24 holdings; 18 were of the market garden type; on 15 poultry-keeping was combined with market gardening; there were four specialist pig holdings; the remaining 16 were more varied. Most holders (48) had an agricultural background. Only 15 were drawn from industry; seven had been tradesmen, and the remaining seven had had miscellaneous previous occupations. Of the 77 tenants, 47 worked entirely on their holdings, 16 had an additional full-time job, and 14 worked away from the holding for part of the time.

Two groups of holders were considered separately. Group A consisted of 45 holdings entered at Martinmas 1935 with a negligible opening valuation (nothing but small tools and equipment), so that the holders were in effect starting from scratch. Group B—the remaining 32—had got their holdings under way prior to Martinmas 1935 or had started with enough stock and equipment to be on a par with earlier entrants. In Group A, 12 holdings showed a net loss in 1935-6, 19 showed a net profit of anything up to £50, and 14 showed a net profit of more than £50. In Group B six holdings showed a net loss in 1935-6, nine showed a net profit of anything up to £50, and 17 showed a net profit of more than £50. Remarks were appended to indicate probable reasons for those who showed little or no profit (e.g. 'Lazy', 'Buys rubbish', 'Little business acumen'). The general data was also broken down by average entry capital, amount of experience (indicated as 'much', 'some', or 'little'), other employment (i.e. how many had full-time jobs, part-time jobs or no other jobs), and type of holding.

A general survey of the returns did not suggest that the amount of capital available on entry bore any particular relation to the results achieved. Nor did the possession of a full or part time job away from the holding appear to have any effect on the progress made. Similarly, there was no particular correlation between the type of holding and results achieved. The one significant factor that did emerge was the importance, in the early period of settlement at least, of experience. Of the 31 holders making a net profit of more than £50, 24 were listed as having had much experience, while of the 18 holders incurring a net loss only five were held to have had much experience.

There was one other study, of a more wide-ranging character. In April 1934 Lord Astor's Committee on Land Settlement requested information on the Scottish situation; the committee was considering how land settlement might help to relieve unemployment. Though the study did not in the end have any real relevance to this question, a good deal of interesting

TABLE 2
Previous Occupations of Holders Settled

		%
Agriculture	2960	66.5
Fishing	431	9.7
Mining & quarrying	88	2.0
Metal working	148	3.3
Building, stone, slate and glass trades	102	2.3
Wood & leather working, paper-making, painting	128	2.9
Food, drink & clothing trades	98	2.1
Transport & communication	261	5.9
Commerce, finance, insurance	155	3.5
Public administration & defence	47	1.0
Professions	35	0.8

material emerged from the Economics Officer's analysis of departmental records.[35]

The report began with a table showing the previous occupations of 4453 applicants settled in new holdings up to 31 December 1934 by the Department of Agriculture for Scotland (reproduced as Table 2). For the next table (Table 3), showing the reasons for changes of tenancy, information was only available for the 2639 holders who had been settled on the Department's own estates. Over a period of 16 years changes of tenancy had occurred in 642 cases.

The report then went on to a more detailed analysis of 436 holdings on fourteen of the settlement schemes which had been in existence for the longest period. Over the period 1919-1935 the 436 holdings had been occupied by 704 tenants, an average of 1.6 tenants per holding. Approximately 9% of tenants left to take up another holding or farm; another 2% left because of dissatisfaction with the terms of agreement. There were 76 failures, 11% of

TABLE 3
Reasons for Changes of Tenancy

Failure	167
Dissatisfaction after taking entry	33
Change of mind before taking effective entry	25
Failure of health	44
Left for larger farms, emigration, other employment	161
Renounced to relatives	29
Death	69
* Miscellaneous reasons	114

*e.g. domestic reasons; too old, or renounced on being pressed to reside on holding. In the majority of these cases, no reason given.

all entrants, with another 5% relinquishing their holdings and turning to some non-agricultural occupation.

These reasons for change were analysed against the agricultural experience of the tenants: 416 (59%) were classified as having 'all agricultural experience', 175 (25%) had 'part agricultural experience', and 113 (16%) had 'little agricultural experience'. About 66% of the tenants with all agricultural experience were still in occupation, against 62% of those with 'part', and only 48% of those with 'little'. Amongst those with less experience there were proportionately more failures and changes to other occupations while those with greater experience were more likely to have changed to other holdings or farms. The average capital at time of application for those still in occupation was £343 and for 'failures' was £238. In this study it was therefore surmised that lack of sufficient capital was a cause of unsuccessful occupation.

More than half the 704 tenants were settled between 1919 and 1923. Naturally the proportion of those still in possession was smaller than that of tenants settled in later years. Among the tenants settled after 1926, no failures were recorded, but an appreciable proportion moved to other holdings or farms. The average number of years the 'failures' occupied their holdings was 5.6, and interestingly this average hardly varied for the different years of settlement.

The report concluded by pointing out the dangers of applying the findings to more recent land settlement activities, as the situation in the post-war period differed completely from that in the mid 1930s. ('In these circumstances, it is wise to consider this piece of work solely as an analysis of the settlement history of certain small holding schemes.') Although Lord Astor's Committee on Land Settlement are unlikely to have found anything of much use to them in the report, it certainly does provide some interesting insights into the history of land settlement.

Although in this period most attention was paid to Lowland areas where the industrial depression was biting, the plight of Highland smallholders was also made known. In 1935 a petition by 693 smallholders in the counties of Sutherland, Ross & Cromarty, Inverness and Argyll was presented to the Secretary of State for Scotland. Accompanying and supporting the petition was a 44-page memorandum prepared by the Rev T.M. Murchison, minister of Glenelg, Inverness-shire.[36]

Sheep stock clubs, in particular, were suffering great hardship. These cooperative ventures, where all the holders on a particular settlement held their sheep stock in common, were supposed to pay a dividend at the end of each year. However, during the depression years far from making any profit they had great difficulty even in repaying the government loan which had allowed them to take over the stock on entry. In 1933 a two-year moratorium had been granted on repayments of interest on capital debt. Unfortunately, 1933 and 1934 being agriculturally very lean years, very few farms had been able to clear even their working expenses, so that the moratorium had done nothing more for the holders than ease them temporarily of the Department's recurring demands. In 1934 there had been an almost complete failure of the harvest in Skye, but the Department had refused to make any concessions which would have allowed holders there to use some of their rent money to purchase foodstuffs to keep their stock alive; the Department's attitude had led to a number of protest meetings.[37]

The poor position of sheep stock clubs was seen as arising from the abnormally high valuation of sheep stock at ingoing, due to the ephemeral agricultural boom of the immediate post-war years, and the high interest rate of 5% on the unredeemed capital of stock loans. The two main remedies suggested were therefore a revaluation of the sheep stock and a reduction of interest charges. Details of the exact position of several sheep stock clubs were provided in the memorandum in support of this.

Murchison then went on to the other chief grievances of the smallholders: rents and building annuities. Holders in Skye and the Outer Isles insisted that their rents were too high because the poor soil and climate had not been taken into account when the rents were set. Even occupants of large arable holdings in the Inverness area, in Easter Ross and in Sutherland, complained that their rents plus building annuities amounted to an annual burden far in excess of the possible income of their holdings. It was, of course, the Department who decided the rent, and appeal could not be made to the Land Court until seven years had elapsed. The recent reply of a divisional technical land officer of the Department in a Land Court case was quoted to explain the sense of grievance which the holders felt. The officer had said that there was no principle in fixing rents: 'One depended on common-sense, knowledge and experience, but there was no definite principle which could be explained.' It was also alleged that the Department over-valued many old buildings leading to excessively high building annuities. It was suggested that the rule that rents could be revised only septennially should be waived temporarily and that the powers of the Land Court should be extended to allow them to decide on reasonable payments.

The M.P. for Sutherland and Caithness, Sir Archibald Sinclair, had recently pointed out that in Scotland over the previous fifteen years less than £3,000,000 had been spent on land settlement, as compared with over £10,000,000 on roads and more than £15,000,000 in grants from the Unemployed Relief Committee. Murchison continued

> If a really generous and far-reaching policy in land settlement had been adopted in the early post-war years, the agricultural depression, serious though its effects might be, would not have caused the present grave situation. But the policy that was adopted—on a strict actuarial basis, as if farming, especially in the Highlands, can be made to fit office policy and red-tape regulations—was such, we submit, that even should a serious depreciation in agricultural values not have occurred, the situation would be grave enough to warrant investigation, and only in the improbable contingency of prices remaining at immediately post-war levels could the holders be expected to pay their way. But it is now too late to bewail a policy that might or might not have been adopted fifteen years ago. The just and honourable thing to do now is to face the present situation courageously and generously, and, before proceeding to further land settlement (which is urgently needed), to come ere it is too late to the rescue of those already settled.

He again emphasised the precariousness of the position of many smallholders at that time and pleaded for a Commission of Inquiry to investigate the whole situation and report on ways of alleviating the plight of Highland smallholders. He also asked for a further moratorium, covering not only stock loans but other obligations as well.

The petition was briefly discussed in the House of Commons in June 1935.[38] Sinclair argued the case for the Highland smallholders, but the Secretary of State for Scotland (Sir Geoffrey Collins) saw no reason for an official inquiry and insisted that a decision on a further moratorium could not be reached until the course of prices were known. Anyone who made further enquiries about the petition was simply referred to the Secretary of State's remarks in the House. However, the moratorium did in fact continue; it was still in force during World War II.[39]

A review by the Department of Agriculture of land settlement during the previous half century,[40] included in their annual report for 1938, did not mention the difficulties under which Highland smallholders were labouring. Instead, stress was laid on the relief of congestion and improvements in living conditions in that area. Nor was any attempt made to utilise the studies which had been carried out on the small intensive holdings in the Lowlands; the review merely commented that it was too early to assess results. The point about a smallholder being his own master was once again emphasised. Since 1912 the Department had settled 5725 applicants in new holdings and 2083 in enlargements. The area involved in land settlement operations extended to 655,766 acres; added to the 205,300 acres sub-divided by the Congested Districts Board and Crofters' Commission, the total area of 861,066 comprised no less than 4.5% of Scotland. The Department itself owned 449,000 acres. (The geographical distribution of government-created holdings was very uneven. Even in the most densely settled Lowland areas such settlements are only small pockets, while in some parts of the Highlands and Islands, particularly Skye, the Secretary of State is still by far the biggest landowner.)

It is clear from the review that in 1938 land settlement was an ongoing operation believed to have a vital role in Scottish rural life. The Committee which reported on Scottish land settlement in 1944 also recognised the value of smallholdings, and some of their recommendations were incorporated into the Agriculture (Scotland) Act of 1948, which extended the maximum size of holdings and permitted the state to lend up to 75% of working capital to incoming tenants. However, in a determined effort not to repeat the mistakes made after the First World War, land settlement was carried out very cautiously after the Second, with agricultural experience being a prerequisite even for ex-servicemen. The government's intention to proceed with the creation of new holdings throughout Scotland as soon as economic conditions permitted was affirmed in 1951, but between 1950 and 1955 only 36 new holdings were created (although at that time the Department was still receiving an average of 500 applications annually for new holdings), and after 1956 no new holdings at all were established.41

It is beyond the scope of this book to examine the changes in thinking which brought the land settlement programme to an end in the 1950s, and the more recent attempts by the government to sell as many existing holdings as possible to the sitting tenants.[42] The aim of these three introductory chapters has been to present the general background to the individual land settlement schemes which form the subject of the chapters which follow.

CHAPTER 4

Schemes in Sutherland

The Sutherland Clearances were notorious so it is natural that of all the mainland crofting counties this was where demand for land was most persistent. As James Hunter has pointed out, the emphasis on Patrick Sellar and the brutal events of 1816 has obscured the fact that the evictions affected not just a few localities but almost the whole of a very large county.[1] In the post-war social climate, the congested townships of crofters on the edge of large empty sheep farms should have led to a rapid reallocation of land, but it did not happen that way. In fact, most farms in Sutherland took longer to settle than those in any other part of Scotland. As will become apparent below, much of this was due to the reluctance of landowners there to yield an inch of their land and the varied and often devious means which they used to hold on to that land. However, this was by no means the only source of problems in the county.

One problem was simply the incompatibility between the concept of land settlement—which was really geared to creating new holdings and only incidentally to providing enlargements for existing holders—and the situation as it actually existed in Sutherland. In an internal memorandum the Secretary of the Board of Agriculture noted that the real need was to provide a redistribution of land for the benefit of existing crofters

> mainly by way of enlargements and incidentally by way of migrating 'congests' and throwing their existing crofts into adjoining ones. ... It can only be effectively done by treating whole areas as units, each unit comprising a congested township (or townships) and a neighbouring area forming the field for enlargement and re-distribution. And each unit can only be brought under treatment by the acquisition of the whole. This, of course, would burden the State with the cost of acquisition and management of existing townships, as well as the cost proper to development.[2]

Such expenditure by the government was quite out of the question, so acquisitions of land had to be piecemeal.

Another problem was the crofters' lack of capital. Had they possessed the money, the crofters could themselves have become sheep farmers in the nineteenth century, for the claim that the land was ideally suited for sheep was not disputed (only the claim that it had to be the preserve of a small

2 Map of Sutherland.

number of men with enormous herds). It had been the crofters' lack of capital that had forced the Congested Districts Board to divide their first Sutherland acquisition (North Syre) into much smaller holdings than originally intended.[3] With the high prices prevailing during and immediately after the war, it seemed that sheep farming could be a truly profitable line again, even on a small scale, but the dramatic slump which followed put paid to that idea.

In March 1922 the Board's statistics for Sutherland were as follows. By that time ex-service men had been settled on 40 new holdings and ten enlargements; ex-service demand was for 272 new holdings and eight enlargements; schemes in hand would provide for 23 new holdings and 127 enlargements, so the unsatisfied demand would apparently be for 249 new holdings. In February 1923 it was noted that there were also 860 civilian applicants.[4]

Although various Sutherland farms were threatened with forcible possession at one time or another, the only one actually raided after the war was Kirkton in the Portskerra district.[5] This 2748-acre farm, carrying 800 Cheviot sheep, was first applied for in 1912 by the neighbouring crofters of Melvich, whose holdings were a mere one to three acres in size, and who were desperate for grazing land. It appears that before the passing of the 1911 Act the Duke of Sutherland had promised the crofters that when the lease expired they could have the farm as a common grazing; however, after the new legislation was passed he shifted all responsibility for this on to the Board of Agriculture.

The problem was that Kirkton farm had three tenants, who petitioned the Land Court to become statutory small tenants; not unreasonably, the Board decided to await the judgement of the Court before proceeding further. When the war broke out the case had not yet been heard, and in March 1915 six of the Melvich crofters re-applied to the Board emphasising the 'response made by the men of our district to their Country's appeal' and stating that they were making the application on behalf of those men as well. Although it was now known that the three tenants of the farm were actually non-resident crofters on an adjoining estate, so that nobody believed the Land Court would grant their request, the Small Holdings Commissioner was nevertheless reluctant to act until the matter was decided.

By the autumn of that year the case still had not been heard before the Land Court. The estate factor asked the Board whether they proposed taking over the farm as he required a clear undertaking from them before giving notice to the tenants. The Board replied that they could not give such an undertaking until the Land Court decision was known but asked the factor to give notice (which could always be withdrawn later) in order to leave the position open. The Board appear to have suddenly decided that they did want to settle the farm at Whitsunday 1916, as they hurriedly wrote to the Secretary for Scotland asking for his approval. As the applicants had not been interviewed and the Board could not yet provide a detailed breakdown of expenditure (though a rough estimate of £1800 was given), the Secretary for Scotland refused to consider it. The Duke was not prepared to give notice to the tenants without a definite undertaking by the Board, so the matter was left in abeyance.

By the end of the war the Duke had sold the part of his estate containing

Kirkton to a Mr Macandrew, who wanted Kirkton for his home farm. He insisted that he had no record of any promise made to the crofters by either the Duke of Sutherland or the Board of Agriculture. On 28 May 1920 Macandrew received a letter from a group of ex-servicemen advising him that they would be taking possession of the farm, 'it being the only land available for us.' He replied that the farm of Kirkton carried a large and valuable sheep stock which he had taken over at a valuation, and on that ground alone it was impossible for him to hand the farm over even if he were willing to do so. On 29 May he received another letter stating that the men had taken possession of the farm on the 28th and had resolved to give the proprietor until the 14th of June to remove his stock, at which date they would be putting their own stock on the farm. This threat was carried out in grand style. *The Glasgow Herald* reported that the ex-servicemen, having failed to persuade the new owner of the need to honour the promise made to them by the Duke of Sutherland, 'gathered their cattle and sheep and, with flags flying and headed by a piper who played at Boulogne when the 5th Seaforths landed there in 1915, drove their stock on to the farm.'

An interim interdict was served on the men, but they defied the interdict and remained on what they called (with a nice sense of humour) 'the promised land'. The owner's agents were convinced that the raiders did not have popular support and that 'if the land were given to them tomorrow, many of the agitators have not a beast to put on it and it could be of no practical service to them'; they were said to be 'dupes'. Not for the first or last time, the landowning side underestimated the determination of ex-service applicants to get the land they wanted. They were still there in August, by which time there was serious concern that their example would inspire others. It was made a condition for further negotiation that the raiders should first withdraw from the farm, but this they refused to do. Not until October was a breakthrough achieved.[6]

With the intervention of the Board of Agriculture, the raiders withdrew, on the understanding that if they found they could afford the sheep stock on the farm the Board would reconsider the possibility of a scheme. The proprietor remained reluctant to make his farm available but accepted the need to do so. When the crofters renewed their application, with the necessary financial assurances, the Board asked the Treasury (in June 1921) for sanction to settle the farm as a club farm enlargement for 22 men. The estimated expenditure was £8510. The Treasury referred this to the K & LTR. As the considerable number of extensions proposed would 'satisfy the demands for land in that district', and the scheme was within the cost limits laid down, he recommended consenting to it, which the Treasury subsequently did.[7] However, Kirkton was not in the end broken up.

In May 1922 a meeting of some 60 ex-servicemen and tenants was held in Melvich to discuss the Board's plans to turn the farm into a common grazing for 14 crofters. Since the raid in 1920 the proprietor had employed many local men in improving the farm, and these men had petitioned the Board to leave it in his hands. The chairman of the meeting, who had been one of the leaders of the raid, claimed that he would lead another raid if the Board went ahead with their plans, because Mr Macandrew was genuinely concerned with the welfare of his tenantry, and the meeting unanimously agreed to ask the Board to allow Macandrew to retain the farm.[8] This reason for not going ahead with a land settlement scheme is unique in the annals of the period.

Schemes for the Sutherland farms actually settled took a long time to come to fruition. An example is Achinduich, part of the Skibo estate in the Lairg district.[9] The Board first enquired about Achinduich in 1912 and inspected it in 1915. At that time they had received no applications for the farm, so they proceeded no further with it.

In 1919 the Board received applications for enlargements on the farm. (The owner, Andrew Carnegie, had recently died, and the property was in the hands of his trustees.) A sub-commissioner inspected it twice in January 1920, 'with a view to considering how best the farm could be utilised to meet the demands of the people in the District', one difficulty being that 'the people in the District were not agreed on exactly what they did want.' In March the Board formally notified the estate of their intention to prepare a scheme. The estate factor replied that he was negotiating with a prospective tenant. The Board pointed out the strong demand for holdings there; for that reason they could not 'consider the suggestion that this farm might be left untouched by us, as it is very difficult to find enough arable land in that district to provide for all the applicants.' The proposal for the 4750-acre farm (of which only 60 acres was arable) was to form two new holdings and 18 enlargements.

However, in August the Board formally withdrew their notice, to the anger of the estate, which had lost its prospective tenant when the intimation notice had been served, and the fury of the applicants who, at the Board's suggestion, had set up a committee with a view to forming a club to take over the farm. The secretary of this committee demanded an explanation and insisted, 'This arbitrary, autocratic and reactionary policy of the Board, is not to be allowed to go unchallenged.' The Board's honest reply was that 'the funds at present available for land settlement are not more than sufficient for schemes to which the Board are committed.' The secretary of the crofters' committee insisted that the cost to the Board would be practically nil as the applicants would stock the whole farm themselves. If the Board refused, the committee would be forced to adopt 'more drastic measures to obtain their legitimate demands'. The Board strongly deprecated the threat of violence but refused to take further action.

In the spring of 1921 the sub-commissioner was able to advise the Board that at a meeting of the crofters' committee 'the decision was that they could not take over Achinduich as a club.' He continued, 'The probable price of the sheep, the demand by the Board for one fourth of the price within a month, the probability of a drop in prices long before they had paid up the ten annual instalments, frightened them.' And he concluded—with a very obvious sigh of relief—'I think we can safely say that the applicants got every opportunity of accepting a very fair proposal, but they could not see their way to accept it.' But this was not the end of the story.

At the beginning of 1923 some 26 crofters renewed their applications for enlargements on this farm and advised the Board they would be willing to take over part of the stock as club stock. Only five of the applicants were ex-service men, which gave the Board an excuse to postpone further consideration of a scheme. In November a sub-commissioner reported that a scheme was only viable if the whole farm was taken, and even then the scheme had nothing to recommend it. The crofters could not afford to take over the sheep stock, and the estate would oppose it, so in view of the small percentage of ex-service applicants he recommended leaving it alone. At this stage, however, the M.P. for Sutherland & Caithness, Sir Archibald Sinclair, interceded by forwarding letters from the crofters to the Secretary for Scotland. There was further correspondence between the M.P. and Scottish Office during 1924, when the crofters increased their offer to the Board for the sheep stock.

Further agitation took place early in 1925, when the sub-commissioner described the situation thus.

> There is an ex-Service Tenant in occupation ... it must be conceded that the best use possible is being made of this Land at present by mingling shootings, grazings and amenity together.
>
> The compensation due to the Tenant would be about £1,000 and loss on sheep stock and compensation to Proprietor would be a further £1,000. Thereafter a Loan of £6,000 for the sheep stock would, I think, be required.
>
> In the circumstances I consider the difficulties of really proving a case for taking this Farm are very great. The Home Farm question would be raised and might be successfully contended.
>
> On the other hand, this is the only land available for the present applicants. They are hemmed in all round otherwise. Their need is very great, and I anticipate they will continue agitation until sooner or later they will break down the arguments against it and be accommodated upon it. How soon that may be I cannot say, but in the whole circumstances I do not think the time is ripe to break up this Farm unless the Board are satisfied that the Home Farm plea can be rebutted, that it is proper to displace the existing management, and that they are prepared to face the heavy expense.

In the summer of 1926, after more threats of violence, agitation by the M.P., and correspondence with the estate, the Board was advised by the factor that 'the proprietrix [Mrs. Carnegie] is not in sympathy with the proposed scheme, nor are the tenants of the farm.' The Board decided that in view of the estate's opposition no further action should be taken at that time and advised Sir Archibald Sinclair of the reasons.

In the spring of 1931, having seen the farm advertised to let, the Department wrote to the estate office. The proprietrix was abroad at that time, but the Department was told that the farm would not be re-let for another year at least. The Department wrote again at the end of the year and was advised that the proprietrix was still abroad but 'does not favour the suggestion very kindly.' In the spring of 1932 the Department decided it was time to check that a genuine demand still existed; the local sub-commissioner confirmed that it did. A new scheme was submitted to the estate, and after further correspondence and meetings the estate agreed to accept £950 in compensation. Thirteen new holdings were created, and the holders gained entry at Whitsunday 1933, some 21 years after the farm had first been considered for land settlement.

Another Sutherland farm which took decades to settle was Scibercross.[10] Applications for enlargements here were first made by crofters in 1906. After the passing of the 1911 Act they renewed their applications, but the farm had been let in 1907 on a 21 year lease, and the tenant's compensation would have been prohibitively expensive. The crofters wrote bitterly to the Chancellor of the Exchequer that 'it is in vain for Government to pass land legislation if their efforts are to be thwarted by Landlords and tenants demanding exorbitant compensation and thereby rendering the working of the Act abortive'. Questions were raised in parliament, but the fact remained that breaking the lease would have cost the Board far more than the scheme was worth, and so it was dropped.

At the end of 1925, knowing that the lease would expire in 1928, the crofters again renewed their applications for enlargements. In October 1926 Sutherland County Council sent a petition from the crofters to the Board along with their own resolutions.

> The Council considers that the interests of this County demand that immediate steps be taken by the Board of Agriculture to implement their policy of extension of holdings, and that this urgent and reasonable request of the Petitioners be granted. These young men have got a first class war record, and it is high time the State should now, when conditions are favourable, give some tangible recognition of the services rendered, by enabling them to have holdings sufficiently large to live on, and so encourage them to remain on the land.

The Board contacted the estate only to learn that the existing lease had been broken and a new 14 year lease with the same tenant entered into in July of that year. 'In these circumstances', wrote the estate to the Board in November, 'the Proprietor is unable to make the Farm, or part of it, available for the enlargement of existing Holdings.'

At about this time the factor wrote to the County Council: 'The Duke of Sutherland wishes me to say that as far as the proprietor is concerned, no obstacle whatsoever would be put in the way of the Board of Agriculture for Scotland if they decided to proceed, after due consideration, with the scheme.' As the Scottish Office wrote to the Board early in 1927, the letter to the Board saying the estate was *unable* to make the farm available was arguably 'quite consistent with the earlier letter seeing that it expresses no unwillingness or opposition but only inability in the circumstances. Your answer to that may be that the Estate have made it more difficult and expensive to carry out a Scheme because the new lease will involve an increase in the compensation payable to the tenant.' In March 1927 the Duke assured the Secretary of State that he had been personally unaware of any applications for enlargements off this farm when he agreed to the new lease and that the reason for it had been the estate's anxiety to let the neighbouring farm of Clebrig to the same tenant.

As the tenant was interworking the sheep stocks of the two farms, the Board enquired (in April 1927) 'whether, in opposition to the terms of the lease, there is any undertaking by the proprietor whereby, in the event of the tenant quitting the farm, the proprietor or incoming tenant will be required to take over the sheep stock other than the natural stock of Scibercross only.' The reply was, 'There is no undertaking such as is suggested in your letter.' In due course the Board framed a scheme for three large new holdings and 24 enlargements. In view of the heavy financial commitment required by the Board, they sought financial security from the applicants and required them to subscribe a percentage of the value of the stock; a sum of £1716 was duly subscribed by the applicants. In 1928 the Secretary of State and Treasury approved the scheme, and formal notice was given to the estate early in 1929, when both landlord and tenant objected to the proposed scheme.

At the hearing (in April 1929) the estate dropped a bombshell: the existence of an agreement, subsequent to the leases, which made specific arrangements for the working of Scibercross in conjunction with Clebrig. This would mean additional compensation payments by the Board if they went ahead with the Scibercross scheme.[11] The Scottish Office wondered why the Board had previously been informed that there was nothing of this kind to hinder the scheme. 'Is one now to deduce that the proprietor has deliberately introduced further difficulties at a late stage of your preparations?' The Board quoted the exact wording of their query and the estates' reply (see above) and went on, 'This is perhaps a literally correct reply to the question asked, but it does not disclose the fact that at that date there was in existence an Agreement altering the conditions of the leases of Scibercross and Clebrig and providing for the interworking of the Clebrig stock with that of Scibercross.'

The Board then investigated the possibility of framing a scheme for Clebrig as well. Throughout 1929 the M.P., Sir Archibald Sinclair, continued to press the Scottish Office to expedite settlement, and the Secretary of State did not find it easy to provide a convincing explanation of the new delays without revealing the estate's duplicity. Why on earth it was *not* made public does not emerge from the files; there was clearly a political dimension. (It certainly would have provided plenty of ammunition to the anti-landlord faction.)

In late April 1929 a senior sub-commissioner inspected Clebrig farm and found it suitable for the formation of five large individual pastoral holdings.[12] The notice of intention to prepare a scheme was submitted by the Board to the estate in October; landlord and tenant put forward their Representations, and the hearing was held in January 1930. Orders for both Scibercross and Clebrig schemes were submitted to the Secretary of State, who consented in February. But no progress was possible on either or both of the schemes until the Land Court assessed the compensation due.

After this was done—in October 1930—the Secretary of State decided to approve Scibercross but not Clebrig. In December the Department asked to be allowed to proceed with the Scibercross scheme to although no completed agreement had been reached with the landlord and tenant, since it was felt that 'the Court could not reasonably award compensation in excess of that indicated by them.' The Secretary of State approved this course of action, and the way was finally clear for the establishment of five new holdings and 22 enlargements on a farm which had first been asked for in 1906.[13]

One part of Sutherland where demand was great was Strathnaver, notorious for its Clearance episodes. (The strath itself had been resettled at the beginning of the century, but there remained some large sheep farms in the hands of single tenants.) The story of the settlement of the farm of Rhifail in that district is a complex one.[14] The Board initially enquired about this farm in 1915 when they learned that it was let on a 19 year lease from Whitsunday 1904 and so was not available under the 1911 Act. In April 1919 the Association of Discharged Soldiers and Sailors asked the Board to break up the large sheep farms of Strathnaver into holdings for discharged soldiers and sailors of the district, 'who claim to be the rightful descendants, of the people, that were so unjustly evicted from Strathnaver about a hundred years ago.' Rhifail, the most suitable farm for smallholdings, had been sold, but the tenant's lease did not expire until 1923. Although the crofters were dismayed by the long wait, especially as no other farms in the district would become available earlier, the proprietor did at least intimate his agreement to smallholdings being created on his estate.

By the beginning of 1923 an agreement had been reached on a scheme for seven new holdings on the northern section of Rhifail. The Secretary for Scotland approved on 2 February, and after some initial objections the Treasury also gave their sanction. But the proprietor had excluded one particular triangular area, and when the scheme was presented to the applicants with a view to their settlement at Whitsunday, they unanimously refused it because the area offered was now too small. The Board were thus obliged to take over and manage the farm themselves, while continuing to negotiate with the proprietor.[15]

In the spring of 1924 Strathnaver crofters petitioned for enlargements on the southern sections of Rhifail. The proprietor's agent responded to the Board that those portions of the farm could be made available provided the farm of South Syre (which crofters had also applied for) remained in his hands as his home farm. But then the proprietor changed agents, which was most unfortunate for the Board since they had built up an extremely good relationship with the former agent and now had to deal with agents who appear from the tone of their letters to have been actively hostile.

In the spring of 1925, when the Board were still managing north Rhifail themselves and no further progress had been made with the southern section, the agents made a new suggestion. The proprietor was prepared to hand over the triangular section of north Rhifail, allowing the scheme there to proceed provided south Rhifail was left alone, as the proprietor had now decided to retain it in his own hands. The Board replied that they were not entitled to make such a promise. After considerably more correspondence—and continual questions by the M.P., Sir Archibald Sinclair, about the delays—the Board in November 1926 sought the Secretary of State's approval of the expenditure for managing the farm until Whitsunday 1927. They also asked for approval to proceed with a scheme under compulsory procedure if the proprietor failed either to accept the scheme as prepared by the Board or the compensation of £300 which they were offering him.

The formal compulsory scheme notice was issued by the Board on 11

February 1927. Representations against the scheme were made by the proprietor's agents, and a hearing took place on 18 March. The Board amended the scheme after considering the representations and asked the Secretary of State to consent to an Order confirming the scheme. They realised that the agents would oppose the Order, and indeed the estate factor had already accused the Board of all kinds of mismanagement ('The Board of Agriculture for Scotland have too much power and are not required either by Proprietors, Crofters or the State'). The Board responded with a long letter to the Secretary of State, relating the complete history of the case and refuting all the allegations made against them.

During this period the Board anxiously tried to find men willing and able to take possession of the holdings at Whitsunday. The local sub-commissioner was more than a little dismayed at this, because the best men were unlikely to be able to commit themselves at such short notice, but quite apart from the undesirability of having to manage the farm themselves for another year the Board clearly felt they would be in a stronger position if they could name men ready to take the holdings at Whitsun.

On 5 April the Chairman of the Board asked the Under Secretary to expedite approval of the Order, 'as we are confident of being able to settle four out of the six holders at Whitsunday first.' Doing so would mean proceeding without knowing the amount of compensation payable, but the Board was convinced it would not be excessive. On the same date the proprietor's agents wrote to the Secretary of State, opposing the Order. Internal Scottish Office memoranda commented: 'There seems to have been a good deal of misunderstanding in the negotiations and it is conceivable that if the matter were held over for a year a settlement by agreement would still be reached. The Board, however, probably think that no progress on such lines would be made with the present Agents, and there will be considerable agitation (see the Sinclair correspondence...) if further delay takes place.'

On 29 May 1927 the Secretary of State consented to the Order confirming the scheme and agreed that it could proceed before compensation was settled. The local sub-commissioner provided details of six applicants whom able to take at least nominal entry at Whitsun and also named ten others who seemed suitable. The Board submitted this list to the proprietor, who named the six he favoured (they all worked for him during the sporting season); the applicants accepted the holdings, and the farm was at last settled.[16]

In view of all the problems which confronted the Board in connection with privately-owned land in Sutherland (Part II schemes), one may ask if it would not have been easier for them to purchase estates there under Part I of the 1919 Act. And, indeed, one trouble-free purchase was made under the Congested Districts Act before the passage of the later statute. Applications had been received by the Board for enlargements on Armadale farm in 1913, but the landlord was implacably opposed to any action being taken under the 1911 Act, and as the lease had been entered into before 1906 the farm was not available without the proprietor's agreement. In 1919 the applications were renewed. The farm was to be auctioned in July, and the Board wished to purchase it. A sub-commissioner suggested to the Chairman, 'This is an important case, partly from the extent of the subject [40,300 acres], and partly owing to the probability of forcible seizure if early action is not taken. Some 50 families whose need is pressing would be benefited if a scheme proceeded.' The Secretary for Scotland acquiesced and the farm was purchased.[17]

A second Sutherland estate purchased at that time—Eriboll—later proved a great embarrassment to the government.[18] In the summer of 1925 a minute to the Land Committee noted

> At Whitsunday, 1922, and Whitsunday, 1923, the Board endeavoured to find applicants—16 in number—who would be prepared to take holdings on the area in the Board's hands and who would provide 25% of the price of the sheep stock. The holdings were advertised and notices posted in Post Offices, etc., but the applicants were not forthcoming, the real difficulty being want of capital to produce the initial cash payment for the stock.

This lack of capital was not the only problem, according to a letter from the Chairman of the Board to the Under Secretary for Scotland in September. The estate was isolated and the prospective holders were unwilling to be responsible for the erection of a house and buildings. (He noted a distinction between Sutherland men and Hebrideans, the latter being accustomed to building their own houses.) A scheme providing a 100% loan would cost the State £6000 for each family settled. Under these circumstances land settlement did not appear justified, and the Chairman therefore suggested selling the estate. 'The objection to sale is the difficulty of meeting the outcry which will arise when the proposal is known.' The Under Secretary noted that this was an important question of policy. The Secretary for Scotland's reaction was that the farm clearly should not have been purchased in the first place, 'and now the proper course is to sell the property as the cost of forming these holdings is quite indefensible.'

Why indeed was this farm purchased? Eriboll had been offered for sale at a reasonable price in a county where pressure for land by demobilised soldiers and sailors was great, so understandably but unwisely the Board offered for it without stopping to consider its suitability. In partial defence of the Board it could be argued that they could not have foreseen the disastrous slump in post-war sheep stock prices, a slump which also played havoc with many other schemes.

At the end of December the Treasury sanctioned the Board selling the estate for £12,000, but there were no offerers. The price was lowered to £11,000 and then £10,000 with no offers, to the Board's despair. (The Treasury were by then past caring about the price; their only object was to get rid of what an internal Treasury memo referred to as 'this expensive incubus'.[19]) Finally, in August 1926, the Board managed to sell the farm (at disadvantageous terms) for £10,000. As anticipated, there was an outcry in press and parliament, especially when it became known that the sheep stock for which the Board had paid over £43,000 seven years earlier was now valued at just over £9000. The attacks continued for well over a year afterwards, but the Board managed to weather them.

In an interview with an old man in the district, it emerged that there is still some bitterness in the district over the sale, as it was felt the government should have been able to offer crofters holdings on this farm without demanding such prohibitive terms. And—ironically, in view of the enormous difficulty which the Board had in getting rid of it—the local belief was that it was sold only because the man who bought it (the cousin of a government minister) was so keen to have it.[20]

In the above case the Board rushed into an ill-considered purchase. The case of Keoldale was quite different, as the Board first received applications for enlargements on this farm in 1912, and after the war the applicants kept pressing the Board to take action.[21] The owner—a pluralist farmer who had been the sitting tenant—was completely opposed to a Part II scheme and was not keen to sell either; the price he asked for the property in 1919 (£20,000) was approximately double what the Board considered its value. However, in March 1920 he became very ill and was advised not to live at Keoldale; the asking price was lowered to £15,500. The senior sub-commissioner for the district noted, 'So far it has been possible to prevent actual seizure but unless a definite undertaking is given to the people soon I anticipate very serious trouble.' Preliminary approval to negotiate for purchase was obtained from the Scottish Office, but that year saw the nadir of the Board's finances, so there was a delay with consequent mutterings of broken promises from the crofters.

In February 1921 the senior sub-commissioner produced a scheme for six new holdings and 38 enlargements. The owner had died, but his brother, on behalf of the widow, was now willing to dispose of the property, and in April the Treasury sanctioned purchase. The K & LTR wrote

> This scheme will have to go on in some way, as the proposal is the result of a Meeting Sir Arthur Rose [Director of Land Settlement] had with the malcontents in the Durness district, who were on the verge of raiding and in a nasty humour. He did not undertake to get holdings, but said he would do his best to get them; and on being threatened, told them that the only promise he would give was that 'no man who raided would get any help whatever from the Government with his consent, or if he could help it.' This firm attitude had a good effect, though it was a bit doubtful whether he would be stoned or not before he got away.[22]

In August a crisis arose. The crofters had agreed to pay 25% toward the stock, but after it had been valued they refused to do so. Their spokesman wrote that they considered the valuation 'altogether exorbitant and unreasonable'; the amount represented by 25% was far in excess of the crofters' expectations and they were unable to meet it. The Director of Land Settlement replied that their attitude had disappointed him greatly: 'we received the definite assurance of the applicants that they would take over the sheep at the price the Board would have to pay and on this basis alone did I authorise the completion of the purchase of Keoldale on behalf of the applicants. The intimation you now send...is therefore a distinct breach of the agreement we arrived at.' He asked the local minister, the Reverend Adam Gunn, to intercede, reiterating his feeling of disappointment: 'it shakes my hitherto strongly held conviction of our old Scottish honesty, and, if I have to run the risk of this sort of thing, the work will be quite impossible.' The crofters replied simply that 'they regret as much as the Board their inability to face the responsibility of taking over the Keoldale stock at the inflated prices arrived at by the Valuation.'

In August 1922 the Board asked the Treasury to sanction a loan of £25,000 to the prospective holders, representing about 90% of the value of the sheep stock. They forwarded a letter written by the Reverend Adam Gunn to the Secretary for Scotland.

> The farm and stock were bought just a few months ere the slump in prices took place. The Board is not to blame for the purchase at that unfavourable moment. They were urged from three quarters to do so: the force of public opinion directed against their dilatoriness, the eagerness of the applicants themselves, who were on the point of raiding the farm, and the willingness of the representatives of the owner and occupier to effect a sale.
>
> Sir Arthur Rose did his level best to warn them of the high prices then obtaining, but the men who for 30 years to my own knowledge were agitating for a portion of this farm...would brook no delay, and gave him a verbal assurance in public meeting to pay 25% of the purchase price of the stock.

The 25% amounted to nearly £7000 and meant an initial payment of £150 per applicant. Ten of the applicants had come up with this amount, but the majority had failed to do so. They had all lodged whatever sums they could manage in the bank, but were quite unable to pay the balance in the near future.

> Now, Sir, what is to be done in the circumstances? The Board's threat...is to let the farm on lease to a tenant able to meet the whole amount, and thus recoup themselves so far as possible for the expense already incurred. This would be a fatal step to take—involving a loss of £18,000, without a single ex-soldier benefitted. I hope it is not beyond the power of legislation to find some way out. That the men are capable of managing the farm, if once they get it, is not questioned. They have managed their own, on club-stock principles, so well that the Board's officials issued leaflets to crofting townships based upon the Durness regulations, as a sample of how things ought to be done. They are looking for no share of profits from the farm, until they have fully paid their share of the purchase price. It is quite beyond the power of most of the applicants to raise £150 at once. So eager are some of them that they have actually sold some of their present stock to place £15 and £20 in their name in the Club-stock Co-operative Society, and are hopeful of being able to contribute other £15 and £20 next year without receiving a penny out of the Farm, until the £150 is paid.

The Treasury were anything but happy with the proposal, but the K & LTR thought that 'the Board make out a good case for special consideration', and Treasury sanction was reluctantly given.[23]

In the 1935 memorandum on the plight of Highland smallholders, the position of the 43 Keoldale holders was shown as being fairly desperate, since the club owed the Department about £14,000 which they had not the remotest hope of paying.[24] However, an article written in 1964 about crofting in Sutherland referred to the Durness crofters jointly controlling 'the famous Keoldale Club Farm, which is worked as one large integrated unit'. In the 1980s Keoldale was the only remaining sheep stock club in Sutherland, and the shareholders earned an annual dividend of about £700. However, the original idea had been lost sight of, as the shareholders had no need to go anywhere near the land.[25]

A later Sutherland scheme in the Brora district reveals that objections to schemes on privately-owned land had by no means ceased by the late 1920s. Applications for enlargements of existing holdings on the farm of West Kintradwell were received by the Board in February 1926.[26] The problem was that arable land would have had to be converted to pasture, which would have led to criticism of the Board. They therefore advised the applicants that nothing could be done at that time. The local M.P. took up the matter, and the Scottish Office became involved. The senior sub-commissioner for the area felt that a proper resettlement of the district would require a comprehensive scheme involving two large farms and the crofting area as well. He suggested that a local inquiry be instigated.

The local inquiry went ahead, and in due course a sub-commissioner produced a very detailed report on the town of Brora and the various types of holdings in the district. He did not think there was anything the Board could do about the larger-scale problems, but he believed that if a scheme were effected for West Kintradwell enlargements, 'the pressing demand from the locality would be dealt with.' He also reported that the tenant was converting the farm to permanent pasture, which removed the main problem over the crofters' application.

By April 1928 the Board had finalised a scheme and received the Secretary of State's approval for it. In August they served the formal notice on the proprietor, who opposed it (as did the tenant). The scheme was said to be 'unnecessary and unbeneficial, as also it is uneconomic, subversive to public policy and the expense thereof would be unjustified by the results'. The hearing was held on 19 October. It was a long and abrasive affair, with many points debated at length. One of the main objections was that three of the thirteen applicants were in arrears of rent (the Board subsequently confirmed that this was true of two of the applicants, who were therefore dropped). Another was the proprietor's insistence that the applicants did not possess enough animals to stock even their own holdings, let alone the enlargements; it was eventually admitted that the animals referred to were horses and cattle, and that there was no paucity of sheep.

By August the Board had amended the scheme to take account of some of the objections, and the Secretary of State approved the Order on 16 October. However, on 5 November the senior sub-commissioner advised the Board that only nine of the applicants were willing to go forward, although he had warned them that eleven signatures were necessary for the scheme to be implemented. The nine were very disappointed, and he therefore suggested an amended scheme. The estate agent wrote to the Board on 11 November,

'I am not at all surprised to hear that some of the applicants have withdrawn from the Scheme. The Estate has all along been opposed to this Scheme, and I cannot assent to your suggested amendments.' However, there was nothing he could do about it, for the Secretary of State approved the amended Order on 12 December, and the applicants got their enlargements.

This chapter has so far dealt with land settlement schemes only up to the stage where the confirming order was signed; little has been said about how the holders fared in the years that followed. For the most part this is unavoidable. Settlements on privately-owned estates were outwith the control of the Department, while for state-owned farms the sheer volume of files makes it almost impossible to build up a coherent picture. However, although it remained in private hands, there is enough documentary material—supplemented by oral history—on the 16,000-acre farm of Shinness, offered by the Duke of Sutherland to the Board of Agriculture in 1916 for the settlement of ex-servicemen, to piece together that story.[27]

Thirty holders were given nominal entry at Martinmas 1919, although the buildings were nowhere near completed, nor had a decision been made on the terms under which the holders were to take over the sheep stock. The Board's local officer reported that when he balloted the men for the holdings, they expressed surprise and dissatisfaction when they learned he was unable to give them any definite information about the cost of sheep stock and annuities on buildings. They agreed to the ballot on the understanding that they would have full information on these points before they took possession and would be at liberty to withdraw if they considered the terms unsatisfactory. In fact, the conditions were not arrived at until Whitsunday 1921, so when the holders took entry in the spring of 1920 they still had no idea what they would have to pay.

When, at Whitsunday 1921, the terms for the sheep stock and building annuities were announced, five men left their holdings, and all the others refused to sign agreements, grant bonds, or agree to sheep stock conditions. There were a number of applications for the five holdings now vacant; when the applicants were told the conditions some withdrew but 14 replied they would be willing to take the holdings on those terms. A shortlist was drawn up and submitted to the proprietor's agents, and five men were selected. In December 1921 the men were invited to meet the sub-commissioner at Shinness, and the senior sub-commissioner reported

> They went over the ground, saw the holdings, buildings, etc. and appeared to be satisfied with everything, but!——when asked to pay the £112 due as 25% value of the sheep stock and to grant bonds for building loan, every man refused contending that the price of the sheep was too high and the amount of annuity out of all proportion to the value of the holding.

The senior sub-commissioner did not agree with them about the sheep prices but thought annuities were indeed much too high.

In March 1922 a minute to the Board noted that the holders had not yet been registered as landholders because they had not paid any deposit for the sheep stock nor signed building loan bonds.

> In order to expedite the settlement of holders, the buildings were erected prior to the signing of bonds. Mr Coles reported on 20th December, 1918, that he had discussed the question of cost of the dwelling house plan with the Chairman and suggested that, owing to high costs, a revised plan might be necessary. He was instructed to make no change as the Secretary for Scotland was emphatic that a good house should be given to the ex-soldiers and was of opinion that a grant-in-aid towards any extraordinary cost, owing to war prices, would be made by the Government in forthcoming legislation. ... The holders' objections to the signing of bonds are due to the high cost of buildings and the consequential high annuities.

In the spring of 1923 the holders agreed to take over the sheep stock at Whitsunday at a price fixed by the Board, and they subscribed the necessary initial cash payments at that time. As to the annuities, it was agreed to apply to the Land Court for a revaluation of the buildings.

In April 1928 the Shinness Sheep Stock Club Co-Operative Society were in financial difficulties and asked the Board for assistance. The Board took no action, so the holders' M.P. lobbied the Secretary of State for Scotland on their behalf. He did so again in the summer of 1929, but still without success. The holders therefore took matters into their own hands; in October of that year they sold enough of the stock to pay off the balance of their loan to the Department. The Department made a fuss about this as it had been done without any authorisation and contravened the terms of the Bond. Internally, however, it was admitted, 'The Club have presented us with an accomplished fact, but the results and prospects are...satisfactory.' In fact, their timing had been perfect, the stock was quickly built up again, and the transaction made all the difference to the holders' financial position.[28]

In view of the initial high prices for the buildings, one might have expected them to be of high quality. Yet as early as April 1921 one holder was already complaining about the terrible state of his house, and in August of that year the local officer wrote to the senior sub-commissioner that the shepherds' houses were in such a bad state one man had threatened to leave. In one house, he reported, 'the roof is so bad that they have to move the beds in wet weather', while in another 'the front door step is so badly worn that the rain drives right into the kitchen'.

Additional expenditure was sanctioned shortly after this, but the simple fact was that the houses were very shoddily built, for the high prices demanded by the contractors had been nothing but profiteering. In 1931, after a complaint by a holder, his house was inspected. As the brickwork was found to have deteriorated, all the houses on the scheme were subsequently inspected, and a number were found to be in various stages of decay. (Problems were also discovered in buildings erected in the immediate post-war period on three other schemes—Arabella, Gagie and Gretna—although none of the necessary repairs came to anything like the cost of Shinness.) A submission was approved by the Secretary of State in 1932 for expenditure on all these buildings.[29]

In 1937 the local M.P., Sir Archibald Sinclair, wrote to the Secretary of State about the Shinness water supply (many of the holdings still had no piped water) and about the condition of the houses and steadings. He insisted that though he heard complaints from holders on various estates, 'nowhere...do I hear a fraction of the complaints which reach me every year at Shinness.' He added

> You refer...to the fact that the holders are heavily in arrear with payments due to the Department in respect of building loans. I am afraid this is true, but it is also true that the tenants feel deep resentment at having to pay for houses which let water in freely and are almost uninhabitable and for steadings in which they cannot even keep cattle. In short, they are paying for equipment which is almost useless to them and which ought to be entirely renewed and reconstructed. Yet the reconstruction of their houses and steadings with the aid of loans from the Department of Agriculture would mean that they would have to go on paying interest on the money borrowed for erecting the old and useless dwellings and steadings, in addition to paying interest on the reconstructed houses and steadings. Not only would that be unsound in principle but in practice it would be impossible for them to pay interest at these rates because their land is too poor.

He concluded by suggesting that an independent investigation be held into conditions at Shinness.

The Department advised the Scottish Office, 'It would be impossible to agree to a special inquiry without creating a precedent which could not fail to be exploited by holders with any plausible case, however ill-founded.' They suggested that the Secretary of State's reply point out that the fact that there were no vacant holdings and no changes of tenancies hardly suggested the scheme had been a failure.

In response, in February 1938, Sinclair wrote that against the point that there were no vacant holdings must be weighed 'the undoubted land hunger in Sutherland, the fact that there are very few vacant holdings in the county, and that there is a long waiting list of applicants for new holdings.' He was convinced the only reason holders remained at Shinness was that they had nowhere else to go. As to the claim that there had been no changes of tenancy, Sinclair enclosed details of no less than nine changes of tenancies, along with a memo by the holders, which stated that 'as a matter of absolute fact there would be a general exodus from the Shinness Holdings if anything that promised an existence was available.'

Petitions by the holders in the course of 1938 did at least force the Department to consider the situation at Shinness. Internally it was admitted, 'The general impression is that the construction of the buildings (by contract) was not altogether satisfactory.' However, it was claimed there was also some evidence of neglect by the holders, and to what extent conditions reflected that neglect or defective construction would be difficult to establish. 'In any event it will be dangerous for the Department to undertake wholesale remedial works.' The Department's smug, arrogant, and self-righteous memo concluded by summing up the position thus

> Shinness may not be a good scheme but on the other hand it is not a failure. Probably more holders were settled than the ground could reasonably carry—and this was a feature of settlement immediately post-war—but the holdings are at least of a higher standard than those in the locality. The tenants have continued with exceptionally few changes for a period of almost twenty years. They have not fulfilled their obligations to the Department in the matter of annuity payments and they have consistently made complaints regarding equipment. At the initial stages of the scheme, i.e. before 1923 there were serious difficulties in completing the settlement and there has all along been a suggestion that whilst some good men were settled at Shinness, there were a number of not very satisfactory settlers. Combining all these considerations one might say that the scheme, not by any means perfect in its construction, has never really been given a good opportunity to develop. It is not a scheme which requires or merits radical alteration or further heavy expenditure and I suggest that the proper course is to make certain limited provision for improvements to the water supplies, as already promised, and to allow the scheme a further opportunity to develop.

I spoke to the woman who had been the first teacher at the new school built for the Shinness settlers. She had no criticisms of the crofters but quite a bit to say about the poor land and the hardships suffered by the settlers. And she remembered all too well how awful the houses had been, describing them as jerry-built: 'In fact some of them fell down before they were built right. They were just put together with inferior stuff and then covered over ... there were a lot of complaints. They were cold and they were draughty and not very well designed. ... A very poor house altogether.' It was only after World War II, when substantial grants became available, that the houses were rebuilt, and the settlers got an adequate water supply.[30]

The story of land settlement in Sutherland after World War I is an unedifying one. The resistance of landowners to having their farms broken up, the bad mistakes made by the Board of Agriculture, and the post-war slump in sheep prices made land settlement in that county fraught with difficulties. However, the Shinness case demonstrates just how powerful Highland land hunger really was in the generation who survived the First World War. By any economic criteria crofting in Sutherland in the 1920s and 30s appears to have been a disaster, yet there was still not enough land to satisfy the applicants willing and eager to take up any vacant holding.

CHAPTER 5

Schemes in Other Crofting Counties

Argyll

Argyllshire, which includes the islands of Islay, Mull, Coll and Tiree, belongs firmly in the area covered by James Hunter's *The Making of the Crofting Community*, but the story of land settlement there differs from that of Sutherland, Skye, and the Outer Hebrides. This may have been partly because before the war the Duke of Argyll did not share the implacable opposition to land settlement which characterised so many of his contemporaries, and the settlement of at least some of the farms on his estates under the 1911 Act (see Chapter 1) clearly made a difference. Most of the land settlement schemes in Argyll, like those elsewhere in the West Highlands, resulted from actual or threatened raids, but, as will be seen, the scope of the demand in that county was much weaker than in Sutherland or the Hebrides.

The case of Ormsaigmore in the Ardnamurchan district is an example of a scheme which could not be implemented under the 1911 Act but which was brought to fruition under the 1919 Act.[1] A scheme was first mooted early in 1914. The 1437-acre farm was considered suitable for five new holdings from $4\frac{1}{2}$-$12\frac{1}{2}$ acres with a common pasture of 1394 acres. The cost at that stage was estimated at £1255. The landlord was not unwilling but insisted on his compensation claim being settled by arbitration.

The Land Court Order was not issued until December 1915. By the time the Board discussed the advisability of carrying on with the scheme early in 1916 they knew they had to pay a number of heavy compensation claims for loss of letting value. At Ormsaigmore it was the cost of arbitration rather than the anticipated award that the Board were worried about. The Small Holdings Commissioner believed the scheme should be abandoned immediately, while the Chairman argued that as it was such a desirable scheme (the five holdings being of a size and character likely to ensure success) it should go forward. The matter was put to the Secretary for Scotland who decided it was to be abandoned. In their Report for 1915 the Scottish Land Court gave this case as an example of how arbitration proceedings affected a scheme: 'It appeared that in the circumstances...the compensation to which Mr. Rudd might have been found entitled would not be very large; but the course adopted would have involved the Board in an arbitration in an outlying district of the country, the cost of which might be serious, and out of all proportion to the advantage which the constitution of five new holdings would confer.'[2]

In the summer of 1918, with the demand for holdings in Ardnamurchan said to be 'urgent and increasing', the Small Holdings Commissioner recommended that the scheme be revived, and the Board entered into fresh correspondence with the estate's agents. There was further disagreement over the question of compensation, but in April 1919 the Board was advised that the whole estate had been sold and the new owner was agreeable to the proposals. A sum of £750 was agreed for the settlement of the proprietor's compensation claim, and the Small Holdings Commissioner recommended that the scheme be proceeded with as 'the demand for holdings on this farm is intense.' In September the estate expressed their concern at the delay in settling the farm in view of the proprietor's agreement: 'a wave of discontent and suspicion is very prevalent among the applicants that they are badly treated and will be deprived of the holdings. ... The good faith in the Board is fast dwindling away and mistrust setting in at a very fast pace.' In December the Board advised the applicants that a decision had not yet been taken on whether the scheme would proceed.

The reason for the procrastination was that expenditure was now estimated to be around £3000. However, by February 1920 the Board wrote to the Under Secretary for Scotland. 'After carefully considering the question of costs in this case, the Board are agreed that the pressure for small holdings on the farm in question is so great as to make it desirable for them to proceed with the scheme even on the present high estimates.' This was approved by the Secretary for Scotland.

In October 1921 the Treasury asked the K & LTR for his observations. The latter noted that for a scheme of pastoral holdings the limit imposed after the Cabinet Committee Report was very much exceeded but added that the case had been brought specially to the notice of the Secretary for Scotland because of the insistent demand for holdings in the district. 'I am informed that the work is well on toward completion. It seems useless to criticise now especially as plans would be made and part of the work carried out before the limit was imposed.' By this time the scheme had been altered to provide only three holdings, and when the Treasury gave their sanction they expressed surprise and regret that a scheme of this kind should involve 'an expenditure on adaptation and equipment of £917 per holder and an annual deficit of about £44 per holder for twenty five years.'[3]

The scheme for Achalic & Lagnakeil in the Oban district settled only two holders and is unusual in having been instigated by men who were already on the land.[4] Their solicitor wrote to the Board in June 1920, stating that Mr McArthur, whose forefathers had been tenants of these farms for generations. and his son-in-law, Mr McPhee, had received notice to remove at Whitsunday 1921, and were anxious to continue their tenancy. 'They would be satisfied with a much smaller place than they have at present so long as they are allowed to retain a home in the district.' The solicitor asked if the Board could enquire if it was possible to create smallholdings on the farms, which were being taken over by the landlord. This was the period when the Board's finances were very straitened, and they declined to act.

The solicitor wrote two further letters to the Board, pointing out how much easier it would be if the men could remain rather than being removed and later brought back, but the Board remained obdurate. The North Argyll Liberal Association then took up the cause. The Board's response to the Secretary for Scotland's request for an explanation was that they did not think they should 'spend any of the limited balance of Land Settlement funds in protecting the tenants from removal under ordinary process of law.' But the North Argyll Liberal Association refused to drop the matter.

In December it was reported that the proprietor, a Mr Sinclair, was 'taking over all three farms on his estate and intended settling ex-service men on a profit sharing co-operative basis on the land.' The North Argyll Liberal Association wrote to the Board in February 1921

> They consider it unreasonable that the whole estate of Lerags should be resumed for experimental purposes, the scheme for which at present appears to be in a very nebulous state. No details of the scheme have been made public, and it is not known whether any ex-service men have definitely been asked to participate in it. There are already five ex-service [men] on the estate, and they do not appear to have been invited to cooperate; although with their local knowledge one would consider they would be the most suitable men for a scheme of this kind.

The Association also pointed out that very little expense would fall on the Board as the present tenants would take over the buildings and equipment they needed.

Whether it was this last consideration, or simply the political pressure being put on them, is not clear, but later that month the Board issued a notice of their intention to prepare a scheme for all the farms on the Lerags estate. They advised the Secretary for Scotland it was hoped this would induce the proprietor 'to show whether his proposals for the employment of ex-service men on the Estate on a profit sharing basis are made in good faith ... the reports made to the Board indicate that it is doubtful whether the landlord has any real intention to go on with the cooperative farming scheme.' Early in March the District Agricultural Committee for North Argyll sent a report on Sinclair's proposals but advised that owing to his serious illness 'the scheme may have to be considerably altered or even abandoned'. When the agents wrote later that month Sinclair was still very ill. They had advised him he might successfully contest the whole scheme, but in view of the state of his health he was willing to agree to the Board's carrying out a scheme on Achalic & Lagnakeil. (By this time Mr McArthur, one of the two original applicants, had died).

There was much more correspondence between the Board and agents before agreement was reached, the agents always insisting that 'any concessions we may make in the whole matter are made under compulsion and because Mr Sinclair's life is threatened by any excitement.' (He died soon after.) On 25 May the Secretary for Scotland's approval was urgently requested in order to settle the farm at Whitsun. After his approval was given it went before the Treasury who asked for the K & LTR's observations. Sir James Adam replied he had taken exception to so much arable land being absorbed by just two holders but had learned that the soil was very inferior and stony; also one of the new holders had an ex-service brother living with him, so that actually three men would be settled. 'The figures are within the limit laid down for average cost of arable holdings, and while these are partly arable and partly pastoral, it might be judicious to agree, as there is a good deal of unrest in the neighbourhood of Oban and it is very difficult to obtain any place there for land settlement.' He added, 'It is anticipated that if this scheme is put into operation, it will indicate that the Board has good intentions and will probably obviate any chance of disturbances.' The Treasury sanctioned the scheme. The amount of time and money expended on this scheme, and on Ormsaigmore, is a good indication of the way in which pressure to be seen to be doing something affected the policy of land settlement. The settling of a mere five men did not have any real impact on demand, except to show that the Board were trying.

At least the scheme for Balephetrish, Tiree, provided for a fairly large number of men.[5] As was seen in Chapter 1, most of the Duke of Argyll's estates on the island of Tiree were settled before the war, but there were exceptions, this farm being the most notable. The problem was the tenant, who ran the farm in conjunction with two other farms, Reef and Crossapol, and who insisted that the land asked for on Balephetrish could not be taken without damage to all three farms. At the Land Court hearing, which took place on 30 April 1913, the following interchange took place.

> **Q.** You cannot suggest any bit of land suitable for crofters or small land holders which the Board might apply for and which you would not object to? **A.** No, there is none whatever. **Q.** All your 3,000 acres are absolutely necessary to you to enable you to carry on the farm? **A.** Yes, in the way it has been for a very long time.

The Board amended the scheme, but in the months that followed the crofters grew increasingly restive at the delay and threatened forcible possession. The Land Court Order was issued on 15 December 1913, and a second Order, for amended conditions of let, was issued on 13 May 1914. But the Board had still not decided whether to proceed, as the tenant was claiming compensation of £3890. Even the amount awarded by the Court in June—£1243—seemed excessive to them, and they continued to dither. Meanwhile the crofters had actually begun cultivating the lands which they considered had been promised them, and when the Board decided to abandon the scheme the tenant's agents reacted with fury

> Your department pegged out the ground, selected the Applicants and told each applicant what he was to have and his rent and we understood gave them so long in each case to take or leave the land. They accepted the land and took possession. In this and other ways, your department went on with the scheme,

> and led all concerned to believe that it was being proceeded with. It was only after great trouble to our client that he afterwards got the applicants to leave the land and had to give them other concessions to get them to do this.

The Board did nothing, and in January 1918 some cottars took possession of a thirteen-acre field on the farm. Although they were old men with sons on active service, the Duke of Argyll took legal action, and they were imprisoned for ten days.[6] The Balephetrish 'raid' was remembered by two local men who were interviewed in the 1970s. As a boy one of them had helped to keep cattle off the illegally-planted ground. He recalled that at the time they were imprisoned the men had been asked to swear they would not break the law again, but they had refused to do so.[7]

Not long after the raid the tenant agreed to the Board taking control of 22 acres of land which was let as allotments to 22 landless cottars. A similar arrangement was made on Crossapol farm. This caused some difficulty after the war, because very few of the men, all of whom were keen to retain the land they held, had service qualifications. By that time the tenant had died, and the Duke of Argyll offered the Board all three farms for smallholdings. A scheme was formulated in 1920, and a report of March 1921 noted, 'It is well known that the Duke has offered the Board those farms for small holdings, and were anything to occur to prevent the carrying into effect of the settlement at Whitsunday 1922 considerable trouble might be expected.' No major obstacles were encountered, and the final scheme consisted of 38 new holdings and eight enlargements. However, the second Tiree man interviewed said that after the farms were broken up for crofters 'the majority of them weren't occupying the crofts at all, they were just letting them, letting the grazing and working at sea or working away from there.'[8] As will be seen in the next chapter, this situation was not unique to Tiree.

The above schemes were all carried out on privately-owned land, but the Board did purchase one large estate in Argyll, Sunart.[9]. Although by no means the complete disaster of Eriboll in Sutherland, the property still proved something of a white elephant. The reason for the purchase was the notice which the Board received at the beginning of 1918 of a 'strong and dangerous feeling existing on the land question' in the Strontian district.

The 50,000-acre estate of Sunart was entailed and therefore had to be sold as a whole. It was primarily a sporting estate, with even the agent admitting that only one-twentieth was arable: 'the great bulk of it is mountains and rocks'. Even given the fears of raiding and lawlessness, why did the Board consider such an estate? The sub-commissioner who reported in May 1919 seems to have got rather carried away with its supposed potential. He wrote enthusiastically, 'The Board of Agriculture can convert the whole territory into a valuable and economic asset to the nation by utilising the grazing to the fullest extent and increasing the sheep stock by some 10,000.' More mundanely, it was an undoubted fact that there were some 90 miserably small holdings on the estate and the holders were pressing for enlargements and threatening forcible possession if they did not get them.

There was by no means unanimity within the Board about the advisability of purchasing Sunart, but the Chairman was in favour, and so the Board submitted the scheme to the Secretary for Scotland. The three main advantages were said to be that (1) at least 80 new holdings and 90 enlargements could be provided (the only suitable lands for the latter were either part of the home farm or rented too low to be available under statute, so purchase was the only way of providing them), (2) there was no stock obligation, and (3) purchase and the creation of smallholdings would 'relieve unrest in the district'. The Board continued to dither, but in January 1920 they made the estate a formal offer; this was approved by the Secretary for Scotland after he was assured by the Chairman that it was 'a thoroughly sound and cheap proposition.' The Board then asked for Treasury approval. The K & LTR's response to the Treasury's request for his opinion was a lengthy one which concluded

> To me this seems the most uneconomic purchase the Board have yet put forward, as the creation of small holdings in the areas proposed will eliminate the sporting value of that portion of the property, and in addition to that I am informed that practically every alternate house of those at present standing will have to be pulled down, and a new one erected elsewhere, so as to make the very small holdings presently existing into holdings of reasonable size, in which case the future development will be extremely costly. On the other hand, you have the question of policy, and the Board is in a 'blue funk' as to what may occur if they don't acquire land and create holdings. All up the West Coast in the congested areas (where the population went to the war to a man), the people are relying on the Government's promise that land would be provided for them on their return, and as it is only very partially available for them as yet, there is very great discontent, and in many places they are raiding farms, and putting up houses on them for themselves. How far it is necessary to make uneconomic purchases of land to implement the pledges given by the Government is not for me to say, but it certainly looks as if there would be considerable trouble if the people do not get the holdings they expect, and maintain were promised to them.[10]

The Treasury gave their sanction but objected strongly to the Board's having already made a formal offer to the estate. The Board replied that the offer was made 'solely in order to keep matters open, and to prevent the sale of the Estate to another party before a decision could be reached by Their Lordships'.

In the summer the local M.P. began agitating because nothing had yet been done about settling the estate. At the same time an inspection was carried out by a new sub-commissioner. He began his reporting by stating, 'I read through the file and observed that in the Submission to the Treasury and the Secretary for Scotland it was given as a reason for the purchase of the estate that at the least 150 economic holdings could be made in place of 90 uneconomic holdings which were at present there. I cannot see any prospect of such an estimate being realised'. In March 1921 the M.P. was again agitating. The Board supplied the Secretary for Scotland with the following reply

The Board tell me that while this Estate was bought by them at Whitsunday, 1920, none of the leases has yet expired, the first falling out at Whitsunday next. This is why no holders have yet been actually settled.

I should tell you frankly for your own information that Sunart is not an easy scheme under present conditions. The property was bought by the Board because of the reported position in North Argyll and especially in the Strontian area, where at the time there was much local agitation and threatened seizures. Enquiries which the Board made show that the demand from ex-service men, to whom the Board are now practically restricted, is not by any means so acute as was represented.

Had the proposal to buy the property only now come up for consideration, it is probable it would have been rejected, and as it is the Board may have to reconsider the position to the extent of re-selling part or the whole of the Estate subject to the right to provide for the effective ex-service demand.

By the spring of 1922 four of the nine Sunart farms had been taken over by the Board on the expiry of their leases. They sought approval for a scheme of nine new holdings and 11 enlargements, pointing out that the position had significantly altered since their original proposal had been submitted, because the conditions imposed after the Cabinet Committee report restricted expenditure to £500 per holding. Also, the Board were now limited to ex-servicemen whereas the original demand had come from crofters on the estate wanting enlargements of their small and poor holdings, and few of these men had service qualifications. The ex-service demand, it was again admitted, had proved more apparent than real, and the schemes now submitted were expected to satisfy this demand. While discussions about the possibility of selling off the three farms held under long lease continued, in the summer of 1923 Treasury sanction was sought and given for expenditure in connection with schemes on six farms.

Sunart may not have been one of the wiser purchases made by the Board, but at least it did not have to be re-sold, and viable schemes were eventually carried out on the farms. The question of why—in such marked contrast to Sutherland and the Hebrides—the scope of ex-service demand in Argyll should have proved so much less than anticipated cannot, unfortunately, be answered here.

Inverness-shire[11]

This county is entirely Highland, but much of it belongs to the central and eastern Highlands rather than to the west (in his map of the area in which the crofting community was made, James Hunter included only the western part of Inverness-shire). Because communication between the central Highlands and Lowland Scotland was comparatively easy (and Gaelic was giving ground to English) depopulation had been a gradual process. For the most part the people had been able to go elsewhere in easy stages without the trauma of forcible eviction. Thus there was not the same pressure to regain the land as existed to the west and north. Where demand for holdings existed, it was usually expressed in archetypal Highland fashion, i.e. for a specific farm and accompanied by threats of forcible possession. However, the threats were rarely serious, and the situation never got out of hand as it did in the western Highlands.

An important landowner in Inverness-shire was Lord Lovat, who has been encountered in earlier chapters as a strong opponent of land settlement. After the war such an attitude, if made public, would have been considered unpatriotic, but there were indirect ways of hampering land settlement, and Dell farm provides a classic example.[12] The property was inspected in March 1921 when the sub-commissioner reported

> This Farm is very suitable for Small Holdings as the proportion of arable is exceptionally large for a hill grazing Farm. The land is easy to work, being practically level. If cultivated a considerable number of cattle could be reared, and the pastures improved for sheep stock. Both land and buildings have been shamefully neglected, and at present there is not a man or beast on the Farm, although it is capable of carrying a breeding stock of 300 Ewes, besides cattle and horses. The Farm could be divided to form six holdings, and already there are suitable applicants for them.

Although the lease did not expire until 1930, the tenant, who also occupied three other large farms in Inverness-shire, was apparently willing to facilitate a scheme.

The scheme for six holdings was submitted to Lord Lovat, who insisted he agreed in principle, but the correspondence with his agents dragged on for months while he quibbled over various points. At the end of December Lovat wrote direct to the Director of Land Settlement, Sir Arthur Rose, proposing a new scheme, for only three holdings. An internal memo by one of of the Board's officers to Land Division in January 1922 concluded: 'In my view the Estate are trifling with the proposal & I consider the Scheme as drafted should be pushed forward to the Board. Otherwise Lord Lovat will, as is usual, turn round & blame the Board for leaving the Farm derelict in his hands.'

By May the Board agreed to Lovat's proposal to restrict the scheme to three holdings. However, the three men selected by the proprietor refused the holdings, the first because the land was already occupied by a friend for whose disabled nephew the holding was originally intended and the second and third because the holdings were too large for the amount of capital they possessed. The local sub-commissioner reported that he had heard in Inverness that 'there is a feeling in the district that Lord Lovat had really proposed the 3 holding scheme to defeat the ends of the applicants who were all satisfied with the 6 holdings scheme.'

On 7 June the farm was raided. This was reported in *The Glasgow Herald* on that date and in *The Scotsman* and *Inverness Courier* on 9 June, by which time Lord Lovat had arrived on the scene. *The Scotsman* said 'The news of the land raid in Stratherrick, Inverness-shire, has caused something of a sensation among the inhabitants of that quiet and scattered district. The raid was carried out by four of the ex-Service applicants for the farm of the Dell who, at the close of their day's work, proceeded to the farm and drove into the ground pegs with their names on them.' The *Inverness Courier* insisted that the whole thing had been exaggerated because 'an attempt is being made to work up a land agitation in the North, or, at the very least to create an impression that a dangerous atmosphere exists in the Highlands.' During the 45-minute wait for the train south from Inverness Lord Lovat had provided the *Courier* with his version of the story, and the paper laid full blame on the Board, praising Lovat for the number of ex-servicemen he had settled on his lands.

The local sub-commissioner advised that after innumerable discussions 'Lovat practically agreed to almost revert to the Board's old Scheme'. The Secretary of the Board wrote privately to the Scottish Office, 'So far as I can find out Lord Lovat must have hurried north whenever he heard of the trouble; and while I think he has done the right thing at this juncture, his incentive was as much to save his own dignity as anything else, because the compromise which he now suggests is a perfect climb down.' During the rest of the summer endless meetings took place with the crofters and estate factor, and by the end of September agreement had been reached for four holdings with a fifth applicant making arrangements for a holding direct with the proprietor.

The story of Balloch farm did not have such a satisfactory ending.[13] On 20 January 1921 a senior sub-commissioner advised Sir Arthur Rose that the farm was likely to be on the market as the tenant had died, and that the local sub-commissioner considered it very suitable for smallholdings. He also informed the Director of Land Settlement that the agents for the Culloden Trustees had on three previous occasions when the Board were interested in farms on the estate 'hastened to put them out of our reach by either selling or letting.' The local sub-commissioner believed they were already trying to let the farm without advertising it so that unless a formal notice was served immediately this farm would also be lost to the Board. Even while writing this the senior sub-commissioner received a telegram from the local man advising that 'offers are being invited privately and will be considered on Saturday'. The formal notice was served by the Board on 21 January.

After inspecting the farm the sub-commissioner reported, 'There is a keen demand for land in the neighbourhood of Inverness, and as it is seldom that such a change occurs in the tenancy of such a suitable subject, and so conveniently situated, I strongly recommend that the opportunity should not be lost of formulating a scheme here.' This was not, however, going to be an easy matter, for the agents insisted the farm had been let before the notice had been served (which meant high compensations costs would be payable to the tenant), and they refused to cooperate in any way. The Board nevertheless decided to press on with the scheme to the stage of a hearing, and after various requests for postponements by the agents, and other delays, the hearing finally took place on 26 September 1922, when the estate raised numerous objections to the scheme.

On 26 October the Board asked for approval to proceed, and the Under

Secretary for Scotland explained to the Secretary for Scotland: 'This is an opposed scheme and the Board are preparing and will submit in due course a Compulsory Order. The proprietors will probably make representations to you against the confirmation of the Order, and at that stage you will have to consider whether or not you will confirm the Order. Approval of this submission merely means that you authorise the Board to submit the scheme to the Treasury. If the Treasury turn it down on financial grounds, that of course is an end to the matter. If, however, they approve, it will still be for you to decide whether the Compulsory Order is to be issued.'

The Treasury asked for the opinion of Sir James Adam, the K & LTR, who replied, 'There is a considerable amount of compensation to the landlord and tenant involved in this scheme. In regard to this the Board say that there are about 300 ex-service applicants and that there is the greatest difficulty in getting the necessary land in that district.' At this stage the Secretary for Scotland decided it was worth investigating purchase of the farm, making it a Part I scheme. Correspondence dragged on with the agents through 1923 and 1924, during which time the farm acquired a new owner, but the asking price was more than the Board was willing to pay, and the scheme was abandoned.

There is a postscript to this story, for in 1937 the idea of purchasing the farm arose again. The senior sub-commissioner recommended that the Department go ahead with it, as it was in a district 'where suitable available land is *very* scarce and where the demand for holdings is very strong.' However, once again the asking price was too high, and the scheme was abandoned.

A third Inverness-shire case illustrates how much time and trouble could be spent on a scheme for just one or two holdings; it also provides elements of unintentional comedy not often found in this material. Applications for the farm of Kincraig on the Mackintosh estate were received from two men, Peter Stuart, an ex-serviceman and a cottar on the estate, who asked for some arable land near his cottage, and Donald Mackintosh who was considered suitable for a new holding.[14] After a great deal of correspondence in the course of 1919 and 1920, the Board advised Donald Mackintosh that the estate would not agree to his becoming a landholder but was willing to lease land to him; his reply was that he 'will have nothing to do with a Holding under the proprietor's regulations.' The scheme was abandoned. Both Stuart and Mackintosh threatened forcible possession.

In January 1921 an internal memo concluded, 'In view of the strong feeling in the district and the Proprietor's hostile attitude toward Land Settlement, the Senior Sub-Commissioner recommends that the correspondence be placed before the Director of Land Settlement that he may know the position and decide the course of action.' In February the Board wrote to the estate re-opening negotiations. The eventual outcome of these was that Donald Mackintosh was to be registered as a landholder but Peter Stuart was not.

In December 1921 Stuart wrote to the Prime Minister, complaining about his position. The Board provided the necessary information for the official reply. 'As Mr Stuart has received a reasonable offer of a holding, outside the provision of the Landholders Acts, they would not be justified in pressing his application further against The Mackintosh ... Mr Stuart would be well advised to accept the offer made to him. In any event, the Board have no compulsory power over the lands offered to Mr Stuart by The Mackintosh, in order to obtain the former's registration as a new holder.' On 29 July 1922 Stuart sent the following letter to the Board

> Sir, I hereby beg to intimate to your Board that I am at an early date to take possession of the field on the left hand side of the County Road as you go North on the Farm of Kincraig and just opposite the field I have at present.
>
> My reason for this is first, I have got neither road nor water supply where my steading is at present. All enquiry made by letters as to this are left unanswered; second, this ten acres arable which I have got will not keep me going and no other work in the district. I don't see why I should not share in the land that is going to waste. I should not have done this if I had been fairly dealt with. I am now forced in more ways than one to take action. There is only a leader required in Badenoch to set the heather burning, you and others had full warning. I am taking all responsibility, quite prepared to go to Prison or bear any punishment the law may pass on me, but that's not going to get you out of trouble, wait and see. ... If I had anything like fair play I would be struggling along with it, but seeing I am only laughed at and not even answers to my letters. No that's not going to do the old Soldier. I may be led, but they are not in Scotland that will drive me. You can bring your Shooting Party if you like.

The Board attached no importance to the threat. On 22 August they advised the Under Secretary for Scotland that they had just received an unsigned telegram: 'Stuart has raided Kincraig Farm to-day'. They were fairly certain it was Stuart himself who had sent the telegram after he had taken occupation of the field in question. They further advised the Under Secretary that they did not consider it necessary to 'take any action in the matter of this "raid", but they are instructing their local officers to make discreet enquiries and to keep them advised as to the developments which take place.' The *Daily Record* printed the story of 'A One Man Land Raid', as did the *Aberdeen Daily Journal*, with the sub-head, 'Ex-Soldier Seizes Field in Inverness-shire'. No one else took any notice. Stuart continued to agitate, and in 1923 the local M.P. took up his case again. The Board advised the Under Secretary for Scotland that they 'do not consider that Mr. Stuart is occupying the ground under any real disadvantage, and they cannot see that any useful purpose will be served by reopening discussions either with the factor or Mr. Stuart.'[15] So Peter Stuart's raid on the field did not produce the desired result.

The case of Ardersier Mains, near Inverness, provides a good example of a proprietor ultimately offering to sell rather than have a Part II scheme imposed on him.[16] The farm was considered an excellent one for smallholdings, as the land was all of good quality, and it was considered that at least ten self-supporting holdings could be formed. In March 1920 Secretary for Scotland approval for a Part II scheme was given, but there ensued a battle with the Treasury over whether the proposal to pay the proprietor in respect of existing buildings from money allocated for the adaptation of the land was competent. Sir Kenneth Mackenzie's comment (as K & LTR) on the proposal shows very clearly his attitude toward land settlement policy

> This scheme, considered an exceptionally good one by the Board of Agriculture, illustrates well how destructive to the country is this policy of creating small holdings. Here is a farm which in its present state brings in £393 a year. After spending £7575 of public money on it, its return for taxation purposes is to be only £293! On the other hand it comes within the limits allowed and I suppose you must agree.[17]

Meanwhile, the proprietor objected strongly to the Board's proposals. The formal hearing was held in December. The proprietor's main representation was that some large farms should be left on his estate for smallholders to aspire to. The Chairman of the Board wryly noted, 'this argument is somewhat invalidated by the fact that the last occupant of Ardersier Mains was a pluralist farmer. In any case', he added, 'the proportion of large farms throughout the county will provide for many years sufficient scope for the ambitions of small-holders.' The Chairman approved of the scheme going ahead, and a Confirming Order was issued on 31 January 1922. The proprietor's agents objected, but the Secretary for Scotland eventually consented to the scheme.

Some months later, when agreement could not be reached over compensation, the agents suggested the Board should acquire the farm by feu, which the Board thought a good idea. The Under Secretary advised the Secretary for Scotland, 'This is a case where the proprietor has agreed to a feu rather than have the 1911 Act tenure imposed upon him.' Acquisition of the farm under Part I of the Act was approved by the Secretary for Scotland and sanctioned by the Treasury in November.

In the case of Beolary in Glenelg parish, there was no difficulty in purchasing the farm, which was offered to the Board by the Forestry Commission in May 1922, but a great deal of difficulty in settling it.[18] In June 1923, a year after the Board took entry, the sub-commissioner advised that there was no local demand for holdings of the type intended for Beolary and carrying a large sheep stock. The Board first offered the holdings to Kintail applicants who refused, then to ex-service applicants in Skye, where the local officer advised that it would be difficult to find suitable men to go to a farm on the mainland where there were no houses.

The Board were forced to go on managing the farm for another year. A revised scheme was put forward by the senior sub-commissioner, but this actually increased the average cost per holder from £756 (already well over the Treasury limit of £500 for Highland pastoral holdings) to £768. Nevertheless, the Board 'felt that the acquisition of the property by the Forestry Commission and the development of their plans for its utilisation left them no alternative but to proceed with the scheme of land settlement.' In view of the cost per holder, and the fact that the Board now intended to ask for no more than 10% in cash of the total sheep stock, it was necessary to return to the Treasury.

One member of the Treasury certainly gave vent to his feelings in his internal memo on this proposal: 'It's really outrageous that the Board should rush us into a half-baked scheme, and then let matters drag on and expenses mount up, until we are finally confronted after 2 years with the same scheme at more than double the cost.' He thought the K & LTR ought to be consulted about abandoning the scheme. One can well imagine what Sir Kenneth Mackenzie would have had to say, but his successor, Sir James Adam, was a very different character.

> I fear the Board are fully committed to this scheme. The original scheme on the papers seemed all right and originated with the Forestry Commission as a joint scheme for afforestation and small holdings. The difficulty of getting qualified ex-service men is undoubtedly their objection to going to this outlandish place and the only way out seems to be to allow the applicants from a distance or from Skye to migrate. ... The Board were rushed into this scheme by the desire to co-operate with the Forestry Commission and this of course is hardly an excuse but unfortunately the commitments were made.[19]

The Treasury gave their reluctant sanction in April 1924. Nine new holders were eventually found, six from Skye and three from Glenelg (two of the latter had been shepherds on the farm). Of the nine, only four were ex-service men.

The difficulty, clearly, was that the Board had purchased the farm because the Forestry Commission had offered it to them, rather than because applicants had asked for holdings on it. In densely-populated Highland areas there were always more applicants than holdings, but Highlanders did not share the willingness of their Lowland counterparts to move to another area in order to get a holding; their attachment was normally to a particular spot where they insisted on remaining. It was because in most parts of Inverness-shire there did not exist the large numbers of landless men found in the western Highlands and Islands that land settlement in this county followed a different pattern.

Ross & Cromarty[20]

In common with Inverness-shire, only the western section of this county figures in James Hunter's *The Making of the Crofting Community*; however, unlike eastern Inverness-shire, Easter Ross was geographically lowland and English speaking. So, although the whole of Ross & Cromarty was considered administratively to be a 'crofting county', in practice the two sections were treated very differently. The Highland section of the county resembled the more western parts of Inverness-shire, areas about which Hunter wrote that if those straths remained deserted it was because the evictors there had been more thorough and ruthless than in the Hebrides.[21] Easter Ross was treated in the same way as Lowland counties in that schemes were normally carried out on farms which had been purchased rather than on privately-owned land.

Point farm in the Gairloch district is a good example of the Highland situation there.[22] The proprietor was none other than the former K & LTR, Sir Kenneth Mackenzie, who was approached by the Board in August 1921. At that time the tenant was in bad health and Sir Kenneth wanted to wait and see if he recovered before taking matters further. In January 1922 the Board were informed that the farm would become vacant at Whitsun. It was considered suitable for five new holdings and seven enlargements, and a notice was duly served. Sir Kenneth's proposed holders were not ex-servicemen, but he agreed to take others as long as first chance was given to ex-servicemen from the Gairloch estate. The scheme appeared ready to proceed when, on 24 May, the Board suddenly withdrew their notice. Sir Kenneth was absolutely furious as arrangements had been made for the tenant to quit the farm. No explanation was given to him for this action, though an internal minute advised that the time available had been too short to obtain Secretary for Scotland and Treasury sanction.

After further correspondence and animadversions by Sir Kenneth on the Board's conduct, it was agreed that a scheme would be put forward to commence at Whitsun 1923. At this point there was a further snag as Sir Kenneth insisted on receiving the value of buildings and fences from the Board with the holders' rents to be in respect of bare land only, although this went against a recent legal opinion that buildings should remain in possession of the landlord whilst the holders paid rent for land plus buildings and other permanent improvements. The Treasury were most unhappy about Sir Kenneth's attitude—his former office of K & LTR made it worse in their eyes—but eventually they capitulated and sanctioned the scheme.

In March 1924 the senior sub-commissioner sent a minute to Land Division: 'Inform the Estate Factor that every effort has been made to find ex-service tenants from the Gairloch Estate and Parish for the holdings, but without success. Ask in the circumstances if they would agree to give the holdings to Harris ex-service applicants.' A memo to the Board advised

> A number of ex-service applicants resident in the Parish of Gairloch declined the holdings when offered. Further efforts to obtain holders were made by advertising in the Press and by posting up particulars of the holdings at Post Offices in the Gairloch area, but without satisfactory results. The reason for this lack of demand would appear to be the want of housing accommodation provided under the scheme. Only one of the five holdings has existing buildings; the tenants of the others were to be assisted to build houses with the aid of £100 loans. The farm is 11 miles distant from the village of Gairloch.

The senior sub-commissioner proposed that huts be erected on the four holdings without buildings to provide temporary accommodation. Expenditure for this purpose was sanctioned at the end of May. However, in September the Board advised the Secretary for Scotland that suitable candidates still had not been found and additional financial sanction was required for the Board to continue managing the farm themselves. In April 1926 the Board wrote to the Secretary for Scotland

> notwithstanding the provision which was made for temporary accommodation...and notwithstanding their continued and widespread efforts, the Board have failed to secure suitable applicants for the holdings. It would appear that the remote and isolated situation of the farm...is the cause of the refusal of applicants to take up these holdings.

The Board's proposed solution was to form a single holding, for which they had an applicant in mind. This was approved by the Secretary for Scotland, but Sir Kenneth Mackenzie refused to consider the idea. In view of his opposition, the Board made a fresh attempt to find men from Harris, but without success. In December a sub-commissioner reported that 'the feeling among the applicants was that so long as there was land available in Harris they were not prepared to go to Gairloch.'

In March 1927 the Board advised Sir Kenneth that efforts to secure holders from Harris had failed and asked him to reconsider allowing the single-holding scheme. Once again he refused. In May the Chairman of the Board wrote to him personally, admitting that the demand had proved 'illusive' and concluding his letter by saying that the Board could not go on managing the farm indefinitely, and if agreement could not be reached on the current proposal they would have to embark on a compulsory scheme. In July Sir Kenneth replied

> It is freely stated in Parliament that you have vast numbers of applicants for such holdings. If you can't get them to Point wouldn't it be wise to tell Parliament quite frankly that as far as this area of Scotland goes, the small holding idea is 'bust'. The people themselves know (just as well as you and I) that going into these places on money borrowed for stock and buildings from your Board means starting with a millstone round their necks and a life struggle of hopeless poverty. ... I am not surprised, therefore, that you find it difficult to get tenants, but this is your job which the Legislation in its wisdom! has provided you with and you are expected to live up to it!

By the end of December he very reluctantly agreed to the single-holding scheme, but his misgivings proved to be only too well founded. In 1929 and 1930 the estate factor advised the Department that the tenant owed two years rent and had never resided on the farm, 'in which apparently he takes little or no interest.' In fact the tenant also owed the Department a considerable sum for buildings and charges incurred on his behalf. Legal action was eventually taken against him.

This story once again points up regional differences in the demand for holdings. No applicants had asked for land on this farm, which was a clear indication that the demand did not exist in that area. It must, however, be emphasised that such a situation occurred only in those parts of the Highlands where there were no crofting townships.

In Easter Ross—the lowland part of the county—the Board made one of its earliest purchases, Arabella farm, in 1918, under the Small Holdings Colonies Acts.[23] The farm comprised 603 acres of arable land and 41 acres outrun and woodland, and the scheme provided 21 new holdings, ranging in size from six to 50 acres. There was also a large central farm which acted as a demonstration centre for the instruction of the holders as well as affording facilities for the hire of horses and implements. Central farms of this nature proved very helpful to holders in the early stages of a settlement but were thereafter unnecessary, and in 1924 Treasury sanction was granted to break up Arabella's central farm into smallholdings. At that time an internal Treasury memo noted, 'The Arabella Scheme, one of the early "commitments", was fabulously expensive.[24]

The Department of Agriculture purchased several other farms in Easter Ross during the late 1920s (e.g. Tomich & Broomhill, Kinbeachie, Kinkell, Radderty), but apart from running battles with the Treasury over cost, settlement of these farms generally went very smoothly.

Caithness

Because Caithness lies adjacent to Sutherland in the far north, it is often mistakenly thought of as Highland in character. In reality it is very flat, and its cultural background is Scandinavian, not Celtic. The characteristic which Caithness did share with its neighbour (apart from the fact that the same Member of Parliament represented both), was that much of the land had been cleared for large-scale sheep farming. Caithness was one of the crofting counties, and strenuous efforts were made under the 1911 Act to break up some of the large sheep farms into smallholdings. However, although there was certainly a great demand for holdings, the persistent land hunger of Sutherland was not prevalent in Caithness.

It was in Caithness that the Board of Agriculture made one of their earliest purchases, the farm of West Watten.[25] They had first considered the property in 1917; the proprietrix was against a scheme but offered to sell West Watten. It was considered very suitable for ex-soldiers and sailors, but the proportion of arable land (816 acres) to pastoral (2916 acres) made it unavailable under the Small Holdings Colonies Act of 1916 and even the amended Act of 1918. (It is not clear why the Board did not exercise their powers under the Congested Districts Act in this case, as they did in Sutherland; the sub-commissioner suggested they did so, but the suggestion was never taken up.)

Toward the end of 1918 the estate was receiving offers for the tenancy, and the Board advised the Secretary for Scotland that the proprietrix was willing to lease the farm to them for a year from Whitsunday 1919 in order to leave options open for both sides; this was approved and the Board became tenants at that time. With the passing of the Land Settlement Act at the end of the year, the Board began to negotiate for the purchase of the farm. Inevitably the estimates of what the property was worth differed widely: the Board reckoned the price at £12,865 while the estate reckoned it at £17,000.

In the spring of 1920 the Board received authorisation from the Secretary for Scotland to renew the lease for another year. In September Sir Arthur Rose noted the results of his interview with the factor. The trustees were not happy with the Board's offer of £15,000, but it was felt that the scheme should go on, first because it was a good one 'with every prospect of success for the holders', and second because 'the Board having been in occupation for two years their withdrawal now would raise a considerable local storm.' Eventually agreement was reached at £14,000 with a payment by feu or rent charge over a period of thirty years at 6% interest. (The dwelling house and garden and a field of 23 acres were excluded from the final scheme, hence the acceptance of this price.)

The Board then had to convince the Treasury of the viability of the scheme, which provided 22 new holdings at a cost of £1300 per holder (exclusive of the land and loans for stocking). The Board pressed for a decision urgently as 'unless the subjects are bought now, they will be otherwise disposed of by the Estate who are at the moment proposing to sell the property.' However, the Treasury insisted that the Board should reduce the size of the proposed holdings and the capital expenditure in equipment; the Board in reply claimed that 'the proposed expenditure has been reduced to the minimum.'

At the end of December the K & LTR wrote a long critical report on the proposed scheme.[26] He considered the arable holdings on the large side and had suggested to Sir Arthur Rose that it might be possible 'to form several quite small holdings on which settlers might be put, who would make a living by outside labour, poultry, shop keeping, or jobbing work such as carpentry, tailoring or shoemaking.' He went on: 'It seems to me that with the large number of men still awaiting settlement in Caithness, as many as possible should be placed on this farm.' By reducing the size of the purely arable holdings and adding some eight or ten very small holdings, the average cost per holder would be considerably reduced. In view of the K & LTR's remarks, the Treasury continued to press the Board to increase the number of holdings in the scheme.

The Board wrote privately to the factor at the end of January 1921, regretting they did not yet have Treasury approval; negotiations for purchase had been authorised but the scheme itself was not sanctioned. However, in order to allow some progress to be made, Sir Arthur Rose had agreed that the Board should make the estate a formal offer (subject, of course, to Treasury approval). 'Although this is not strictly in accordance with Treasury procedure, I am certain that they will raise no objections to the terms we propose to offer you. It is our scheme to which they object & from enquiries which we have been making I think we shall be able to meet them on this.' The revised scheme presented to the Treasury in February provided for 28 holdings, six of which were allotments requiring no equipment. This was approved although the Treasury still considered the estimated annual deficits 'regrettably high'.

In 1921 a member of the Board reported: 'It can safely be claimed that in no county has a greater number of more satisfactory land settlement schemes been carried through than in Caithness. The holdings are usually of a fair size, about 60 acres, and men of a good type, coming from the crofters and farm workers, have been found for the holdings.'[27]

Shetland

The northern isles, like Caithness, were culturally Scandinavian rather than Celtic. However, there were differences between Orkney and Shetland: 'Shetland comes nearer socially to the Hebrides than to Orkney—the Shetlander being, like many of the Lewismen, a fisherman with a croft, while the Orkneyman is a small farmer.'[28] Perhaps this was why land hunger appears to have been so much fiercer in Shetland than in Orkney. (Orkney land settlement schemes proved so straightforward that they are not discussed here.) The impetus for land settlement in Shetland came from crofters wanting new holdings or enlargements. As will be seen below, acquiring land for this purpose could be a protracted affair.[29]

On 25 April 1914 the applicants for enlargements on the farm of Burrafirth, Unst, wrote to the Board,

> It is now more than two years since the long looked for Small Land Holders Act became law & nearly the same time since our application was forwarded to you and still there is not the least sign of us obtaining the much needed enlargement of our Holdings. And in a short time we will have to reduce our poorly fed stock. ... At a meeting of the applicants held lately the majority would have been in favour of driving our animals on the ground thus taking possession. Please let us know what hope there is of us obtaining the land referred to.

That spring a scheme was prepared for enlargement of common pasture for 27 holders and correspondence was instigated with the agents. However, the agents' terms, involving heavy compensation and stringent conditions, were considered too onerous by the Board, who decided it was not worth doing anything more until the lease expired in 1918. In November 1916 the Small Holdings Commissioner stated

> The applicants have at various times threatened to take forcible possession and I have no doubt that were the Board to take no steps in the matter they will enter on the land at the termination of the present tenancy. Should the crofters, who with their sons have helped to man the Navy and Army, be refused the land they will be in a position to defy the law with impunity, because it can be pointed out that the farm fulfils all the conditions required by the Small Landholders Act.

He added, 'I strongly recommend that if anything is to be done to provide holdings for Shetlanders in 1918 it should be started now, otherwise the inevitable result will be a muddle at the end.'

This proved to be a typical example of the Board's failure to plan ahead for demobilisation, for the Small Holdings Commissioner's advice was not taken, and the next entry in the file, in November 1917, noted that it was most unlikely everything could be settled in time for Martinmas 1918 entry.

Correspondence with the agents was resumed, but in January 1918 little hope of agreement was seen, 'as there is too much difference between the negotiating parties.' In February the Board asked for sanction to apply to the Land Court for a compulsory order, leaving the method of settling landlord's compensation to be left for a later decision. The Secretary for Scotland gave his sanction in May, 'with considerable hesitation', and only because 'the demand seems to be considerable'. At the end of that month the agents came forward with new proposals for compensation, and correspondence began again, without, however, bringing matters any closer to fruition. In November the applicants wrote bitterly,

> After waiting six years for the lease to run, we consider it very unfair of the board to keep us in the dark we therefore again appeal to the Board to give us a satisfactory answer what has our Sons and Brothers fought for and laid down their lives for if those that return are to be denied the land they have so dearly bought.

The letter concluded with a threat of force.

Correspondence with the agents dragged on over the first few months of 1919; at one stage the possibility of purchase was considered but rejected. In August the Board advised the Secretary for Scotland that because they had been considering purchase they had not yet applied to the Land Court. The tenant was still sitting but had given notice to quit at Martinmas next. A revised scheme for one new holding and 31 enlargements had been submitted to the agents and was about to be lodged with the Land Court. In view of the threat of illegal seizure of the farm, the Board requested permission to proceed with the scheme in anticipation of the Land Court Order. The holders were in fact settled at Martinmas 1919, although the compensation question was not settled until 1922.[30]

In December 1917 the Small Holdings Commissioner drew the attention of Land Division to the fact that the lease for Quendale farm, Dunrossness, would expire at Martinmas 1918, and recommended that the estate be asked if they would be willing to make land available.[31] In April 1918 the County Council petitioned for 'land in Shetland for the settlement of discharged Soldiers and Sailors, with the dependants of men who have fallen in the service of the Country during the war.' The Board wrote to the estate, and after initial opposition the estate agreed to make a part of the farm—which was the home farm and therefore not available under compulsory procedures—available.

In November 1919 the estate advised the Board that the following Martinmas would be the most suitable time for entry and the tenant had been given notice accordingly. A scheme was submitted in February 1920, but by September the estate had heard nothing further from the Board and were getting anxious as Martinmas was fast approaching. A telegram at the beginning of October advised the Board, 'Feeling of unrest prevails among Dunrossness applicants with threat of Raid on Quendale unless scheme proceeded November term'. This was the period when the Board's finances were at their lowest ebb, and only schemes to which they were absolutely committed were being implemented. A minute from the senior sub-commissioner advised Land Committee that the Director of Land Settlement thought the scheme should be withdrawn as there was no sanction of any kind. He himself disagreed:

> After fully considering the whole circumstances of the case I recommend that the scheme should go forward at the coming Martinmas term. I do not think the Board can decently withdraw at this stage because (1) The Tenant is under notice to quit at the Board's request, (2) Subject to the scheme proceeding the tenants were selected and although no *promise* of a holding was made to any man, they will no doubt look on the holdings as good as theirs. (3) The maximum total cost of the scheme (which would settle 38 applicants) is only estimated at £1554. (4) Practically nothing in the way of land settlement has been done in Shetland since the war, and only one scheme is proceeding—for 4 people.

The Board did not in fact settle the farm that year, and further threats of forcible seizure followed. In February 1921 the estate wrote to the Board that the actions of 'certain malcontent seditious socialists or Bolshevists', who had threatened forcible possession of the land, had aggravated the condition of the tenant who was 'suffering from a nervous breakdown combined with heart weakness'. That same month the applicants withdrew their threat to raid, and in March the Secretary for Scotland's approval was sought and given for a scheme to proceed; Treasury sanction followed in April.

In May it transpired that there were rival claims to the land, the existing holders wanting enlargements while ex-service applicants demanded new holdings. The views of the latter prevailed. In August the local M.P. sent the Board a petition protesting at the delay. The Board explained that a scheme had been prepared, 'but in response to strong representations made by ex-servicemen in Quendale district, the Board have at present under consideration the question of revising the scheme in order that the claims of these ex-service men may be more fully satisfied'.

As far as the Board were concerned, the three arguments in favour of the new scheme were that a larger number of bona fide ex-service applicants would be settled; the existing crofts were of a substantial size for Shetland and had previously been enlarged by the estate; and the estimated cost was nearly the same as before since the applicants for the proposed new holdings had stated they would provide any necessary new buildings. The scheme—for 13 new holdings and a common enlargement for 13 existing crofters—went forward, and the holders were settled at Martinmas.[32]

As a postscript to this story, the Department received a petition from landholders, cottars and others resident in Quendale district in 1938, asking that the rest of the farm—which would become vacant at Martinmas—be constituted into new holdings and enlargements. The existing crofts were too small to support the holders' families, particularly since the herring fishing had failed in recent years. Also, new holdings would provide employment for members of their families. The Department took the petition seriously, but before a scheme had been prepared the farm was re-let on a 21-year lease, which ruled out any further action by the Department.[33]

The aim of this chapter has been to illustrate the difficulties of breaking up large farms into small holdings within the different regions. Sometimes the landowner held up proceedings; at other times the inefficiency and shilly-shallying of the Board of Agriculture were more to blame. No attempt has been made to present a comprehensive picture of land settlement in various crofting counties, and generalisations would be out of place in view of the many regional differences.

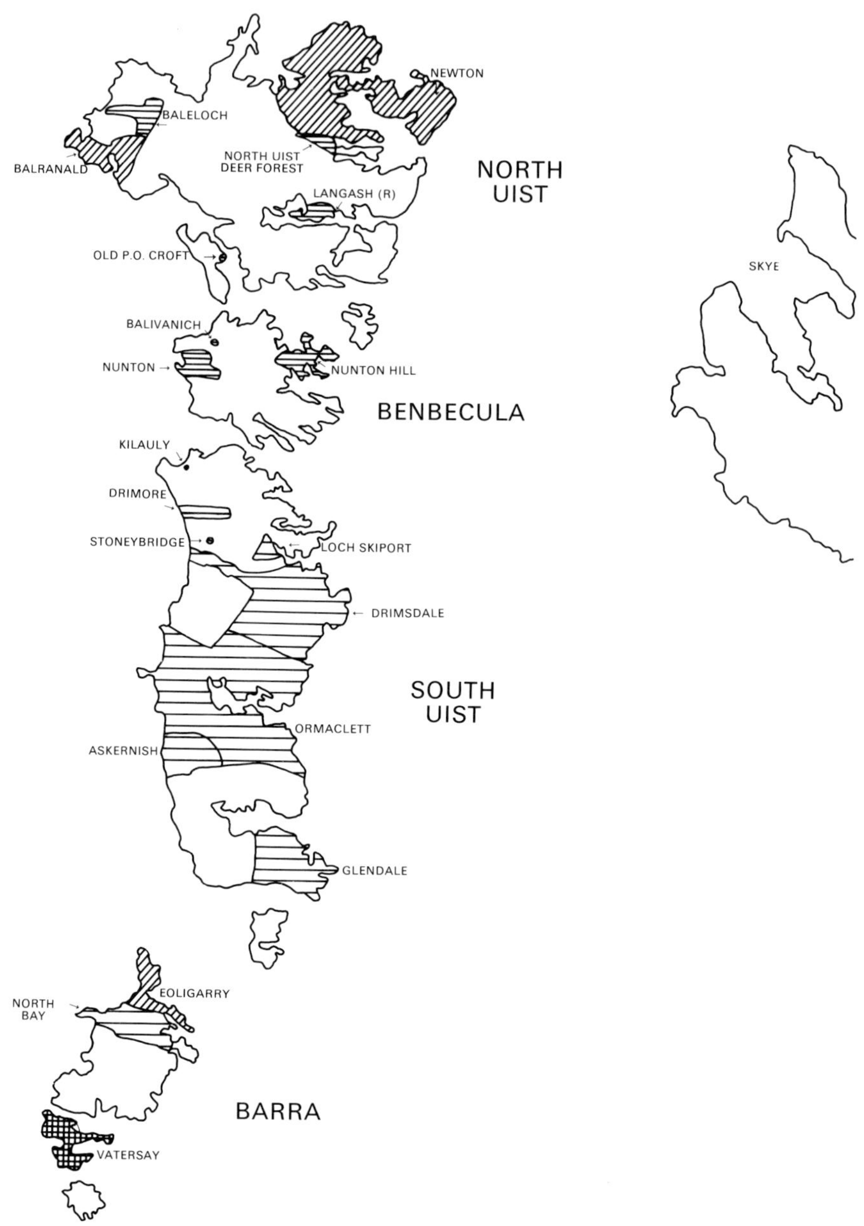

3 Map of North Uist, Benbecula, South Uist and Barra.

CHAPTER 6

Schemes in the Long Island

The chain of islands (now connected by causeways)—North Uist, Benbecula and South Uist, along with the island of Barra to the south—were the scene of some of the most brutal clearances of the nineteenth century,[1] so it is hardly surprising that the backlash in that area was so great. South Uist and Benbecula were owned by one woman, Lady Gordon Cathcart (proprietrix from 1878 until her death in 1932), who was implacably opposed to land settlement on her estates, and the difficulties faced by the Board of Agriculture in settling these estates form the greater part of this chapter. Barra was a somewhat different case, as Lady Cathcart had sold much of the island before the passage of the 1911 Act. North Uist was owned by more than one proprietor so the story there was also different.

South Uist and Benbecula

Lady Gordon Cathcart had already experienced the Hebrideans' determination to gain possession of the land long before the Board of Agriculture was created. There had been agitation on her estates in the 1880s and 1890s,[2] and in the early years of the twentieth century she had succumbed to pressure and allowed some of her farms to be broken up by the Congested Districts Board. However, she retained various farms from which the islanders had been evicted in earlier periods, and the passage of the 1911 Act raised the hopes of landless men that more such farms might be regained.

In May 1912 the new Board of Agriculture wrote to Lady Cathcart's agents, Skene, Edwards & Garson, asking if she was disposed to offer any of her lands for smallholdings.[3] Their reply was that Lady Cathcart had recently broken up various farms at the government's urging and with the cooperation of the Congested Districts Board; at that time she had been told that if fifty new holdings were formed in South Uist the situation would be sufficiently relieved: 'Lady Cathcart formed eighty small holdings, and in doing so she broke up farms which she believes were the only farms in South Uist suitable for small holdings.'

The Board persisted; in September they wrote to the agents stating that after enquiry they were satisfied of the need for more holdings on the island, the most suitable farms being Ormiclate, Bornish and Milton[4] (all of which had been raided in previous decades). The agents responded by sending to the Board a copy of a report by the factor on the disastrous effects which he claimed had resulted from the assignment by the Crofters Commission of hill pasture as enlargements. The agents wrote, 'All Lady Cathcart's experience has gone to prove that under the conditions which exist in the Outer Islands crofters are unable to stock or manage pasture land, and that arable land which comes into their hands is soon run out and exhausted by them.'

Needless to say, the Board did not share the contemptuous view which Lady Cathcart and her agents held of crofters' abilities, and they prepared a scheme for 99 new holdings and 77 enlargements (later amended to 77 new holdings and 35 enlargements) on the three farms. In February 1913 the Board received a letter from the local crofters threatening violent possession if the farms were not settled by the spring. The Board advised them that as the proprietrix was unwilling to negotiate, the case had to be brought before the Land Court. The initial hearing was held in April, with further hearings in May. In spite of Lady Cathcart's objections, the Land Court issued an Order for the constitution of new holdings and enlargements on Ormiclate, Bornish and Milton. There was a great deal of acrimony and disagreement in the wake of the Order, but at least the Board were able to put men on the farms—the only ones in South Uist to be settled under the 1911 Act.

The next South Uist farm to which the Board turned their attention—also in 1912—was Glendale.[5] The applications came mainly from men living on the adjacent island of Eriskay who asked for access to peat moss and for enlargements to their existing holdings. The Board drew up a scheme for six new holdings on the northern part of the farm, with the southern part to be used as an enlargement for 43 existing holders. Amongst Lady Cathcart's many objections was that the men of Eriskay were 'enterprising, well-doing fishermen, who derive a comfortable livelihood from the sea. To impose upon these men additional responsibilities as regards land would be a calamity.' (She could not have been more mistaken; see Chapter 11.)

The applicants threatened forcible possession in 1913 and again in 1914 while the Board's correspondence with the agents dragged on and on. In July 1916 the applicants wrote to their M.P. The Board advised him, 'There would be strong opposition from the Proprietrix and the legal and other expenses which the scheme would involve would not be justifiable under existing conditions.' In October of that year the agents advised the Board that the Eriskay crofters had asked the Land Court to draw up a scheme allowing them access to the Glendale peat moss, which the agents considered 'incompetent and impracticable.'[6]

At the end of 1916 another threat was made to raid the farm, and the Board took up the case again, but the probable excessive cost of compulsory proceedings combined with the cost of financing the penurious applicants to take over the sheep stock, plus war conditions generally, deterred them from taking further action at that time. In 1918 two of the applicants, in desperation, seized some ground at Glendale and built rough shacks for their families there. The Board's local officer wrote in February 1919

> That they acted illegally in so doing is beyond question, and Lady Gordon Cathcart in taking interdict against them on 18th October 1918, was acting quite within her legal rights, and she will also be within her legal rights in proceeding with her complaint for breach of interdict, but the wisdom of her doing so is quite a different matter. Lady Cathcart's hostility to every scheme for the provision of small holdings and the amelioration of the condition of the people on her Island Estates, is too well known not to be recognised by the Islanders, whose feelings are that it is her Ladyship and those who advise her who are the cause of men otherwise law-abiding, taking the law into their own hands by her refusal to meet the requirements of their position, thus compelling them against their own better natures to become breakers of the law. I question if her Ladyship's complaint for Breach of Interdict were to come before a Jury, she would get a verdict of Guilty—certainly she would not get such a verdict from an Outer Island Jury.[7]

The report concluded by recommending that the Board go ahead with a scheme for the whole of Glendale. The Chairman sent this report to the Scottish Office asking whether it was justifiable for the Board to proceed with the preparation of a scheme, since if the estate did not voluntarily agree to the breaking up of the farm they would certainly demand the highest possible compensation.

Before a reply was received, the agents advised the Board that the raiders had remained on the land in breach of interdict. (The sub-commissioner had predicted that they would. 'What else can they do? The whole Island of South Uist belongs to Lady Cathcart. She will not grant them even the site of a house on any part of it.') The agents advised that 'it had been represented to her Ladyship that a serious condition of matters might arise if the proceedings were gone on with ... Lady Cathcart is not sanguine of the success of any scheme involving the breaking up of Glendale farm into small holdings, but if such treatment of the farm would obviate the risk of any disturbance, or rising, among the local cottars etc., her Ladyship would be ready to place the farm at the disposal of your Board, subject to the existing tenant's rights, and subject to the like conditions as if the farm were taken compulsorily by the Board.' In view of this concession, the Board persuaded the men to remove themselves from Glendale.

In May a solicitor representing the two men wrote that they were occupying houses 'absolutely unfit for human habitation, with the result that the health of their young children has greatly suffered.' He felt the delay was intolerable and that the men would be forced to resume possession of their 'sheds' on Glendale land. The local M.P. also took up the matter. The Board's difficulty was that the factor felt his authority had been flouted and so was attempting to ensure that the two raiders were not given holdings on the farm. The factor insisted that if the men interdicted were given the holdings they had illegally seized, 'that fact will become generally known in the Western Islands, and others will follow their example.' But the Board had induced the men to leave those holdings on the understanding that they would be re-established on them legally, and therefore such a condition would have put them in an impossible position.

By August the Board had prepared a new scheme for 29 new holdings (later reduced to 22). Lady Cathcart allowed this to go ahead, refusing to concern herself with any of the arrangements, including the selection of holders, since she still considered the whole idea a great mistake. The holders were finally settled the following year, including the two raiders who had spent the intervening period with their families in what their solicitor described as 'hovels'. But, as will be seen below, the case of Glendale was to be brought up again and again in connection with other South Uist farms.[8]

One such farm was Askernish, for which the Board had also prepared a scheme before the war, opposed by Lady Gordon Cathcart and her agents.[9] Applications were renewed in 1919. In view of the circumstances under which Glendale had just been made available to them the Board felt somewhat constrained, but that summer they prepared a new scheme, for 12 holdings and seven enlargements. The agents' response was that the alleged demand came entirely from young single men who did not really need new holdings.

By the beginning of December a land raid was threatened. The Board advised the Scottish Office that to proceed compulsorily would be costly, and that the farm was not particularly suitable for small holdings: 'but for the strong and insistent demand from ex-service men, the Board would have hesitated to project a scheme in respect of it.' The agents claimed that the threatened raid was 'another illustration of the evil effects of pandering by the Board of Agriculture to lawlessness'. On 9 December some thirty young men marched through the farm, 'headed by pipers and flag-bearers' and marked off holdings. The factor did not take this very seriously, believing it only a ploy to attract press attention. The agents reiterated their belief that there were no cases of real hardship and, 'if the Board of Agriculture dealt with the matter firmly and refused to allow themselves to be coerced, there would be no further trouble as regards Askernish Farm.' The Board angrily retorted that they were 'not the Authorities charged with the maintenance of law and order.' The agents replied at length, insisting that the Board's having given the two Glendale raiders the lands they had illegally seized, against the wishes of Lady Cathcart,[10] had led all the inhabitants of South Uist and the Western Isles generally to the inevitable conclusion that all they need do to gain the land was to raid it.

In January 1920 the agents forwarded to the Board a telegram from the tenant in which he stated that more stock had been put on the farm by a further batch of raiders and that his own stock was in danger of being ruined. In early April the raiders made threats against the tenant if he continued ploughing, and the Board were warned that Lady Cathcart would be seek an interdict. The Board remained adamant that the only solution was for the proprietrix to cooperate in formulating a scheme for smallholdings. At the end of that month the agents wrote that although she still objected as strongly, Lady Cathcart felt 'that it would be useless for her to protest further' and was therefore prepared to make the farm available at the coming term of Whitsun.

The Board were not able to settle the farm in time for Whitsun, and in September the sub-commissioner reported to the Board that a dozen or so young men had 'banded together and seem to have constituted themselves an authority to look after and take possession of Askernish Farm'. He added that many of them had seen little, if any, active service. In October the Board arranged a ballot for holdings on the farm, but the raiders objected to anyone other than themselves participating and disrupted proceedings. However, a second ballot was arranged, and in February 1921 the sub-commissioner reported that he had successfully balloted 31 ex-service men, all of whom had been overseas, for the nine Askernish holdings, and that the raiders had given no further trouble. (An old man who had been a child at that time remembers that the schoolhouse at Daliburgh was used for the balloting, and that, waiting outside, the children knew instantly from the expression on the face of each man who emerged whether or not he had got a holding.[11]) This is by no means the end of the Askernish story, but the settlement of Lady Cathcart's remaining farms will be dealt with before returning to the aftermath of this one.

Enlargements on the farms of Drimore and Drimsdale were also applied for before the war. Two of the three applicants for Drimore lacked sufficient capital, so the Board dropped that scheme, while the Land Court refused the application for Drimsdale in 1914 on the grounds that a two-mile fence would have had to be erected at disproportionate cost. At Martinmas 1917 both farms—along with the home farm of Grogary—were let to a single tenant. When the war was over the demand was not just for enlargements but also for new holdings, and in the autumn of 1919 both farms were raided.[12]

When the Board attempted to open negotiations, Lady Cathcart's agents replied that 'the unfortunate action of the Board of Agriculture in giving holdings on Glendale to the two men who made a raid on that farm has a good deal to do with the present state of matters. Mr Mcdonald [the factor] states that he has frequently heard it said by people in South Uist that the granting of holdings to the Glendale raiders was clear proof that the demand for small holdings would only be met if the law was first broken'. Apart from spreading seaweed as manure early in 1920, the raiders took no further action, and the factor believed there was nothing to worry about.[13] The Board eventually persuaded the raiders to withdraw and continued their attempts to negotiate. They were advised that parts of Drimore might be made available for enlargements; however the tenant opposed any such arrangement. In view of their parlous finances the Board let the schemes drop.

At the end of November 1920 both farms were raided anew. The Board's local sub-commissioner spoke to the raiders: 'They told me they had not the least intention of taking their cattle from there as long as the cattle were fit to stand the weather. They said when they joined up for service that there was a definite and precise promise of land made to them, that if they were in any default of law and order so were others in not fulfilling the promise of land made.' This time the estate took the matter seriously, and the agents asked the Board to intervene, 'with a view to having the lands raided made available for small holders'.

The Board realised that if they agreed to negotiate they would be faced with the usual criticism 'that they are countenancing unlawful action by coming to the help of raiders and so setting a bad example to applicants in other districts.' They felt, however, that they would be putting themselves in a false position 'if they did not attempt to take advantage of the opportunity now offered of meeting part at least of the clamant demand for small holdings which exists in South Uist.' They therefore asked the Scottish Office for authority 'to take up further with the Proprietrix and tenant with a view to carrying out a scheme or schemes for both farms.' At the end of the year the agents wrote to the Board that the tenant was 'almost in a state of despair' as all the best grazing on the farms, which he had reserved for the wintering of his stock, was held by the raiders.

The Board thought it might be helpful if Lady Cathcart's offer to make the farms available were made public and asked her agents if she would allow this. They replied that her attitude had so consistently been misrepresented in the past that she was averse to any further publicity. The Board were bewildered by this statement, and the agents hastened to state that they were not accusing the Board of misrepresentation. However, the public had been given the impression that Lady Cathcart had *offered* Askernish Farm, which was not true. 'Lady Cathcart has never wavered in her opinion that, in the case of Askernish, as in the previous cases of Glendale and other farms, the Board ought not to have given way to lawlessness, and, in her view, it altogether misrepresented her attitude when the House of Commons—and through them the public—were given the impression that she had voluntarily and of her own free will come forward with an offer to make the raided farm available for small holdings, the true position being that she was dragooned into acquiescence in the policy proposed by your Board.'

On 19 January 1921 the Secretary for Scotland authorised the Board to negotiate with the proprietrix and tenants, but as the raiders refused to withdraw from the farms, the Board could not justifiably do so. During the months that followed, the raiders made the tenant's position increasingly difficult, and in April he offered to make the farms available to the Board for Whitsunday entry, but the Board insisted on lower prices for the sheep stock than he would consider. The Scottish Office kept very quiet during this period, and in June the tenant's agents wrote direct to the Secretary for Scotland, expressing their disappointment at having received no response to previous letters: 'The Crofters blame the Government for having promised them the farms, and if the Government really intend to place Crofters upon them, it is most unfortunate that they should stand aloof and allow so much damage to be inflicted upon the *bona fide* tenants.'

In July firm offers were made by both the proprietrix and tenant, on terms which the Board had to admit were very reasonable. A decision was therefore necessary. The senior sub-commissioner advised Land Committee

> The facts are Drimsdale and Drimore Farms are partly held by Raiders who refuse to remove—and in consequence the Tenant is placed in the position of being almost forced to throw up the 3 Farms of Drimsdale, Grogary and Drimore—as he will be without wintering for his stock next winter, cropping having been prevented. The Landlord seems averse to adopting civil proceedings—Both Landlord and Tenant ask the Board to step in and fetch a solution. Although

> the subjects are not ideal for Small Holdings, and great difficulties will probably be experienced in working out a Scheme—and some considerable loss sustained in effecting it—I think there is no course open but to step in and take the burden of effecting a solution on our shoulders.

The Board told the Under Secretary for Scotland that on purely financial grounds they would wish the scheme to be authorised, but the continued presence of the raiders on the farms raised a question of policy which had to be determined by the Scottish Office. The course which the Under Secretary suggested to the Secretary for Scotland was to continue to the stage of getting Treasury approval and then tell the raiders that the Board were prepared to proceed immediately with a scheme but only if the lands were vacated. The raiders would then take their chances along with other ex-service applicants; if they refused to leave then the scheme would have to be dropped, and the proprietrix and tenant would need to resort to legal remedies.[14]

In September Treasury sanction was given on condition that the raiders withdrew. At the end of the month they did so, and the Board took possession of the farms at Whitsunday 1922. However, none of the holdings were actually settled until 1923; schemes proved as difficult to frame as had been predicted by the senior sub-commissioner. For example, it was impossible to get holders for the eastern half of Drimsdale, where the land was very poor, and that area had to be turned into an enlargement for other holdings. The whole operation cost very much more than the original estimates, so the Board had to go back to the Treasury for more money. Not until April 1925 was a formal scheme submitted to the agents, who raised all manner of objections; after the hearing on 24 June the Board agreed to certain minor changes but adhered to their overall schemes.

No further demands were made for any farms in South Uist. This is not to say that all the landless men now had land, but rather that all the farms which could have been broken up now *had* been broken up. That was not yet the case in Benbecula, but before turning to that area it is interesting to note that in 1921 Lady Cathcart seriously considered selling her Long Island estates to the Board of Agriculture, a fact which has come to light through a set of correspondence between James Garson of Skene, Edwards & Garson, and Lady Cathcart.[15]

This began on 7 March 1921, with a letter from Garson advising Lady Cathcart that the Director of Land Settlement had called on him for an unofficial and confidential talk, with the suggestion that the Board buy the estates of South Uist, Benbecula and Barra from her. Payment would be made in the form of a 30-year annuity, for the sum of £50,000 which Garson appears to have plucked from the air. Asking if the idea appealed, he wrote, 'I certainly think it would prolong your Ladyship's life if you were quit of all these worries', and concluded by passing on Sir Arthur Rose's request that this be kept absolutely private and confidential, 'as he thinks it might create difficulties if the matter were to leak out.' Lady Cathcart replied that it would indeed be a comfort to be rid of the anxiety of the islands, but she considered £50,000 to be absurdly inadequate. She presumed that the enormous amount of money that she had spent on buildings and other developments would be taken into account and did not think anything under £100,000 would be worth considering.

Having gone through the figures, Garson then had the unpleasant task of advising Lady Cathcart that £50,000 was in fact the most that could be got for the estate: 'The memorandum shews quite clearly that the Estates theoretically stand in your Ladyship's books as of the present value of round about £200,000. The Treasury will regard this, however, merely as an interesting historical fact, which has no bearing whatsoever on the value of the Estates to a purchaser today.' He pointed out that Sir James Matheson had spent vast sums on Lewis, to no advantage when he came to sell the island: 'the only point which was regarded as worthy of consideration was the present return which a proprietor could get.' By 18 March Lady Cathcart appeared reconciled to the sale, although she still felt she was being rushed into a decision.

> I can assure you that it is a great wrench to part with these Islands. I have taken a great interest in the place and have done all in my power to help improve it and the people, for which I have received nothing but base ingratitude and absolute insolence from the Government, who I think are now in a tight place. I believe that this move of theirs of paying annuities for land is nothing more or less than the thin end of the wedge towards land nationalisation...and on that account and that alone I feel it is wiser to allow the Islands to go.

The correspondence ends abruptly with this letter, and no mention of this proposed transaction has been uncovered elsewhere, so there is no way of knowing if it was Lady Cathcart or the Scottish Office who backed off.

Turning back to Benbecula, applications had been made before the war for enlargements on Nunton Farm, but as the lease had been entered into prior to 1906 the farm was not available under the 1911 Act. After being demobilised, ex-servicemen applied again, and in 1922 they renewed their application. A scheme for this farm would have incurred high costs in providing an adequate water supply, as well as in heavy compensation for the tenant, whose lease did not run out until 1928. The Board therefore decided that 'the scheme should be allowed to lie in abeyance meantime so long as the demand is not great.'

However, the demand was great, as was proved in time-honoured fashion when the farm was raided in December 1922. The agents asked whether the Board had a scheme planned and were told they did not. They asked the Scottish Office whether 'the Government will assist Lady Cathcart to put down lawlessness in the Outer Islands' and were told that 'in the matter of interdict proceedings Lady Cathcart would receive the ordinary protection to which law-abiding citizens are entitled against law-breakers.'

Lady Cathcart duly obtained interdict against the twenty raiders; four of them subsequently committed breach of interdict, and her counsel recommended she bring them before the Court of Session for punishment. In July 1923 she wrote direct to the Secretary for Scotland, Viscount Novar.

She suggested meeting over lunch in London and bemoaned the fact that nearly all her South Uist properties had been taken over and now Benbecula was also wanted. One might have felt more sympathy for her had she not been writing from her home in Berkshire. Then she got to the heart of the matter.

> In ordinary circumstances I would have without hesitation followed Counsel's advice, but I am deterred by what happened in the Strathaird case a week or two ago [see Chapter 8]. The raiders on that occasion were sentenced to two months' imprisonment by the Court of Session, but two or three days later were liberated and promised holdings of land without delay. My Factor informs me that the Benbecula people are jubilant over the Skye incident. I feel therefore it would be folly on my part to incur the expense and the risk involved in bringing the Nunton interdict breakers to Edinburgh, unless I have an assurance of support by the Government in my action, as there is little doubt there would be a repetition of the Skye case in this instance. While it is very distasteful to me to have to yield to lawbreakers, I recognise that we are passing through extraordinary times, and that there is no telling how small an incident may set the heather on fire. In these circumstances I have decided that if the Government approach me with a request to allow the farm of Nunton, including the adjoining farm known as Nunton Hill Farm, to be broken up into small holdings, I will be prepared to enter into an agreement with the Board of Agriculture.

Lord Novar regretted being unable to meet for lunch on the date proposed, and stated, 'I think that in all the circumstances of the case your decision seems to be the best method of meeting the situation'.

In September he authorised the Board to take the necessary steps to secure entry at Martinmas, but in November the Scottish Office jibbed at the cost of the water supply. The Board advised that the farm had always been notorious for its poor water. They had had samples of the water collected from different parts of the farm, and the Chief Analyst had reported that none were drinkable, so the Board concluded it would be necessary to sink wells.

The agents lodged a number of objections to the scheme. The hearing was held in March 1924, and at the end of it the Board decided to adhere to their scheme of eight new holdings and 22 enlargements, but with certain modifications. The agents continued to object at every step, and the Scottish Office still had reservations. The Board wrote that they hoped the Secretary for Scotland understood that they 'were extremely unwilling to take Nunton and Nunton Hill for Land Settlement, and that they only did so because Lady Gordon Cathcart besought the Board to take action when the threats of raiding became serious. The action of the Estate in putting every possible difficulty in the way now is not in accordance with what one might have expected in view of the fact that the scheme originated with the proprietor.' The Secretary for Scotland signed the confirming Orders for Nunton and Nunton Hill on 9 December 1924.[16]

After being settled there were further problems on certain farms, e.g. Glendale and Nunton, but worst of all at Askernish.[17] It will be recalled that the holders were chosen by ballot, Lady Cathcart refusing to cooperate in any way. In November 1922 the Board sent her agents a list of the eleven tenants chosen for holdings on Askernish. They replied that according to her factor, three of the holders had not taken up residence; two of them were on the mainland and one had another holding about nine miles distant. The Board replied that they would arrange to collect rents from the three and would 'insist on the holders in question taking up residence on their holdings without further delay.' In May 1923 the Board sent the agents the application for registration of new holders; the agents replied that there were now *four* non-resident holders, and as the estate had not been consulted on the selection of tenants Lady Cathcart would not concur in the application to the Land Court but would lodge answers to it.

The Board's application and Lady Cathcart's answers were lodged in November of that year. The Board by now had changed their tune and stood on the principle that residence on a holding was not a necessary condition prior to the registration of a new holder. The agents insisted that Lady Cathcart objected chiefly because she considered it 'most unfair that holdings should be allotted to men who do not work them, and who have no intention of working them, while deserving ex-service men who are without land are anxious to get holdings'. (In view of her record, Lady Cathcart's sudden concern for ex-servicemen must have astonished the Board.)

The Land Court hearing was held in December. The Court had great difficulty in coming to a conclusion as to their powers in the matter and suggested an adjournment. After the hearing a meeting was held between a representative of the Board and the agents, and it was agreed that the Board would write to the absentee holders demanding a written undertaking to occupy and cultivate their holdings by 29 February 1924.

The Board wrote to all these men and got various vague promises back from them but nothing firm. In February 1924 they sent the letters to the agents who replied that Lady Cathcart was not prepared to withdraw her objections to their registration.

> In a crofting community, it is essential that each man should do his share of the work connected with common machairs, common fences and drains, common grazings etc., and a few absentee tenants in a township upset the whole routine. So far as Askernish is concerned, we are informed that little or no attempt is made to fulfil these common obligations, the settlers who are on the ground maintaining that they cannot be expected to do anything unless the whole tenants in the township do their fair share of the work. One result of this inaction is that the fences taken over by the Board of Agriculture from the former tenant are tumbling down everywhere, and no one seems to accept any responsibility for their repair. Another result of the present state of matters is that subletting is general on Askernish.

In the autumn one holder, who had been a chauffeur in Inverness, got a job as driver of the South Uist mail van and took up residence on his holding, so the estate withdrew their objection to his registration. However, the general situation had not improved.

In January 1925 the Board's local officer reported that one of the three absentees resided on his father's croft, a second resided in Glasgow, and a third on another holding, Howmore (the one that was nine miles from Askernish). In May the agents wrote that according to the factor 'the state of matters at Askernish is worse by far than exists in any other part of the Western Islands with which he is acquainted. Sub-letting is carried out in wholesale fashion, not only by the absentees, but by most if not all of the registered tenants, who presumably feel at liberty to follow the example of the others.' The factor had also informed them 'that the amount of stock to be seen at Askernish is inconceivable, and the unfortunate result is that the sitting tenants who endeavour loyally to carry out the obligations undertaken by them are swamped by alien stock.' In November the factor wrote direct to the Board about the 'deplorable state of affairs in this settlement', reiterating most of the points made in May and warning that if stern action were not immediately taken the situation would be brought before parliament.

The Board's response was that if registered holders were sub-letting, then the estate could take action against them and have them removed; if the absentee tenants who were sub-letting were registered, then the estate could proceed against them in the same way. The agents replied with a strongly worded letter, and by the end of the year, after some internal discussion, the Board made some concessions. They proposed that since the absentees still had not taken up residence, a meeting should be held between the factor and a representative of the Board to choose new men for these holdings, the non-residents to be informed they were no longer deemed to be the tenants. There was a certain amount of heart-searching on the part of Board members over this, for fear of trouble with the men to whom the holdings were originally given. In any case Lady Cathcart vetoed the proposal, declaring that she would not 'by joint action on the lines suggested by the Board, make herself responsible for a scheme prepared by the Board, which has not so far shewn any prospect of proving a success.'

In March the Board attempted to register Cathelus Macmillan (the man who had another holding at Howmore) in respect of Holding No. 4. The agents were astonished by this since the man had shown no inclination to relinquish Howmore, could not possibly work both holdings at once, and had persistently sub-let the land at Askernish. There is no written evidence of the Board's motives, but presumably they stemmed from the estate's refusal to meet them halfway. They told the agents that at the time Macmillan was successful in the Askernish ballot he was an ex-serviceman without land, and that the Howmore holding had been let to him by the estate on yearly tenure after he had been accepted for Askernish, so the estate was to blame for him having two holdings. They also insisted Macmillan had every intention of building on his holding at Askernish as soon as he could.

The agents replied that 'Mr Cathelus Macmillan, who already has a good house at Howmore, has no intention, and never had any intention, of removing to Askernish and erecting a house there; and that the only use he has made, or is ever likely to make, of the holding at Askernish is to sublet the grazings to all and sundry.' As to the Board's reference to Macmillan's service qualifications, the agents pointed out that the ballot had taken place in 1920 or 1921 and, 'the Board of Agriculture cannot present an Application to the Land Court in March 1926 without some regard to intervening circumstances.' The hearing was held in June; the Land Court summed up the position thus

> The objections of the proprietrix are formidable and deserved the serious consideration of the Board. It would have been more satisfactory for the Court in a case of this kind had they attempted to meet the serious allegations of the landlord, and to justify the selection of this tenant as a new holder. They have contented themselves, however, with standing on their legal position that these matters are committed to their discretion, and that as they have exercised that discretion it is not competent for the Court to consider whether they have done so wisely or not. We are of opinion that we must give effect to this view...[and have] no power to interfere.

Cathelus Macmillan was duly registered as a landholder. Why on earth the estate continued to renew his yearly tenancy of Howmore is a mystery not explained in the files.

In October 1927 the agents advised the Board that the tenants of the neighbouring township of Garryhellie were applying to the Land Court in an attempt to compel the Askernish holders to erect and maintain the march fence between the townships, as the Askernish sheep constantly strayed and destroyed crops. They stated that because the non-residents had not done their share of the common work of the township, and those who had taken up residence objected to bearing the whole burden, the fences were all ruined. Maintenance of those fences, they insisted, was the responsibility of the Board under Section 10 of the 1919 Act. The Board replied that the fences had predated the new holdings, and that if they had since been allowed to fall into disrepair, 'it is for the landlord to take such steps as may be necessary to enforce fulfilment by the holders of their obligation of maintenance.' In December the factor wrote in despair, 'There are hardly any fences left on Askernish, that can be called fences.....Askernish is little more than a Common Grazing for all the Townships within miles of it.' Both Board and agents continued to insist it was the others' responsibility, and nothing was done.

The Land Court heard the Garryhellie tenants' case in October 1928 but did not find it within their powers to take any action. They commented again that it was the failure of so many of the Askernish holders to take up residence that was the cause of all the trouble (even amongst the registered holders several actually lived on their parents' crofts, not at Askernish). They stressed that the obligation for the maintenance and repair of the fences definitely fell on the Askernish holders, 'but the enforcement of the Conditions of Let against the holders must proceed by way of action at the instance of the Landlord'. However, Lady Cathcart did not see why *she* should have to go to the expense of taking action. The one positive result of the Land Court hearing was the appointment of a Grazings Constable.

In January 1929 the Department asked their local officer to report on non-resident holders and the state of fences at Askernish. Six of the 11 holders were absentees, including Cathelus Macmillan, still at Howmore, one man resident with his family in Glasgow, and one confined in Inverness Lunatic Asylum; the Askernish lands were either sub-let or used for grazing purposes by relatives of the holders with nearby crofts. He confirmed the poor state of the fences, and added that the resident holders had at one time made an effort to put the settlement in order but were outvoted by the non-residents. In July he advised that one additional holder was taking up residence, but there was no real improvement in the settlement. 'Probably both the Department of Agriculture and the Proprietor are at fault', he wrote, 'as it is evident that some of the Holders placed here had little or no intention of taking up residence on their holdings from the commencement.'

Faced with a parliamentary question in November, the Secretary of State asked the Department about the current position. He was advised that

> The Scottish Land Court have held that the condition of let relating to maintenance is only enforceable against the holders at the instance of the landlord. The onus of removing the absentee tenants from their holdings similarly rests with the Estate and is a matter in which the Department cannot intervene directly. But the Department have informed the Estate that, if they bring into residence holders who are prepared to fulfil their township obligations, the Department will consider sympathetically an application for the provision of fencing and for assistance towards the cost of putting the drainage system in order.

At the end of December the agents sent the Board a copy of a letter from the factor: 'I was in hope that as a result of a number of meetings which were held by the resident settlers at Askernish within the past month, at the instigation of the Grazings Officer, there would be some developments in regard to the question of repairing fences. It would appear however that all the meetings were more or less a fiasco and it is now clear that nothing is likely to be done by the settlers in the matter of repairing fences or cleaning of drains.' With true-blue loyalty, he could not see the fairness of Lady Cathcart 'being saddled with the worry and expense of taking action in the matter' and thought that as the Department had chosen the wrong men it should be up to them to get rid of those men.

In May 1930 the grazings committee of Milton township, which also bordered Askernish, brought a case before the Land Court concerning the march fences between the townships. At the end of that hearing the Askernish grazings constable announced he had some money in hand and could help with the purchase of materials if the settlers agreed to do the work. Matters appear to have improved considerably after that; the Department also contributed money for fencing material and by February 1932 the factor was able to report that the boundary fences were almost completed, and that the people were enthusiastic and had turned out well to repair the fences.

Before concluding this section, it is worth discussing briefly the subject of absenteeism, which was also mentioned in the Introduction. Temporary migration was a long-established feature of crofting, and during the agricultural depression of the 1920s the need to earn some cash elsewhere may have been pressing. However, the real complaint here was not that the holders were absent but that they had not left anyone behind to fulfil their obligations. The fact that neighbouring townships were complaining, and that the factor considered the situation at Askernish so much worse than elsewhere, clearly indicates that genuine abuse was occurring here.

The story represents the nadir of land settlement schemes. In the chaotic situation after the raids there is no doubt that the Board of Agriculture did not enquire into the qualifications of applicants as they should have done. But it really was indefensible for the estate to go on blaming the Board when Lady Cathcart had so emphatically refused to become involved in any way. Her opposition to land settlement policy did not cease after holdings were established, as is evident from her willingness to cut off her nose to spite her face.

Barra

Between 1900 and 1908 agrarian unrest was particularly strong on the island of Barra. In 1901 the Congested Districts Board bought land for sixty new crofts, but there were still many landless men, some of whom eventually raided the adjacent island of Vatersay and entrenched themselves firmly on it. Lady Cathcart refused to cooperate with the Congested Districts Board in regularising the position of the men there but offered to sell the island at an exorbitant price; in 1907 the government agreed. There is no doubt that the success of that illegal seizure set a precedent for the post-war years.[18]

At the time of the above purchase of land in Barra, Lady Cathcart sold the farm of Eoligarry to the two brothers who tenanted it.[19] In 1912 the Board of Agriculture received applications for part of the farm; the agents insisted it was the proprietors' home farm, but as demand was so great the Board decided to press on. The Small Holdings Commissioner recommended purchasing the estate if it could be got at a reasonable price.

> There is no available ground on the Board's property or on that of Lady Gordon Cathcart. The Barra people will not be satisfied with the proposed settlement and will press for other portions of Eoligarry and as it is the only land available further resumption of parts will mean additional compensation. The present compensation is estimated at £1000, but as the owners will probably resort to arbitration the award may exceed that amount and the expenses may be considerable—and the Board may have to go through the whole thing again.

A great deal of trouble would have been avoided if this advice had been taken, but other members of the Board argued that the intention of the 1911 Act was not purchase, and that buying the property would use up a large proportion of their fund. With Secretary for Scotland approval they therefore applied to the Land Court for a compulsory order. The Land Court hearing was held in May 1913, but the Order was not issued until January 1914. The main objection, that the farm was a home farm, was rejected on the grounds that having no tenants the proprietors could not have a home farm. However, the Court opined that 'purchase of the whole estate would be the most equitable and in their opinion the least expensive solution'. They therefore deferred dealing further with the case in order to give the Board a chance to reconsider this option.

Within the Board it was argued that 'a purchase of any property by the Board, which would have to be exercised in this case under the powers of the Congested Districts Act, is likely to be used as an admission that the policy of the Landholders Act, under which no purchase powers exist in any part of Scotland, has proved itself insufficient to meet the needs of land settlement.' Early in 1914 the brothers offered to sell, but when by July their offer had not been taken up it was withdrawn.[20] The Board therefore asked the Land Court to proceed with the application.

The first threat of forcible seizure of the farm had been made in 1912 and further threats followed. The Board did not press the Land Court to issue a confirming order; it is clear that they were not at all keen to do anything about the farm during the war years. Finally, in 1917, the cottars seized part of the farm.[21] Their solicitor appealed urgently for the Board to act.

> I have done my best to restrain them from violent measures and advised them to exercise patience but I am afraid that they have now arrived at a stage that unless some arrangement is immediately made with them there will be considerable trouble. ... There is no doubt that the people are in dire need of some land. Their housing accommodation is bad and they have had no land unless some of them can get a bit for potatoes from a neighbour. They are all fishermen and since the restriction imposed on them on account of the war came into operation their only means of livelihood has been seriously curtailed while the price of foodstuffs on the islands has increased above 100 per cent.

By June the cottars had erected a fence across the peninsula and the proprietors were unable to use the grazing at the south-east end. After discussion the proprietors agreed not to disturb the cottars that season if they re-positioned the fence so as to allow access to the grazing. But the cottars had no intention of doing so; they wanted to retain the ground permanently and to use not just the potato ground but also the grazings, and to erect buildings. The Board reported this further development to the Scottish Office. 'It is questionable if the Cottars can be restrained indefinitely from putting their threat into force, and it will be difficult to eject them if they once establish themselves on the ground.' The Secretary for Scotland was asked whether negotiations for purchase should be reopened.

In September the men started to build houses, and the proprietors were desperate to sell, but the Secretary for Scotland decided against purchase, and the Board re-applied to the Land Court with regard to the existing application. In November the remainder of the farm was raided, and the 27 raiders were interdicted. The Board advised the Secretary for Scotland: 'The raiders are backed up by every man almost in Barra and they make not the least secret of it that they are merely waiting until it is seen what the Land Court does and will take possession of Eoligarry and divide it up among themselves unless it is granted.' Negotiations for purchase were reopened but broke down over price. In the summer of 1918 the Board realised they were in a cleft stick: if their scheme for part of Eoligarry went ahead, the proprietors could then justifiably claim the remainder as the home farm. They therefore asked the Land Court to dismiss the application, and in the spring of 1919 they purchased the property. The price and conditions were those which the Board had refused to consider the previous year.

Unfortunately, the Board's scheme of 22 new holdings proved unacceptable to the applicants, who demanded at least twice as many. There was also conflict between the 'East side men', who had raided, and the 'West side men' who had not. In May 1920 the Board, finding themselves unable to resolve the conflict, asked the Secretary for Scotland on whether they should carry on with the original scheme, which on merits was certainly the best, or increase the number of holdings to satisfy more of the demand. Ultimately some 38 new holdings were created, and the Board's local officer still had dreadful problems sorting the whole thing out. After finally allocating the holdings he warned that the Board were likely to be flooded with complaints for some time as there were so many more applicants than could be accommodated on the farm.[22]

Eoligarry was then beset by the problem of absenteeism, showing that this could occur as easily on the Department's own estates as on privately-owned lands. In September 1922 the Board learned that four holders had emigrated to Canada or elsewhere.

> These holders have not formally renounced their holdings and if unsuccessful in the Colonies may desire to return to their holdings, but as they were given entry at Whitsunday 1920 and have already had ample time in which to erect dwelling-houses and take up residence on their holdings and have failed to do so, the Senior Sub-Commissioner recommends that their holdings should be declared vacant and relet. Suitable tenants could easily be got as there is still a strong demand for holdings in Barra.

The Board warned the holders that if they did not declare their intention within thirty days of returning to their holdings, those holdings would be considered vacant and would be re-let. Thirty days came and went. In December the fathers of two of the men wrote that their sons planned to return and asked for permission to continue working the holdings meanwhile.

By January 1923 seven men were not resident on their holdings. The Board's solicitor asked if they had signed letters of tenancy. The local officer replied, 'There were no letters of Tenancy signed by the Eoligarry holders when they were put on the holdings, as the rents were not then adjusted & approved at the Head Office...and after the rents were intimated to them, they would sign nothing at all.' By this stage letters of tenancy had in fact been signed by many of the holders, though *not* by the absentees.

In February the Board sent registered letters to all the non-residents advis-

4 Eoligarry shortly after being settled. Photograph courtesy of Scottish Ethnological Archive, National Museums of Scotland.

ing them their crofts would be declared vacant unless the Board received notice within thirty days of their immediate return. The quickest reply was from a man in Aberdeen, stating he had always paid his rent, was getting treatment for war wounds, and was serving an apprenticeship to a trade to enable him to make a living in Barra. (But he never did return.) There were many other letters, most from fathers and brothers working holdings for sons and brothers overseas. One man wrote from Canada: 'I must inform you that I have no intention to lose the croft in anyway what ever I just came across temporary in order to better myself before settling in Eoligarry and my intention is to be back any time now.'

The Board wrote along the same lines in May and received more replies from fathers and brothers. The senior sub-commissioner suggested that in some cases the best plan would be to get the holders to ask for the holdings to be put in the names of those actually working them. A letter from in London echoes the Canadian one and probably sums up the attitude of most, if not all, the non-residents. In response to the demand that all holders return to Eoligarry and build houses there, he wrote

> I don't see how everybody can do that right away, in my case for instance I would like to have a bit of capital before I can settle down there. For there is not enough land there to keep me had [sic] it all the time, so the only thing I can do is to let my father keep it going a while yet the same as he has been doing since I got it, and with what he can get out of it and what I send him out of my earnings he ought to manage pretty fair. But if I go there now, and leave my employment, it would mean that I would have to get a loan of the government, which I would never be able to pay back, whereas if I stop at work for awhile yet will say for another twelve months, then I will be able to make a better start.

The Board faced two problems. Firstly, they were inundated with requests from landless Barra men asking for the apparently vacant holdings. And secondly, as at Askernish, the settlement could not be worked properly when so many holders were absent. In January 1924 the resident holders petitioned the Board to do something; by then there were apparently 17 non-resident tenants so that 'the proper working of the township as a whole is impossible.' In October the senior sub-commissioner reported that

> in absence of some resident official—say a ground officer or some person of that kind—the people take most brazen liberties with Law & Order. If a holder decides on a change he leaves his holding for Canada, Australia or Elsewhere without giving notice of any kind to the Board. He sells any buildings on the holding to the highest bidder and the latter steps in and may or may not inform the Board that he is now a holder! In view of this tendency it is particularly desirable that not a day should be lost in bringing matters to a point where all the holdings I have indicated should be available for re-letting to more desirable holders.

In January 1925 the resident holders again petitioned the Board, this time asking for the vacant crofts to be divided amongst them. The senior sub-commissioner admitted that this would make for a better settlement, but foresaw too much opposition from ex-service applicants who were waiting impatiently for a vacant holding to become available. However, the Board were having the same legal difficulty as at Askernish in that holders had to be registered before the Board could use their statutory powers to remove them. The Board had no objection to registering them and applied to do so, but here a new obstacle arose: the Land Court refused to grant registration to holders who had not given written consent. In November 1925 when the Court's opinion was made known, there were nine such non-resident holders.

In notes marked 'Urgent' or 'Very Urgent' dated 12 August and 25 October 1926, and 28 February 1927, the Board pressed their solicitor to find some way they could act. There was another Land Court hearing in July 1927, but the Court were still of the same opinion. In the interim there had been some returns, some renunciations to brothers, and some complete renunciations and new tenants, but a core of non-residents remained.

A minute to the Board of March 1928 made it clear that absentee holders were not the only problem at Eoligarry: 'From the beginning difficulty has been experienced in the collection of rents and notwithstanding the institution of legal proceedings against the worst offenders, the total amount of arrears outstanding has been steadily increasing. In many cases also holders have failed to cultivate their holdings properly'. In April the local officer provided a full report on the individual holders. Examples of his comments were

> No. 4—This holder is an absentee but the holding is worked quite satisfactorily by his father. Should be written to for payment of the half year's rent.
> No. 16—This man now resides on his holding and conforms to Grazing Regulations. He is heavily in arrears and it is difficult to see how he is to meet the obligation as he has a large young family. His only employment is cockle fishing.
> No. 18—This man...is a very unsatisfactory holder. He defies the Grazing Regulations and is presently overstocked by 14 sheep as well as being badly in arrears. The legal action should be followed up and no leniency shown.

By early 1929 a ground officer had been appointed (it is not clear why this was not done sooner). In February there were legal proceedings against twelve holders: two for recovery of arrears, eight for recovery of arrears and removal in case of non-payment, and two for removal on account of non-residence (these, of course, were men who had signed Conditions of Let). Below are extracts from another report, of March 1929.

> No. 1—This holder is resident on his holding and is a good worker but appears to consider that Grazing Regulations do not apply to him.....A few trips to Lochmaddy Sheriff Court for breach of Grazing Regulations with increased fines will, I think, cure this man. He should then make a good tenant.
> No. 2—This Holder is resident on his holding. He apparently realises that it is a case of residence on the Holding or lose the tenancy.
> No. 33—There is no change here. The holder is still absent. This holding should be declared vacant and re-let.

In 1933 the local officer reported that 'the majority of holders here are now tending to make a reasonable attempt both to observe the terms of their conditions of tenancy and to increase the productivity of their holdings'. Because the Department were themselves the owners of Eoligarry there was none of the nastiness that characterised the Askernish story, but it was still a very unsatisfactory situation. Again, it must surely be blamed on the post-war panic to settle as many holders as possible in the shortest time.

North Uist

The largest landowner in North Uist was Sir Arthur Orde. A scheme for three farms on his Newton estate(Newton, Cheesebay and Clachan Sands) was first mooted in 1914.[23] He did not oppose the scheme, but in July 1918 the arbiter determined Sir Arthur's compensation at £4770. The Board felt they could not justify such an expenditure, and the scheme was dropped.

In April 1919 the Board offered to purchase the estate (under the Congested Districts Act).[24] The proprietor considered the Board's offer totally inadequate, and the haggling commenced. In June 1921 a senior sub-commissioner noted, 'It is very desirable that this matter should be brought to an issue without delay—negotiations are dragging out too long—and the possibilities of raiding are not decreased thereby.' And, indeed, that same month one of the farms was raided. The agents wrote angrily to the Board, blaming them for the delay which had brought about that situation. In 1922 further, more extensive, raids took place.[25] And the negotiations dragged on...and on...and on.

In January 1923 the Board made a formal offer to the proprietor but withdrew it the same month because there had been another raid. Although they realised that abandoning the scheme would penalise the law-abiding applicants, and also that in view of the stage reached in the negotiations the estate would feel very aggrieved, they insisted that they wanted to leave the Secretary for Scotland free to decide whether to abandon the scheme in view of his statement about raiding being an absolute bar to land settlement. This was unncessary, for as the Under Secretary for Scotland rightly remarked to the Secretary for Scotland, 'I am not aware of any instruction which would bar the purchase of a property merely because it happened to be raided. As I understand the position, the standing instruction applies only to raiders.' The Scottish Office worried what to do about the raiders; ejecting them would prove that warnings about the consequences of raiding were serious, but it would also provoke attacks in parliament. Fortunately the raiders withdrew and saved them having to deal with the dilemma; as long as the men did not return it was felt the incident could be considered 'not so much a raid as a demonstration'. The estate was purchased that month with entry at Whitsunday.[26]

At least Sir Arthur Orde still had plenty of land in North Uist, but one of the most notorious land raids was at Balranald, owned by a resident proprietor (Captain MacDonald) whose father and ancestors had been tenants of the farm.[27] He claimed that it was his only source of income and that it also helped to support his five sisters. Applications were made to the Board for the farm of Paiblesgarry on Balranald estate in 1913, but the Board realised the great difficulty and expense that would follow if they attempted to take the farm and therefore deferred the matter. In 1917 crofters from the adjoining townships took possession of part of the farm, subsequently relinquishing it in hopes that the Board would do something about their applications for enlargements. The Board were therefore forced to take the matter up again in 1918. A senior sub-commissioner noted in October of that year, 'in most Congested Districts in the Outer Islands the people are only waiting the return of their able-bodied men from Army and Navy service to take forcible possession of lands and they make no secret of their intentions'; he recommended that action be take with regard to Balranald in anticipation of trouble.

In the spring of 1919 the Board offered the proprietor £8000 for the farm; he demanded £11,000. The Board renewed their offer in the spring of 1920, but he was then asking £12,000. They considered the idea of a Part II scheme for Paiblesgarry alone, but, as with Eoligarry, the remainder of Balranald could then have been declared a home farm 'and therefore outwith the Board's powers for further demands that would probably follow.' If they attempted to use compulsory powers under Part I then the fact that they were dispossessing a resident owner who farmed the land himself would weigh heavily with an arbiter and they would be forced to pay a high price. So an arrangement with the owner was the only solution.

While all this discussion was going on the crofters were losing patience and renewed their threat of forcible possession. The Board took the threat seriously but still failed to agree with the proprietor on a fair price. In December 1920 Paiblesgarry was raided. (Three accounts by raiders agree that it was their M.P., Dr. Murray, who told the men that the only way they would get the land would be by raiding it.[28]) The Board's local officer reported his conversation with the raiders.

> They frankly told me that they thought raiding was now the most probable way of getting a small holding. They instanced how on other estates where raiding took place the applicants got holdings...that the demand was equally urgent and necessitous in North Uist, and the only reason they could attribute to the Board leaving them severely alone was the peaceable and law-abiding behaviour of the applicants there. They stated they were all in the army before conscription came in force, five of them being in France in 1914, three of whom were twice wounded and two once. They also made a considerable point of the Government promise of land and its breach of faith in not fulfilling that promise. That it was no small matter for themselves, and their relatives who had gone under, to have faced the guns in France but they were buoyed up with the hope that if they came back they were to get a holding in their native land on which by their labour and exertion they would be able to make a living. I told them the Board had sent me to warn them of their unlawful action and I asked them to remove from the land raided. They emphatically declared that they would not, and if legal proceedings were taken against them that they were prepared to go to prison.

He added, 'I saw the land raided and it is very suitable for the constitution of small holdings.'

According to the raiders' accounts, the proprietor, Captain MacDonald, attempted to carry on as usual. When he sent his servants to collect seaweed for fertiliser the raiders overturned the carts, and the servants returned home empty-handed. The following day, hoping undoubtedly to intimidate the raiders, Captain MacDonald himself rode ahead of his servants on horseback, but this did not deter the men; the carts were once again overturned, and the raiders knew they had gained the upper hand. The proprietor turned to legal remedies, and in January 1921 an interim interdict was served on the raiders, to which they paid no heed.[29]

Captain MacDonald complained bitterly to the Director of Land Settlement about the Board's inaction; Sir Arthur Rose replied that he fully sympathised with the proprietor's difficult position, but the lack of funds for land settlement made it very difficult to suggest a solution. In January 1921 additional funds had in fact been made available, but this was the period before the Board was reconstituted, and they were incapable of making a quick decision. A local policeman attempted to arrest two of the raiders for breach of the peace in February but was unable to do so 'in consequence of the threatening attitude of the people of the locality'. In order to serve writs on the raiders for breach of interdict it was believed that police from the mainland would be required. The whole matter was turning very nasty.[30]

At the beginning of March the Director of Land Settlement asked the Secretary for Scotland to approve advising the press and Donald Shaw, the crofters' solicitor, that the Board were prepared to reopen negotiations with the proprietor 'in order that the large number of law abiding ex-service applicants should not be penalised because of the unlawful action of the minority.' Three conditions would be attached: anyone still on the farm after 10 March would be ineligible for a holding; the men interdicted would have to appear in Court; and the selection of holders would be by ballot, with no promise of a holding made to anyone.

The Secretary for Scotland approved Rose's suggestion, and the press and Shaw were duly advised. The latter reacted negatively to begin with and further correspondence followed. On 11 March Rose wrote to the Under Secretary for Scotland, 'The difficult situation here has given us all a tremendous amount of worry. ... I am hopeful that the men will leave the land today. Undoubtedly, however, they will only do so for a short time and the position will be very critical.' He feared the Board would have to pay a stiff price for the estate but felt very strongly that 'if we secure the moral victory of getting the men off we should run some risk to arrive at a final settlement'.

Agreement was reached in April, but by the beginning of May, before Treasury sanction had been received, the raiders were back on the land. They had never paid their fines or caution and in early August they were arrested. There was a tremendous outcry in the press, and the Secretary for Scotland declared in parliament that if they promised to observe the interdict in future he was prepared to recommend the prisoners' release. As for holdings on the farm, Rose wrote on 22 August, 'I note the Secretary for Scotland has stated that their raiding will not put them out of consideration. That is my own feeling and as the place is now the Board's, we can proceed to make the best arrangement possible for the good of all concerned without too particularly remembering past peccadilloes.' On 14 September the Board's local officer reported, 'I found the men most courteous and amenable to law and order. Once they understood that the Board had acquired the place for smallholdings they had no desire whatever to be aggressive.' Eight holdings were created on Balranald and eight on Paiblesgarry, a number of which are still in the possession of descendants of the first holders.[31]

One can just imagine how a landowner like Captain MacDonald or Lady Cathcart would have reacted if they had seen the Director of Land Settlement's reference to the land raids as 'peccadilloes', or if they had known that at least one of the raiders numbered his 16 days in prison as 'some of the happiest days of my life. I was regularly brought to my knees with laughter—looking at some with overgrown beards, others salivating because of the absence of tobacco. Indeed I was sometimes feeling physically sick with such laughter.'[32]

It is very clear that in South Uist, Benbecula, Barra and North Uist the demand for land was very strong and urgent indeed, with men willing to break the law and to accept even the smallest plot in the most inhospitable areas (that they did not all subsequently make proper use of that land in no way vitiates this statement). It is also very clear that land raiding in this area did produce the desired results. This was partly because of the militancy of men who had survived the war, but public sympathy for them also played a large part by forcing the government to accede to their demands for the land they insisted had been promised them. Had there been a more efficient Board of Agriculture at the time much delay and friction would undoubtedly have been avoided, but the final result would have been the same.

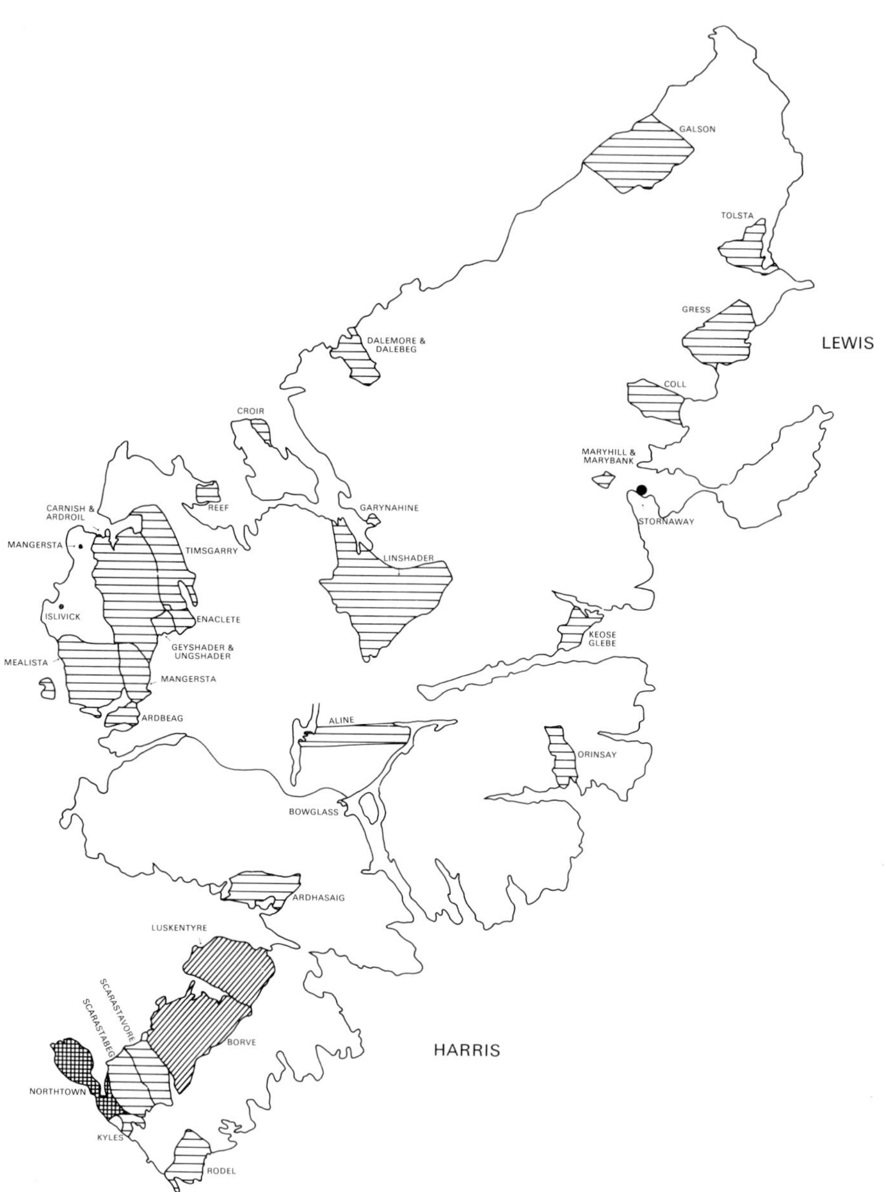

5 Map of Lewis and Harris.

CHAPTER 7

Schemes in Lewis and Harris

Lewis

In the late nineteenth century land hunger was acute in the island of Lewis, and land raids were endemic there in 1887-8.[1] However, from 1912 to 1914 hopes that the newly-created Board of Agriculture for Scotland would be able to break up farms into crofts for the the landless were unrealised. At that time Lewis, like South Uist, was owned by a single proprietor, Major Matheson. Although he had broken up two farms (Aignish near Stornoway and Mangersta in the west of the island), under the aegis of the Congested Districts Board, he was fundamentally opposed to land settlement. He employed the firm of Skene, Edwards & Garson as his agents, and they proved even more effective in blocking land settlement in Lewis than they had been in South Uist.[2] The Board initially proposed schemes for four Lewis farms—Galson, Orinsay & Stimervay, Carnish & Ardroil, and Gress—but because of the agents' stonewalling tactics, not a single one of these schemes was implemented before the war .[3]

The response to each letter of enquiry was that Major Matheson's experiments in forming smallholdings in the past did not encourage him to facilitate the formation of more because rents were in arrears 'and the tenants have run down and exhausted the land by bad cultivation'. The agents did not state that the landlord would oppose any scheme but asked for details of the schemes proposed. The Small Holdings Commissioner provided the details; the agents replied that these were insufficient. The Small Holdings Commissioner wrote back that as the landlord refused to negotiate he proposed recommending to the Board that they apply to the Land Court; the agents denied that the proprietor had refused to negotiate, he simply wanted more information to allow him to make a decision. The Small Holdings Commissioner supplied more information; the agents replied that this was still not sufficient.

After about a year of this fruitless correspondence, the Board finally served statutory notices of their intention to apply to the Land Court. The agents promptly applied for an interdict against the Board's action, alleging that no scheme in the sense implied by the statute had been submitted to them. The Board did not admit this contention but backed down, withdrawing the statutory notices and submitting new schemes in January 1914. In March the agents asked for more information; in May, when the Small Holdings Commissioner pressed for a decision, the agents deprecated the 'attempt to rush the matter into the Land Court without the fullest consideration'.

In July 1914 the Board lodged their applications with the Land Court. The Court heard the cases in March 1915, inspected the farms in June, and reconvened in January 1916 to consider possible amendments. In March the Board were aware that the Court were ready to issue their Orders, but in view of wartime costs and the expensive arbitration that would accompany these schemes, they obtained a sist (suspension of court) for all Lewis schemes. (They could not withdraw the schemes entirely, knowing the agrarian troubles that would certainly follow.) The proprietor challenged this action in the Court of Session, but the sist was upheld and proceedings suspended indefinitely.[4]

In the summer of 1917 the Board were again looking at the Lewis schemes and thought it would be a good idea to pursue them 'at least up to the point of having everything ready to go on with the actual execution at the end of the war'. The Board asked for approval to apply to the Land Court for the recall of the sist and the issue of the compulsory orders in respect of the Lewis schemes. Although there was clearly going to be heavy compensation involved the Secretary for Scotland was satisfied that the schemes should proceed and approved this action in September 1917.

However, the island of Lewis was in the process of being sold, so nothing further was done until August 1918. By then the situation had changed dramatically, for the new owner was Lord Leverhulme.[5] No one could accuse Leverhulme of self-interest. He had radical plans to improve the living standards of the Lewis people by transforming the economy of the island, and he injected large amounts of his own capital in order to do so. His genuine concern for the people was unquestioned. The difficulty was that he had fixed ideas about what was and what was not good for them, and crofting was anathema to him.

In August 1918 the senior sub-commissioner for the region, Thomas Wilson, discussed the situation with Lord Leverhulme. The Board's proposals for the four farms and the certainty of agrarian unrest if schemes were not proceeded with, were put to him. Wilson sent a long report back to the Chairman on 26 September.[6] He found Leverhulme totally opposed to the tenure of Small Landholders Acts and convinced that his various plans (developing the fisheries and establishing a canning industry, establishing weaving sheds and developing a tweed industry, and so on) would solve everything.

> With his aspirations I expressed the most cordial sympathy and approval. I am satisfied his Lordship...has taken up the Lewis problem with the intention of solving it, and he has the energy and resolve to carry his plans to completion. He has great admiration for the Lewis people, who have done such great and noble service for the Country in the War, and I think feels he should do what he can for them. His whole life, however, has been industrial, and I question if his

> experience of three months among the Lewis people has taught him their sentiments or desires. He does not realise that they will never feel satisfied until the farms in Lewis are divided into Holdings and given to them. The Lewisman is not by sentiment, tradition or inclination at all inclined to become a Factory-hand, and the present race cannot be satisfied by industrial methods alone...the older people will not change their present mode of life no matter what his Lordship may do. What the Lewis man wants is a small piece of land for a house site, two cows grazing and potato and corn growing. That is his ideal and it cannot be eradicated—save by allowing the present generation to die out and train up the young generation coming in.[7]

He also suggested that it would do no harm to suspend further consideration of the schemes briefly to give Leverhulme time to assess them. However, Leverhulme was to prove immovable.

When the war was over, the men came back to the island, their ears ringing with promises of land for returning heroes. Leverhulme had achieved great popularity by then, for his various projects were already making a difference to the well-being of the islanders. These developments appeared quite compatible with schemes to break up the large farms into smallholdings, and the Board urged from the beginning that they should go forward concurrently. But Leverhulme had set his mind against the whole idea, and when this was publicly realised—in March 1919—the raids began.

The first farm to be invaded was Tong, which was too small for the Board to have considered for land settlement.[8] More serious was the raid on Gress the following week, when some 40 men pinned out holdings and told the tenant they intended to cultivate them in the spring.[9] An officer of the Board, Colin MacDonald, spoke to several of the most prominent men in Stornoway and was told it had been rumoured throughout the island that the Board intended to abandon their Lewis schemes to give Lord Leverhulme a free hand, and that the men, including demobilised soldiers and sailors, had made the raid as a protest in favour of breaking up the farms into smallholdings. Another farm—Coll—was also raided at this time. At a meeting at Gress which MacDonald attended a few days later, Leverhulme explained his proposals at length to a large crowd, appearing by the end to convince them; but, wrote the Board's officer, 'from the Gaelic remarks which I overheard and from statements the men made to me subsequently I am satisfied that their acquiescence was more apparent than real.'[10]

Later that month MacDonald was surprised to learn that at least one of the influential men of the district was in favour of giving Leverhulme's plans a fair chance. However—and this was the crux of the matter—'At the same time he quite anticipates that any attempt to "drive" the people into accepting that view by summarily rejecting their claims will lead to trouble.' In June a number of Lewis men wrote to the Secretary for Scotland

> We had an interview with Lord Leverhulme at Stornoway on Monday last, and we found no encouragement from him as far as the breaking up of farms is concerned. We believe his Lordship's schemes will ultimately benefit this Island, but at the same time we are convinced that for the reconstruction of the Lewis

> it is best to combine the crofting interests with those of the fishing industry. Life on a small holding in our Island home is one of our inherent ideals. ... We are now as eager for the land as we had been before Lord Leverhulme became the proprietor of this Island; in fact we are convinced that this war has increased the love of the Highlanders for the land of his ancestors.

Many more such letters and appeals were received by the Scottish Office and Board of Agriculture in the following months.

In January 1920 the farms of Gress and Coll, from which the raiders had been persuaded to withdraw the previous autumn, were reoccupied, and the men began to build houses as well. The Board's local man made it clear that this was not a fresh raid but a continuation of what had occurred the previous spring, 'except that this one is more severe and determined than was the case last year'. Rather than take legal action against the raiders, Leverhulme stopped all his works in the district and paid off the men. With about 400 ex-servicemen in the area, only 30 of whom were raiders, this move provoked a great deal of bitterness, although the raiders were happy enough to have the proprietor's unreliability demonstrated.[11]

Leverhulme complained to Robert Munro, the Secretary for Scotland, of the Scottish Office's inaction, and Munro replied on 1 March. He had acquiesced in Leverhulme's requests for a delay in land settlement schemes in Lewis, 'thereby exposing the Government to considerable criticism', to allow Leverhulme time to convince the islanders that their best interests lay in industry rather than crofting. Now, at a time when the government had shown the greatest interest in settling ex-servicemen on the land by passing new legislation, the Lewis people were far from won over to Leverhulme's views, as was clear from the land raids. Munro also pointed out that by Scottish law it was up to a landowner, not the government or police, to instigate legal action against trespassers.

Following this letter, Leverhulme did put the law in force against the raiders, but they defied the interdict. A warrant was issued for their arrest, but before it could be enforced Leverhulme halted the proceedings.[12] Instead he announced that he would stop all his development works in Lewis. This created a tremendous uproar. Scores of appeals and petitions poured in, for whatever loyalty was felt towards raiders by their relatives (the amount of support the raiders enjoyed is something which has never been clearly established) this cessation of all works was obviously going to have a fairly catastrophic effect on many islanders. Fully exploiting this wave of support, Leverhulme informed the Secretary for Scotland that he would resume his schemes as soon as the raiders left the farms. As a compromise gesture he offered to make certain farms on the west coast of Lewis available for smallholdings. In October 1920 the raiders were again persuaded to leave Coll and Gress. They did so believing this would make it easier for the Board of Agriculture to go ahead with their land settlement schemes for the farms, a serious misunderstanding.

However, the raiders having gone, the works started up again, and in January 1921, in the face of the tremendous support manifested for Leverhulme, the Secretary for Scotland gave him the undertaking he had been seeking, that the government would not use their compulsory powers in connection with any Lewis farms for ten years—with the rider that if the development schemes did not proceed the hands of the government would be freed.[13]

In February the Board asked for Treasury approval to go ahead with immediate arrangements for the settlement of the west coast farms which Leverhulme had made available.[14] The K & LTR thought that in view of the situation in Lewis the Treasury must agree to this although detailed estimates were not yet available. He also added a confidential note, 'I don't know why, unless it is on account of the continual issues of fresh capital by Lever Bros., but there seems to be some doubt here as to the financial stability both of that firm and of Lord Leverhulme himself.' Leverhulme's finances were in fact in fairly desperate straits at that time;[15] few people suspected, but the K & LTR's note shows that there must have been rumours. (A curious comment appears in the correspondence between James Garson of Skene, Edwards & Garson and Lady Gordon Cathcart at the time Lady Cathcart was considering the sale of her island estates to the Board of Agriculture. She asked Garson if Lord Leverhulme might not be interested in purchasing these estates; he replied that it was unlikely that Leverhulme would prove any easier to deal with than a government department and added: 'For your Ladyship's own private information solely I may say that I have been told that his Lordships's brain power is not what it used to be, and that one need not be surprised if a mental collapse were to occur. In that case I have an apprehension that all these Lewis schemes might tumble, and end in nothing.'[16])

By the end of June detailed schemes had been prepared for the farms (Mealista, Carnish & Ardroil, Timsgarry, Reef, Dalebeg and Dalemore), at which point another crisis developed. On the 27th the Director of Land Settlement wrote personally to the Treasury.

> When our officers arrived in Lewis they found things in a state of turmoil. They had direct information that some of the farms included in the agreement were to be raided at once. Acting on the instructions passed on by me from the Secretary our officer [Thomas Wilson] took the only practicable course of avoiding a further breach of the law with its inevitable consequences of a further rupture with Lord Leverhulme and renewed difficulties for the Government. He mapped out the holdings, selected his men by ballot, allocated the holdings, and made agreements with the Tenants. Technically all this was provisional and subject to the approval of the Board, the Secretary for Scotland and the Treasury. In point of fact, however, it is impossible to go back upon it; but I want you to understand that while we may appear to have been "outrunning the constable" here (so far as the Treasury is concerned) the position is quite exceptional and there was really no other way, if we were to avoid a situation that would have been embarrassing to the Government.

It appeared to the K & LTR 'that the best has been made of a difficult job, and that credit attaches to Mr. Wilson for his grasp of the situation and for the peace which has resulted from his allocation of the lands.'[17]

The incident must have been kept very quiet for it is not mentioned by either Nicolson or Hunter. However, by the spring of 1921 attention was centred on the farms near Stornoway, which had once more been raided.[18] As a result Leverhulme announced the closure of all his development works in Lewis; unless the raiders withdrew and all raiding ceased, henceforth he would concentrate his efforts on Harris. (He admitted, however, that his reasons for retrenchment were also connected to the worldwide trade depression.)

The Secretary for Scotland took the view that since all development works had been suspended, the government was released from its undertaking. He advised Leverhulme of his plans to go ahead with land settlement schemes, hopefully with the cooperation of the proprietor. Leverhulme was deeply upset by what he regarded as a breach of the understanding between them, but by the end of October he had to admit defeat. 'My views on the evils of crofting are not in any way altered', he told Munro; but, rather than have farms compulsorily taken piecemeal, he offered the whole of Coll and Gress, and part of Orinsay.

The Treasury were not at all happy about the cost of these schemes, but in view of the 'exceptional conditions prevailing in the Island', they did give their sanction. Meanwhile, the Board were involved in heated correspondence with the solicitor representing the men who had raided and then left the farms; he insisted they had been promised holdings if they withdrew, which the Board denied. The Board's officer responsible for settling the farms also experienced difficulties. In February 1922 he wrote to headquarters

> Since coming here I have been told by several parties that I was likely to meet with some opposition in settling the applicants on the holdings. Today I have been in touch with some of them and I find them quite emphatic in their divided opinion as to who should be selected for the holdings some of the raiders insisting that whoever will get holding they must get them, others insisting that all the applicants must come from the townships immediately marching with one side of the farm and giving no chance whatever to the applicants equally needful from the township marching on the other side of the same farms.[19]

Leverhulme wanted the raiders barred from any ballot for holdings, but here too he was defeated, and raiders were chosen for holdings on all three farms. For many months after the ballot unsuccessful applicants bombarded their M.P., the Scottish Office, and even the Prime Minister with letters of protest.[20]

One large Lewis farm, Galson, still remained intact.[21] In the summer of 1922 it was reported to the Board that this farm would probably be raided the following spring. In view of the Secretary for Scotland's public declaration that raiders were not to be given holdings, and the near impossibility of enforcing this, the Board were particularly anxious to avoid further raids at this time. They therefore approached Leverhulme's agents, but the reply was that Lord Leverhulme was utterly opposed to the idea of a scheme.

6 Stacking the hay crop at Gress Farm. Photograph courtesy of Scottish Ethnological Archive, National Museums of Scotland.

By December 1922 the Board were convinced of the genuine need for land in the district, and that the only way to satisfy it was by settling Galson. They had prepared a scheme for 57 new holdings; in view of the proprietor's attitude this would have to be carried out under compulsory powers. The Secretary for Scotland (Lord Novar) wished to avert the complete break with Leverhulme that this would entail, and asked the Board to leave it in abeyance temporarily. But there were continued threats of raids, and in January 1923 the Board sent the Under Secretary a report by their supervisor at Stornoway. 'This report confirms the Board's understanding that all Lord Leverhulme's development works in Lewis have practically ceased so that in the event of any further land settlement schemes being proceeded with it could not be argued that the present cessation of development works was due to schemes of land settlement.'

The Under Secretary felt that the embargo on compulsion in Lewis should be lifted. Otherwise there were likely to be further raids, which would be embarrassing for the government if the proscription of raiders was to be maintained. Novar agreed and authorised the Board to proceed with a scheme for Galson, using compulsory powers if necessary, on 7 February. The K & LTR advised the Treasury, 'A prompt decision should be given in this case as the district is dangerous', and Treasury sanction was granted on 20 February.

Leverhulme expressed his 'deep disappointment and regret' at the use of compulsory powers 'to carry out a policy to which I am wholeheartedly opposed'. Both he and the farm tenant lodged objections to the scheme, (which was slightly modified after the hearing) and then asked the Secretary for Scotland not to confirm the final Order; however, the Order was confirmed and the scheme went ahead.[22]

In 1924 Lord Leverhulme attempted to dispose of all of his Lewis estates.[23] The farm of Linshader was sold to a sporting syndicate. A raid had been threatened on the farm in November 1923, and the Board therefore, had considered it for a scheme, but as a sporting property the proprietor's compensation claims would have been prohibitively high. However, Colin MacDonald, the Board's officer, reported that the syndicate were not at all opposed to a scheme.

> In fact they are quite willing to put forward a scheme of their own and submit it to the Board for official blessing. Their idea is to put in ten (or so) holders who would act as their ghillies. I think the idea is an excellent one. If only Lord Leverhulme had shown such an understanding of the people of Lewis his success in that Island would have been as great as his failure has been ignominious.

Linshader is therefore an unusual example of a scheme going ahead on the owners' initiative; arrangements took somewhat longer to complete than expected, but the new holders were settled by spring 1925.[24]

The files on the Board's settlement of several other Lewis farms also exhibit features of interest, but for reasons of space they are not discussed in this book.[25] One other case is worth mentioning, however, because it illustrates how long the memory of the wartime promises of land lasted in the Hebrides.

Applications were made for a stretch of land which was part of another township's grazings. When the Department advised the men nothing could be done in this case, they responded

> We cannot readily forget that while we were serving and suffering through the Hostilities from 1914 to 1919, and even after that, the cry was the land for the people and the men for the land, but now we find ourselves, a bunch of able-bodied men, applying to where we consider the proper quarter, for a bit of land owned by a group of sportsmen, we find that that Department has no power to grant us a few acres each.

This was in November *1933*. The men went on to ask for land on Garynahine farm, which was held at a rent less than £50 per annum and therefore available only by agreement with the proprietors. In January 1934 the men threatened to raid; after long negotiations the proprietors agreed to make 130 acres available, and the new holders obtained entry at Martinmas 1935.[26]

The memory of the Leverhulme period is still potent in Lewis. One man said that when he had been involved in a development scheme in Stornoway they were frequently told 'it's a waste of time, look at what happened to Lord Leverhulme.'[27] Donald Smith, factor of the Stornoway Trust Estates, believes that Leverhulme had been 'forty, fifty, sixty years ahead of his generation', and that Lewis would be a very different place now if he had been allowed to carry his plans to fruition, although Smith added that 'of course the people who actually raided they had been promised land.'[28] When I asked the Rev Donald Macaulay, former convener of the Western Islands Council, whether he agreed with Nicolson's view that the majority of Lewis people had been on Leverhulme's side he replied

> A lot of people could understand what he was trying to do. But it was really at the wrong time. It was an unfortunate timing. To inject capital into this place was just what was wanted at that time, but the plan was a huge plan which included the reduction of the number of crofts, which conflicted with the opinion of many people. And the land—when they went to war you see the government promised the boys coming back from the war that they would get more crofts, build a house and get married and settle down. And Lord Leverhulme's plan while it was good and more like the kind of plan you'd have in modern times, it was ill-timed because it was the wrong time for it; the boys had just come home from the war.[29]

Those who believe that Lewis would have been transformed if Leverhulme had been left alone to get on with his plans have not looked at Harris, where Leverhulme turned his attention after he gave up on Lewis.[30]

Harris

Before Leverhulme had turned his back on Lewis and begun to concentrate on Harris Ardhasaig farm had been settled by the Board.[31] In 1913 it had appeared unsuitable for smallholdings; the land was poor and, as it was a sporting property, the cost of compensation and providing deer fences would have been prohibitive. In 1915 the farm was raided; the raiders were offered work building a new road, and the trouble died down for a time.

In 1919 Ardhasaig was raided again. Rather than take legal action the proprietor, Sir Samuel Scott, asked the senior sub-commissioner for the area, Thomas Wilson, to come up and investigate. Wilson reported on a meeting with him in August, concluding, 'It is a difficult problem as almost every inch of land in North Harris which could be utilized for Small Holdings is already in the hands of Crofters—and to interfere with the remainder inevitably leads to heavy financial loss.'

By the end of September Wilson had worked out a scheme for 15 new holdings, which he advised the Board to approve as soon as possible. He added, 'I should mention that the action of Sir Samuel Scott in agreeing to the above proposals is most generous, and he should receive the Board's recognition of this. Undoubtedly had compulsory powers been resorted to he would have received very large awards for damage to the Forest Shootings and Fishings—probably so high that it could have proved impossible to proceed with any scheme of small holdings.' By the time the scheme went ahead the estate was owned by Leverhulme's Lewis and Harris Welfare and Development Company, but no difficulty was put in the way of settlement by the new proprietor.

It was in South Harris that Leverhulme planned to build his new harbour of Leverburgh, but first he was determined to prevent any repetition of the events in Lewis. As a preliminary to starting the works he demanded that no applications for holdings be made to the Board of Agriculture, and no farms raided, until a ten-year trial had been given to his schemes. The pledge was given, and for the most part carried out, although there were two raids on Rodel farm, in 1921 and 1922; in the first case the men were sentenced to forty days' imprisonment while in the second the local people persuaded the raiders to withdraw.[32]

But in 1925 Leverhulme died and his trustees immediately stopped all his development works. Once the employment offered by the development works in Harris was no longer available the demand for land there grew fierce. The most desirable lands were the lush machair lands on the west coast which had been cleared in the 1820s.[33] When Leverhulme sold his estates this unpopulated west coast was disposed of in small lots, with the northern portion used as a deer forest. .

Two farms on that coast—Kyles and Rodel—were settled by the beginning of 1926. The Board wrote to the Treasury that the applicants for Kyles were

> neighbouring feuars who, on the understanding that the late Lord Leverhulme's development works would continue for a period of ten years at least, took up feus from the Estate and erected permanent dwelling-houses on the adjoining lands of Kintulivaig. These men are now left with little or no prospect of employment and having incurred comparatively heavy expense in the erection of their houses for which, in the altered circumstances of Leverburgh, there can

> be no sale, they are more or less tied to the district with no sufficient means of support. In the circumstances the need of these applicants for land is particularly pressing and unless early provision is made for them, they will doubtless take forcible possession of Kyles Farm as they have already threatened to do.[34]

A scheme was agreed between the landlord and applicants, with the Board merely paying for fencing, and the matter went smoothly.

Rodel farm was also sold. The new proprietor found it 'rather embarrassing to be immediately confronted with the prospect of making the land available for small holdings', but he bowed to the inevitable and allowed the Board to effect a scheme.[35] The Treasury were irked by the Board's warnings of raids if the scheme were not approved, one member commenting, 'As this is well within our limits we can agree without any reference to the abject surrender to terrorism apparent in this application.'[36]

A third scheme—for the farm of Scaristavore—encountered more in the way of difficulties, but it too was finally settled in 1928.[37] This was the farm on which Finlay J. MacDonald spend his childhood; his trilogy (*Crowdie and Cream*, *Crotal and White*, and *The Corncrake and the Lysander*) is a vivid evocation of life on a Hebridean croft in that era.

However, the above schemes were not enough to prevent all raiding in South Harris, and the Scaristaveg saga rivalled anything that happened in Uist, Lewis or Skye.[38] When a scheme—for six new holdings and enlargements for 35 crofters in the neighbouring township—was first drawn up by the Board in 1925 the farm was part of the unsold portion of the Leverhulme estate. However, by the end of that year it had been purchased by the man who had tenanted it until 1921 (when the estate had taken it into their own hands). He suggested a scheme of only three new holdings, one of them for his daughter, plus the enlargements. The Board were willing to go along with this, but the compensation claim was considered unreasonable. The proprietor ignored the Board's warning of a probable raid, and matters were at an impasse when, in March 1926, five neighbouring cottars did raid the farm.

This forced the landlord to rethink his compensation demand, and the Board told him they would carry on with his suggested scheme of three new holdings and 35 enlargements, 'on condition however that the farm was clear of raiders and no promise was to be given that any of the men who raided the farm would receive holdings on it.' The senior sub-commissioner for the district, Duncan Stewart, visited the farm on 17 March and reported

> To a certain extent the Proprietor is himself responsible for the burst of lawlessness at this particular moment. I find that he has been making injudicious remarks by informing the community he was to have his own selection of the two new tenants who were to hold along with his daughter.....Further it was evident common intention to raid this Farm for some time, and I believe they were held back by the knowledge the Board were attempting to secure the Farm for Land Settlement. The Cottars came to the conclusion they were to be left out of reckoning. That is about the correct way of looking at the Raid. Now that they are in possession, however, the neighbouring community are supporting

> them and I am convinced they are being legally advised in every step. The Cottars have made up their minds as to the serious consequences of their continued lawlessness. They have sketched out their programme, and I at least am of opinion they will continue to the bitter end.

Later that month Stewart wrote to the proprietor's agent with a new suggestion: that he should apply to the Land Court for registration of the five men, plus his daughter, as his tenants, thus allowing the scheme, including the enlargements, to go ahead. The proprietor refused, on the grounds that giving the raiders the holdings would be unfair to other applicants and an encouragement to lawlessness. On 24 April the Board advised the Under Secretary for Scotland that the agent had come up with a new proposal to ballot the five raiders along with five other applicants of the proprietor's own choosing. The Board asked for instructions, and a meeting was subsequently held between members of the Board and the Secretary for Scotland, Sir John Gilmour.

This Secretary for Scotland was determined not to follow in the steps of his predecessors. Robert Munro, after announcing in December 1921 that raiding was to be an absolute bar to land settlement, had capitulated and granted holdings to the Raasay raiders. Similarly, his successor, Lord Novar had reaffirmed the policy, but had been forced to give way over the Skye raiders. Sir John Gilmour was determined to stand firm; the raiders were to be removed from the Board's list of applicants, and a scheme for Scaristaveg was to proceed only if other applicants could be found.

The proprietor instigated interdict proceedings; the men ignored them, and on 31 March 1927 they were sentenced to two months' imprisonment. Inevitably, the press reported fully on this, and questions were asked in parliament. The proprietor's agent suggested that negotiations be reopened 'now that this obstacle has been removed', but as the men had prepared and seeded the ground, and stocked the grazings, the Board did not see how vacant possession could be given to new holders. The Secretary for Scotland's main concern was that 'neither the Board nor its officers (officially or unofficially) should take any action or make any statement which could be construed as indicating a weakening on the definite decision that the raiders are not to be settled under any scheme of the Board either at Scaristaveg or elsewhere'.[39]

After a fuss in parliament, the men were released from prison at the beginning of May, having given an undertaking that they would not return to the farm. However, four of them promptly broke their word (the fifth had been given a croft on a neighbouring estate). They were cited before the sheriff court in December; two appealed and did not appear while the other two were again imprisoned.

In March 1929 the Department agreed to go ahead with the three-holdings scheme, and the proprietor chose two ex-service men to take up holdings (his daughter was still to have the third). But although the two men who had been imprisoned a second time had not returned to the farm, the remaining two were still there until the end of May when they were sentenced to four months' imprisonment. More questions were asked in the House of Commons, and much was made of the fact that the men had first applied for holdings in 1912 and still had not been offered any.

At the end of April Duncan Stewart sent a report on the situation at Scaristaveg.[40] The new holders apparently tried to plough.

> The raiders' wives had attacked the workers. The work was started under police protection but it then became a kind of melee. The women threw odorous waters upon the ploughmen and they fled from the field. The policeman is said to have lost his temper and struck both women and one is now bedridden, but the men were first ejected from the field and parts were duly seeded by the women.[41]

Two days later he advised the Department that the families had planned a campaign whereby if the wives were imprisoned younger members would carry on. In mid May he described two further incidents, involving sticks, stones and dogs. In mid June one of the wives and the daughter of the other stopped the new holders ploughing by lying down in front of the horses. (Women's involvement in late nineteenth-century Highland land agitation was very common, but this is the only instance found in the post-World War I era.)

By August the Department had decided to purchase a neighbouring estate, Luskentyre, and settle the raiders on it (there was by this time a new Secretary of State for Scotland—W. Adamson—who held less hard-line views). The Department attempted to abandon Scaristaveg entirely, but the agent protested so strongly that they had to go on with it.

Luskentyre was a part of Borve deer forest. Applications—and threats of forcible possession—had been received in 1920 and 1921, but at that time the Board were trying to avoid a rift with Lord Leverhulme and did nothing about it. In 1929, when the Department were attempting to extricate themselves from Scaristaveg, they commissioned a report on Luskentyre, which was considered suitable for eight to ten holdings. They wrote to the Secretary of State, the proprietor (the Leverhulme trustees and then the new Lord Leverhulme), and the tenant (Lord Venables) in August advising their intention of using compulsory procedure under Part I of the 1919 Act to expedite purchase of the property so that entry could be taken at Martinmas. The proprietor had no objections to the compulsory procedures being followed, and the main controversy in the press related to the fact that this was the first time a deer forest had been taken for smallholdings.[42]

The Department proposed to retain full control of the estate for three to five years to build up an acclimatised sheep stock, clear the estate of the rabbits with which it was over-run, drain and improve the machair and potential arable ground, erect fences and make roads. During that period the prospective holders—including the two Scaristaveg raiders—were given temporary lets for cattle grazing and small cultivations, and were employed by the Department in the above-mentioned works. I asked John MacDonald, the son of one of the raiders, if his father had minded being given a croft on Luskentyre instead of Scaristaveg, and he replied, 'Well, he was only just wanting a piece of land that he would call his own. They were quite willing to take any place.'[43]

Borve itself was the last estate suitable for land settlement purposes left in South Harris.[44] It had been raided more than once, and in 1926 the proprietor contemplated legal action, but in 1927 he sold the estate. The new owner was more interested in fishing than stalking and shut his eyes to the constant encroachment on his deer forest of stock belonging to crofters and cottars; by 1933 there were an estimated 400-500 sheep on the land. In that year the proprietor decided to sell and the Department feared that a new owner would attempt to stop the trespass, 'with consequent renewal of agitation and possible lawlessness and disorder on the part of those affected'. They therefore asked for sanction to purchase the estate.[45] The Treasury requested the views of the K & LTR, who advised

> The Department make no pretence that this is an economic scheme; it is simply a means of averting an anticipated outbreak of land-raiding. The Kings Writ hardly runs in Harris, and if land-raiding starts, the situation will get out of hand. ... The money is being paid to buy off disorder; whether the bargain is a good one is a political rather than an administrative decision.[46]

When this was put to them, the Department admitted they had received no pressure from applicants since the estate changed hands in 1927, but 'it has to be borne in mind that the stock of those who previously desired settlement has been in unchallenged occupation of the land since then.' They also feared that a speculator might acquire the estate and put the law into effect against the trespassers, whereupon the resulting public and parliamentary pressure would force the Department to pay an inflated price for the property. The Secretary of State advised the Treasury that much as he shared their regret that 'political and social considerations should make it necessary to proceed with schemes of this character when the money available might perhaps be used to better purpose', he thought the situation necessitated approval.

There was also the question of the type of scheme to be effected. The report of the senior sub-commissioner (Duncan Stewart) of 13 June made it clear that they were dealing with the poorest type of land and the most indigent and least able applicants ('The many schemes we have had in the district as well as the migration scheme to Skye [See Chapter 8] have left us with the weakest of the population to choose from'). Yet the demand was there and this was the only land available. Stewart concluded: 'However difficult the scheme may be to bring to fruition it appears to me to be truly of the nature of land settlement for which the Department was primarily constituted.'

The argument implicit in Nicolson's book is that the Lewis raiders were wrong in demanding land first and foremost without giving Leverhulme's plans a chance. In view of what happened in Harris this argument cannot be sustained. Development works in Lewis would not have continued after his death any more than they did in Harris, and it was the land which provided subsistence to the many crofter families like Finlay J. MacDonald's throughout the harsh years of the Depression. In the past Lewis has been treated in isolation, as a unique case, but Leverhulme's benevolent plans were ultimately irrelevant, for the pattern of events in Lewis and Harris was not fundamentally different from that on all the other Hebridean islands where the men returned from the war determined to get land.

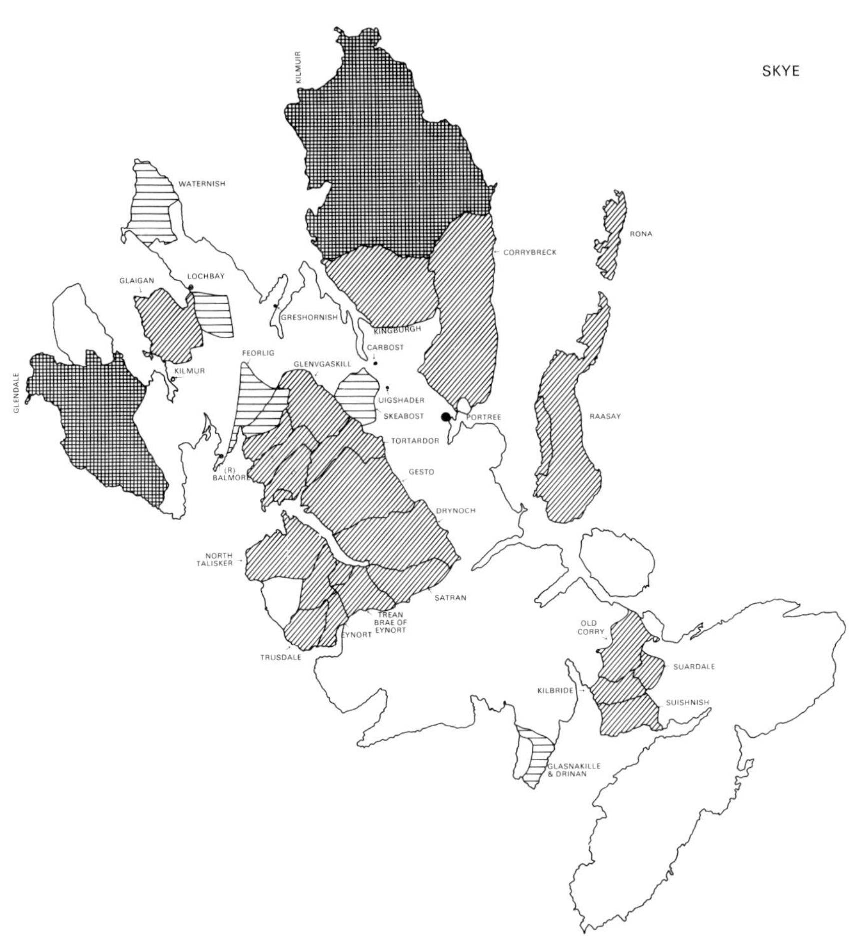

7 Map of Raasay and Skye.

CHAPTER 8

Schemes in Raasay and Skye

Raasay

Looking at a map of the Western Isles, Raasay appears so small and insignificant it may seem surprising to find a section of a chapter devoted to it. However, the Raasay land raid provoked so much controversy that the story requires telling.[1]

The first applications for land on this island—which encompasses about 18,000 acres—were received by the Board in 1915. A scheme was drafted, but the proprietors, William Baird & Co, Ironmasters, would not cooperate because the farms were situated over valuable iron ore deposits.[2] Further applications were received in 1916, 1917 and 1918. In 1919 the Board began to consider purchasing the island (with the mineral rights reserved to Bairds). Then, in 1920, Raasay was raided.

The seven men involved came across from the islet of Rona, where their ancestors had gone several generations earlier when they were evicted from Raasay. The Land Court reported in 1920 that the conditions of the tenants on Rona were 'miserable in the extreme'. The land was of the poorest quality, 'and the housing accommodation and sanitary arrangements are of the most primitive description'. The Court had great difficulty in fixing fair rents for holdings which were 'situated on an island entirely unsuited for a settlement of small holders'. Given these circumstances, there was a great deal of public sympathy for the raiders. Nevertheless, the proprietors had them interdicted.

In July 1921 the raiders were found guilty of contempt of court and breach of interdict because they had not left Raasay or appeared in court. The attitude of the Board at that time is evidenced by a letter from the Director of Land Settlement to the proprietors: 'I have been watching with much interest your endeavour to establish law and order in Raasay and in an unofficial way have been glad to note that the particular form of law-breaking which troubles you in the Island is being vigorously tackled, as I am sure it will ultimately help the work of the Department.'

Naturally the local M.P. took a different view, telling the Scottish Office in September it was dire necessity that had forced the raiders to act as they had. ('They consider it would have been a much more serious matter had they allowed their wives and children to die in the insanitary hovels formerly occupied by them on Rona.') The Board meanwhile were continuing to negotiate with the proprietors, but the essential question of the mineral rights had not yet been settled; they were reluctant to press for a decision while there were raiders on the land.

On 19 September the men were arrested and kept in Portree prison for several days until their solicitor (Donald Shaw) protested; they were then released on bail with an order to appear in court on 6 October for sentencing. Their M.P. implored the Scottish Office to grant them at least temporary accommodation; the Board advised the Scottish Office that they did not believe intervention at that stage was desirable and insisted that the supposed need for temporary accommodation was not really very acute. They had also discovered by then that only one of the men had a service record, a point which they reiterated in the months to come.

In response to further pressure by the M.P., the Director of Land Settlement commented to the Scottish Office, 'while I quite recognise the awkwardness of our position, I am afraid I cannot agree that any weakening of our attitude would improve matters. ... There is a growing feeling throughout the west that the only way to get the land is to raid it, and from everybody's point of view a stand should be taken against the idea that raiding can be undertaken not merely with impunity, but as a sure means of achieving the raiders' ends.' He thought the raiders' agent had exaggerated their plight.[3] 'I have no doubt that the holdings at Rona are very poor but that is a condition of things that exists at other places besides Rona and in my view it would be very unwise of the Board to allow themselves to be stampeded into action by each agitation that comes along.'

The men were sentenced to six weeks imprisonment. One of the raiders remembered that time: 'Oh, they were so good to us. You see we weren't criminals. We weren't treated like criminals at all.'[4] Public sympathy was very much on the side of the raiders, and letters appealing for the men's release from prison, as well as questions in parliament and press reports, kept the case very much to the fore in the weeks that followed.

Two things happened in December. First came the Secretary for Scotland's public announcement that land raiding was to be an absolute bar to land settlement. Second was the visit of the senior sub-commissioner, Thomas Wilson, to the men in prison. His brief was to persuade them to obey the interdict by taking their families back to Rona so that the Board could conclude their negotiations with the proprietors.

Wilson sent back a long report. Had it been midsummer the men would have gone to Rona, but to take their families, cattle and fuel supply across at this time of the year was not possible, and they would not promise what they could not perform. They had begged to be allowed to remain where they had settled in Raasay and promised to obey any order the Board might give them. 'They looked pale from their imprisonment and wearied like, and were subdued in their manner and bearing, yet courteous and anxious to have a settlement without further trouble.' Wilson provided a five-point summary of the position. The first point was the men's insistence that a return to Rona in midwinter was impossible; the second was that they would therefore return to Raasay after their release. He continued

> (c) That repetition of the process of breach of interdict followed by imprisonment again and again will not cause any alteration in the minds of these men, and will not lead to a solution of the problem.
> (d) That the circumstances are such as to necessitate a breaking away from the ordinarily accepted methods for obtaining good government, which here cannot be successfully applied, and
> (e) That having served their sentences their offence should be held as expiated, and as equivalent to fulfilment of the Law's requirements.

On 21 September the Director of Land Settlement advised the Under Secretary for Scotland

> To-day I have (in my private capacity!) had a talk with some of Bairds directors, and have more or less concussed them into assisting in what appears to me to be the only way out of the mess. They would be prepared, as proprietors, to allow the seven families of raiders to occupy seven of their empty houses for the time being, provided they got a pretty clear indication from the Board or from me as Director of Land Settlement, that the Secretary for Scotland would be prepared to push through the purchase scheme. Technically, this would mean the end of the raid and leave us free to proceed with negotiations. ... You will understand that, under this scheme, the Board does not appear till the removal is effected, the arrangement being on the surface an *ex gratia* act on the part of the present proprietors.[5]

The Secretary for Scotland approved this course of action, and the Board approached the Treasury. The latter did not acquiesce easily, for Part I of the 1919 Act had been designed specifically for ex-service men while this scheme provided mainly for civilians, and furthermore civilians with virtually no capital (a 'horrible proposition' was how one member of the Treasury described it). The K & LTR was no help to them. 'My only observation', he wrote in February 1922, 'is that the transaction should be carried out as soon as possible'. And it was.

A postscript to this story concerns the small island of Rona, the place of origin of the Raasay raiders who had found conditions there intolerable. The Board acquired Rona at the same time as Raasay. In October 1924 they expected all the existing holders to have gone by Martinmas and were trying to decide whether to let the place as grazing for a single tenant, or as an enlargement to the crofters in the north end of Raasay. However, by December there still existed eleven holdings 'where there is no sign of them being vacated.' In January 1925 the senior sub-commissioner reported on the individual holders, most, but not all, of whom wished to go to Raasay or elsewhere when accommodation became available. He concluded by stating that all the holders 'will be compelled to leave Rona by force of circumstances, all the young men having left.'

Yet in March 1926 the Board were advised that the five holders still in residence 'show no signs of any intention to move, though we have on a number of occasions offered them vacant holdings or houses on other parts of the Estate.' A scheme for Rona had been deferred until all the holders left, but now interim measures were sought. Arrangements were made for a let of the grazings for a year. In 1929 the five holders were still there and the Department had to try and arrange seasonal lets of the grazings. Dr Alastair Maclean recalls that two sisters left only because of ill health, and that the Macrae brothers remained as landholders in Rona until the Second World War: 'Of course the Macraes were a law unto themselves and it would be a brave man who would try to make *them* do anything they didn't particularly want to.'[6]

The tenaciousness of this small group of crofters in clinging to crofts on an islet which the Land Court had considered unfit for human habitation, despite all attempts to dislodge them, emphasises the strong attachment the older generation still had to their place of birth. And ironically Dr Maclean believes that the Raasay men would have been better off if they had stayed where they were: 'Rona with its harbour would have been a marvellous place for fishing. If they'd stayed there they'd have been much more prosperous than they were up in Raasay where there was no fishing.'

Skye

It is a curious fact that the area where the Board of Agriculture settled the greatest numbers—the Isle of Skye—was also the area where land raids culminated in an extraordinary amount of parliamentary agitation and a whole new set of instructions for the Board in dealing with land settlement in the Highlands (for more on this see Chapter 2).

The Congested Districts Board had effected large-scale land settlement schemes in Skye before the Board of Agriculture replaced it, and at least one scheme was completed before the end of the war under the 1911 Act. Some 36 smallholdings and enlargements for six existing holders were constituted on the farm of Balmeanach & Feorlig, part of the MacLeod estates, with no opposition from MacLeod of MacLeod.[7] Another pre-war scheme was prepared for the farms of Glasnakille & Drinan, part of the Strathaird estates.[8] This did not go smoothly because the estate was sold before the Land Court Order had been issued, and the new owner had not been informed of the Board's plans to break up the farms until he was already committed to buy. Understandably enough, he felt very bitter about this, and a good deal of acrimonious correspondence ensued, his agent attempting to persuade the Board to withdraw their application from the Land Court. But as far as the Board were concerned, congestion in the district was so acute this had to outweigh all other considerations. In spite of the proprietor's appeal to the Secretary for Scotland, the Land Court issued their Order in June 1918 for the constitution of 21 new holdings.

When the holders were chosen in the summer of 1919 ex-servicemen complained because only one of their number had been selected. The Board advised that most of the men settled were longstanding applicants and that for the remaining holdings the proprietor had objected to all but one of the ex-service applicants because they were too young and inexperienced for the type of holdings constituted. The scheme had pre-dated the war and had never been intended for ex-servicemen.

However, the Board certainly did keep in mind the likely demand in Skye from returning soldiers and sailors. The farm of Kingsburgh on the MacDonald estate was purchased under the Congested Districts Act with entry at Whitsunday 1919, and sixteen new holdings were constituted on it. The largest purchase which the Board made was the Bracadale estate from MacLeod of MacLeod.[9] This comprised some 60,000 acres with numerous farms, and the Board advised the Secretary for Scotland in March 1920, 'The demand from ex-service men for small holdings on this estate is intense and repeated threats of seizure have been made.' The individual farms were settled piecemeal over the next few years as the existing leases ran out.

One of the most interesting of the Bracadale schemes was the migration scheme from Lewis and Harris to North Talisker in 1923, which is discussed later in the chapter. A very different type of scheme was effected on another Bracadale farm. The proposal for Drynoch was for eight large self-contained holdings from 528 acres to 1920 acres with rents varying from £27 to £48. The Board's problem here was the best way to present the scheme to the Treasury. For most Hebridean schemes they had insisted on the necessity of creating a large number of very small holdings on the grounds that it was almost impossible to find ex-service holders with the capital necessary for the larger type of holding. The line which they took for this scheme was that while true with regard to the type of holding normally constituted in the area, i.e. worked on the club sheep stock principle, the Board had ascertained that 'for holdings of the Drynoch class, which have individual hirsels, there will be sufficient demand from qualified first preference men.' Subsequently the Board decided to create only seven holdings and submitted revised estimates to the Treasury. The K & LTR wrote on 13 March 1924 that he had no objection to larger holdings as 'there should be more prospect of a decent livelihood'.[10]

The farm of Scorrybreck on the MacDonald estate was also purchased by the Board. (The estate was under Trust as Lord MacDonald was incarcerated in what was then termed a lunatic asylum.) This transaction encountered a hitch in 1920 when the Board's funds were at such a low ebb they could not proceed further. They recommenced negotiations after extra funds had been made available, early in 1921, when the K & LTR advised the Treasury, 'There is considerable need for some sop being given to mitigate the land hunger in the Isle of Skye, and I think it is one of the most reasonable proposals the Board have yet put forward.[11]

The cases which culminated in the House of Commons debate were those of the 'Strathaird raiders' and, to a lesser extent, the 'Kilbride raiders'. It will be recalled that two farms on the Strathaird estate, Glasnakille and Drinan, had already been settled by the Board. The seven Elgol crofters who raided a Strathaird farm in November 1922 were unsuccessful applicants (the Board advised the Secretary for Scotland that the raided land had been included in the original scheme, but in view of the proprietor's representations they had left it out and it was therefore not available for smallholdings).[12] The men were interdicted but ignored the interdict; in January 1923 the Board warned that their names would be removed from the list of applicants. Following this, the Scottish Office was flooded with letters from the raiders' agent, Donald Shaw, and their M.P., and there were many press reports as well; at the end of February the matter was briefly debated in the House of Commons.[13]

Why was there such a furore about these seven men? In fact the men themselves were fairly irrelevant; what mattered was their symbolic status as ex-service Highlanders who had waited since the end of the war for the land they had been 'promised' until forced to unlawfully seize that land. The landowner was very bitter about the whole situation, insisting that the raiders had been offered crofts elsewhere in Skye. He wrote several letters to the Scottish Land and Property Federation, and *The Scotsman* published a letter from the Federation on his behalf on 1 June, but public opinion was too strongly on the crofters' side for him to gain much sympathy.[14]

The men had been summoned to appear before the Court of Session on 12 May but did not do so (their counsel said it was because they 'had not sufficient funds to pay their way to Edinburgh'). On 26 May the raiders were present in Court and were sentenced to two months imprisonment for 'confessed and wilful breach of interdict', after which the storm broke afresh. On 30 May there was a long and impassioned debate in parliament, with a great deal of rhetoric about men languishing in Calton gaol because they had trusted the government at the time of the war.[15] There were no dissenting voices to the view that the men should be released from prison and given holdings. On 1st June the Scottish Office wrote to the Board

> We were informed that Mr. D. Shaw, The Land League, and similar people, are out to exploit this case for inter alia their own ends. The Labour M.P.s after Wednesday's debate were in a reasonable mood and gave the Government credit for reasonableness. It was therefore thought expedient to come to terms with the opposition before they were got at during the week-end. The first two points were (1) apology and withdrawal of the raiders (2) conveyance of any undertaking by them to the Court by Secretary for Scotland in a friendly spirit. ... The main promise, so far as the Board is concerned, is that the raiders are to be offered holdings in Skye next year. Next year was stated deliberately instead of next spring in order to give you more time. 'In Skye' was specified so that the offer might be in any part of Skye and not necessarily in the neighbourhood of Elgoll.

The announcement was made the same day in the House of Commons,[16] and the men were released from prison on 4 June after apologising to the Court and promising to obey the interdict. The Board wrote to the owner of the Strathaird estate in the hope of getting him to yield land on which they could settle the men, but he replied angrily that he had been told very definitely by one of the Board's officials that if he gave up Glasnakille and Drinan no more would be taken from him, and he reiterated his determination that under no circumstances was he prepared to give up any more of his estate. The Board therefore decided to offer the men land on Kilbride estate.

Kilbride was part of the MacDonald estates.[17] At the time of the uproar in the House of Commons the Board had already been negotiating for some time with the proprietor's *curator bonis*, Arthur Kerr, for the purchase of five farms (Old Corry, Kilbride, Swordale, Suisinish and Borreraig). After various threats of forcible possession a section of the estate was raided in March 1921 and then again in November 1922, at which time the Board suspended negotiations for as long as the men were in possession. This appeared to the curator manifestly unfair; he was perfectly happy for the raiders to go on a black list but saw no reason 'why the scheme should not go on for those deserving Crofters...who through the Board's action in the past had been led to suppose that they would have additional land.' He pointed out that the raid was a small one, and that the delay was causing great inconvenience to innocent parties and to the estate as a whole. But the Secretary for Scotland remained adamant: nothing would be done while raiders remained on the land.

In January 1923 the tenants of the raided farm had the men interdicted (the proprietor played no part in this). Three of them ignored the interdict. On 6 June the Scottish Office noted with regard to the Kilbride raiders: 'So far as their position vis a vis the Board is concerned the logical consequences of the Strathaird case seems to be that if and when these men have withdrawn and purged their offence against the Court they will be restored to the Board's list of approved applicants and (if suitable 1st preference ex-service men) will be offered holdings in Skye by the end of 1924.' The Board advised the raiders' agent that if the Court's orders were obeyed, the men would be offered holdings in Skye the following year. Shaw insisted that the holdings must be on Kilbride farm, which the Board refused to promise.

In August 1923 the Board advised the Secretary for Scotland that they intended to use their compulsory powers under Part I of the 1919 Act to acquire Kilbride estate. The regulations (which had, in fact, been drawn up by the Secretary for Scotland only the previous month) called for public advertisements of this to be made in the press—and that was the first the MacDonald estate heard about it. The curator was horrified, because the obvious inference which the public would draw was that it was the estate which had held up, or even opposed, the proceedings. The Board insisted the only reason they had used their compulsory powers was to expedite the settlement. This was undeniably one reason, but it was also clearly an attempt, in the wake of the House of Commons debates, to demonstrate to one and all that the Board were acting decisively when it came to settling Skye. Internally it was admitted that there was perhaps something to be said for the curator's 'contention that the public may suppose that the Estate were not willing to facilitate a scheme.' However, in reply to the Kerr they disingenuously insisted, 'The introduction of the compulsory procedure was not intended to imply that the Estate were responsible for the delay which had occurred, nor in the Board's view is it possible to regard it as open to that interpretation'.[18] The use of compulsory powers may have been justifiable, but keeping the estate in the dark certainly was not.

The Board then had to prepare schemes for the farms. Controversy followed later that year when the Strathaird raiders were offered holdings on

Kilbride, their agent insisting that this land was unsuitable and that they should be given lands on Strathaird; the Board had to remind the Secretary for Scotland of their undertaking to the proprietor of Strathaird when he gave up Glasnakille and Drinan that no more land would be taken from him. Eventually, after the whole thing had dragged on very much longer, three of the men accepted holdings on the estate; of the remaining three it was said, 'it is extremely doubtful whether they now want Crofts at all'—an ironic anticlimax to all the heartrending speeches in parliament about their desperate need for land. Calum Robertson, whose father got a croft on Drinan in 1926, said that 'as far as the Elgol people were concerned I don't think they were really that desperate for land, I think they were just making a point',[19] which confirmed my own feelings about the *symbolic* importance of that raid. (The Kilbride raiders, however, were in deadly earnest, and two of their sons are still on the original crofts.)

There remained two Skye farms which the Board had not yet tackled. Claigan was another MacLeod property.[20] It was considered by the Board before, during, and immediately after the war, but then they began negotiating with MacLeod for the purchase of Bracadale and left Claigan alone for the time being. A threat to raid the farm was first made in 1919 but was not carried out because the men still hoped the Board would settle them.[21] A deputation of ex-service applicants explained this to the Board's local man in April 1920, who asked them if they would take holdings on Bracadale

> but they stated emphatically that they would not saying 'why should we leave our own Parish and suitable land for Small Holdings in our vicinity, and leave that land in possession of a man who has three other "led" farms already, and who took Claigan for his son when he was of military age to get him exempted from the army'. This seems to embitter the applicants more than anything else.

In June, however, the Under Secretary for Scotland wrote to the Board, 'Is not this a case of letting sleeping dogs lie?', and nothing was done about it.

In the summer of 1923 the Board revived their proposal for a Part II scheme on Claigan. When schemes had been mooted in the past MacLeod of MacLeod had blown hot and cold; on this occasion he announced himself implacably opposed. Formal intimation of their intention to prepare a scheme was submitted to the estate in May 1924. The factor sent the Board a diatribe, in the margins of which someone from the Board pencilled in comments. MacLeod of MacLeod had willingly offered Bracadale to the Board, said the factor, and it seemed 'unduly oppressive that the Board should revive the Claigan proposal having in view the sacrifice [underlined by the Board] which MacLeod of Macleod had already made'. 'To propose settling crofters within a few hundred yards ['about 700!' is pencilled in] of the Castle is extremely harsh'; also, this had always been looked on as the castle home farm, 'although circumstances compel its occupancy by a tenant farmer as a temporary expedient ['over 10 years!' pencilled in]'. However, when the seven holdings near the castle grounds were left out, MacLeod's objections were dropped, and a scheme went ahead. (The aftermath of the Claigan settlement is discussed later in the chapter.)

The last estate to be settled—Waternish—was not raided, although there were the usual threats. This was one of the most long drawn-out and convoluted cases of all.[22] The farm was owned by the trustees of the late Captain Allan Macdonald. In fact, only one of the trustees, A.R. Macdonald (sometimes styled 'Captain' himself, at other times styled 'Waternish'), still survived, and he was also the owner of the adjoining estate of Geary.

Applications were received in 1919, and by 1921 the Board decided it was time to do something about the place. A scheme was prepared, embracing some 5000 acres and providing for 24 new holdings and 56 enlargements. Although the proprietor would have been willing to sell the whole estate, the Board would not consider it, and he was implacably opposed to a Part II scheme. One reason he gave was that there were empty crofts on his own estate, so he did not believe the demand for holdings on Waternish was genuine. A sub-commissioner noted he had repeatedly told the proprietor that 'the sole reason for his difficulty in getting tenants for vacant holdings on his Estate is their smallness, that they are not worth taking. While they *had* to do so in former days, the advance of time has opened the eyes of crofters to the necessity of having sufficient land to eke out an existence.'

In June 1922 the Board sent the proprietor a formal notice of their intention to prepare a scheme. He objected, and at a formal hearing in October insisted there was no real demand. The Chairman replied that in view of the Board's limited funds, 'you may take it from us that we would not be moving in this part of Skye or any part of the West Highlands unless we were obeying a demand.'[23] During the months that followed the Board made various amendments to the scheme in accordance with the proprietor's representations, but when they were submitted to the proprietor he was still not satisfied. This went on for nearly *three years*. Finally, in the spring of 1925, agreement appeared to have been reached, when suddenly the estate dropped a bombshell. Macdonald called at the agent's office with his younger son who had become 25 years of age on 26 April, at which age, under the will of the late proprietor, the estate was to be made over to him.[24]

The Chairman of the Board was shocked and disappointed for this meant that they effectively had to start all over again. In October 1925 they sent the formal notice of their intention to prepare a scheme. The new proprietor insisted there was no evidence of any demand in the area; also, he claimed that without the land demanded by the Board the remainder of the farm could not be worked profitably. The Board did not believe a word of this, but as they had no report more recent than 1923 the local man was instructed to enquire into the demand. He replied that although there might be some difficulty in finding enough ex-service applicants on the estate because so many of the proposed holdings were of the larger type and the applicants lacked the necessary capital, by going outside the estate, or including civilians, he was certain all the holdings would be filled.

In December the local M.P. asked why Waternish was not yet settled. The Board advised him, 'The Estate concealed essential facts regarding the ownership of the property until recently. This concealment caused at least a year's delay.' (Such openness is in marked contrast to the later Scibercross story in Sutherland, where the estate's duplicity was never made known.) A formal hearing was set by the Board for mid February 1926. The proprietor, needless to say, lodged representations. After the hearing the agents sent the Board a note of the considerable modifications which the proprietor wanted to make to the scheme, greatly curtailing its extent. The Board found most of them unacceptable and decided to go ahead with an Order confirming the original scheme with only slight modifications. In June the Order was sent to the Secretary for Scotland who also received the landlord's representations. In their Answers to these representations, the Board wrote that they believed 'the amendments now desired by the Estate are framed with a view to making the scheme of little real effect and negligible so far as its purpose of meeting the demand for new holdings is concerned.' They therefore considered compulsory procedure justified.

The Secretary for Scotland referred the matter to the Land Court for inquiry. In November the Court produced their report. They were of opinion that 'no undue hardship would accrue to the beneficiary in the Trust, if he is left with this portion of the estate in his hands.'[25] They also felt that a better scheme could be effected if the whole estate were purchased. The Board did not disagree, but (as mentioned at the beginning of Chapter 5) they endeavoured 'to avoid the use of monies provided for land settlement purposes in the acquisition of property already fully occupied by crofting tenants.' The Land Court's suggestions really amounted to a complete rearrangement of the existing townships, which would have cost a great deal more public money than any government could have contemplated.

The Secretary of State still had not come to a decision after the Land Court's report and had a meeting with Captain Macdonald in February 1927. The Scottish Office then asked for the Board's observations on two of the points raised by Waternish: that the proposed fair rents were too low and that many of the holdings on the estate were lying vacant. The Board provided evidence that the rents were not too low and advised the Secretary of State that they had investigated claims of vacant holdings more than once and found them all occupied. Finally the go-ahead was given; the Board took entry at Whitsunday 1927 and prepared for the holders to take entry at Whitsunday 1928. But this was not the end of the saga.

The problem was that there simply were not enough applicants with sufficient capital to take over the sheep stock. In April 1928 the Board asked the Treasury for sanction to reduce the cash contribution required from 25% to 10%, and this was approved.[26] However, in March 1929 the Department noted that 'a sufficiency of suitable applicants was not obtained for settlement at Whitsunday, 1928. The Department are at present examining the question of varying the number of holdings, either by reducing their size and so accommodating a greater number, or by increasing the size and decreasing the number. In this connection enquiries are still proceeding as to the demand for the different sizes of holding, but no decision in the matter can yet be made.' The estate must have been chortling at this vindication of their stance.

How did holders subsequently fare in Skye? The combination of a detailed report which Colin MacDonald made on the Talisker settlement at the end of 1924 and interviews by me with two people who grew up there means that the fullest information is available for that migration scheme. North Talisker was settled at Whitsunday 1923, temporary accommodation being provided for the Lewis and Harris migrants by the Board of Agriculture. (The holders were not charged rent or rates that first year.) Of the 68 holdings in the settlement 43 were tenanted by Harris families, 20 by families from Lewis, and five by Skye people. They took over a club stock and were expected to build their own houses and byres.

According to Colin MacDonald's report, by the end of 1924 only three holders had built permanent dwelling houses (all three were merchants).[27] In 1925 the Board asked the Treasury for sanction to increase the amount of the individual building loans from £100 to £150. The K & LTR commented: 'the real trouble is the occupants of these wooden houses who came from Harris and Lewis find themselves in very much more comfortable circumstances than they were ever in before and are in no hurry to fulfil their obligations as to building houses.'[28] One woman I spoke to, Mrs Liz Sutherland, who grew up at Talisker, had a clear recollection of their house being built, but that was not until 1928.[29] On the other hand, unlike the Shinness houses, built by contractors, the Hebridean stone houses have lasted; even where crofters decided to build more commodious accommodation in recent years, the original houses still serve as farm buildings.

The idea of the Talisker sheep stock club was that any profits would be paid out as dividends to the holders, but for most of its history there were no profits and hence no dividends. A report at the beginning of 1930 noted: 'The management of the North Talisker club sheep stock has not been altogether satisfactory, and it has been found necessary to exercise careful supervision. Many of the holders are inexperienced in the management of sheep and they do not co-operate well.'30 Until the early 1970s there were two full-time shepherds employed, and most of the income went to pay their salaries. By 1988 there were no shepherds employed, as a group of keen able-bodied holders had decided they were better off doing the work themselves. Whoever works on the hill or at the fanks gets paid for it, and what is left over at the end of the year is paid as a dividend to the shareholders, a system which has proved very satisfactory.[31]

Sheep therefore made no real contribution to the holders' incomes for most of the settlement's existence. In the initial stages the scheme works provided good wages to most households (Colin MacDonald noted at the end of 1924 that some £6000 had been paid in wages), but when those came to an end other ancillary employment had to be found. For the Lewis people it was mostly fishing. Liz Sutherland remembered her father going every season.

> When they went to the fishing they went in May or June and they were home at the end of August, that was the summer season. And then, in October, they would go away to the winter fishing down south, down in Yarmouth and that...and they were away until November. And then he was home in the win-

> tertime but he had a small boat himself and him and my brother did white fishing and lobster fishing and they sent the lobsters to Billingsgate.
> The ones that went to the herring fishing it was all Lewis people, but nearly everyone of the Harris people *and* some of the Lewis people went to the salmon fishing in Perth in the summertime.[32]

The families who came from Harris concentrated more on tweed-making than on fishing. At the end of 1924 Colin MacDonald noted that 31 families were carrying on tweed-making. Each one aimed at manufacturing annually at least one web for sale, about 80 yards: 'but as they require to buy the wool at around 1*s*.2*d*. per lb and pay 5½*d*. per lb for carding it, and as the market for Harris tweed is meantime very slow, the profit from this source is not great and is rather precarious.' But in 1950 the author of an article on Skye wrote: 'There is only domestic fishing, but the community is busy and prosperous from the hand weaving of tweeds'.[33]

Colin MacDonald described the diet of the holders as follows.

> for *Breakfast*—Porridge and milk, tea and bread and butter.
> *Dinner*—Potatoes and fish (mainly cuddies and lythe, but occasionally cod, haddock or herring) tea and bread and butter.
> *Tea*—Bread and butter.
> This may be regarded as the standard diet, and although plain, is really very good. Some of the holders who can afford it have better or more varied diet.

Danny MacLeod, who grew up at Talisker in the thirties, remembered 'they would eat herring on Monday, Tuesday, Wednesday, Thursday, Friday, Saturday and then meat on Sunday.' Of course, they had potatoes too.

> They did a bit of fishing as well. In those days you could get fish, you could go to the lochs and fish off the lochs, you were bound sure to get fish. If you had a boat, and if you didn't you could go out with a neighbour who had a boat, you could be sure of getting fish.[34]

Colin MacDonald noted, 'It is significant that the women of the settlement are in the main contented and consider their present position a decided improvement.' This came across very strongly in the interview with Liz Sutherland. She had often heard her mother say that when they were in Lewis they were crowded together so closely that 'when the hens got out they went in my grandfather's corn'. There had not been anywhere to graze the cow so her grandmother had to take her to the shieling some thirty miles away. Coming to Skye where they had so much space was a liberation for them. She also remembered what a happy community spirit there was until she left in the 1960s.

The Claigan scheme, carried out in the teeth of landowner opposition, had

8 Talisker schoolchildren. Liz Sutherland in tartan dress.

a very different outcome.[35] In 1925 the Board had had great difficulty in finding 15 suitable tenants, mainly because the holdings required substantial capital. The first list of chosen applicants was rejected by the estate as so many of the the men came from other areas; MacLeod of MacLeod wanted to know why Dunvegan applicants had been passed over. The Board's problem was that there were civilian applicants on the MacLeod estates with the necessary capital, but they had been turned down in order to settle ex-servicemen. Yet of the nine ex-service applicants from the estate, one 'was the only man who threatened to raid Claigan, yet he now refuses the chance of a holding—maintains that he has not the capital'; one had gone to New

Zealand, one to Canada, one to southern Scotland, and the rest had no capital. In April 1926 the restriction in favour of ex-servicemen was dropped; even then a memo of 1927 noted that of the 15 holders first selected only six actually took up holdings.

As a Part II scheme, once the holders were settled at Whitsunday 1926 that should have been the end of it, but in 1936 the number of vacant holdings forced the Department to look into the matter. At Whitsunday of that year three holdings were vacant; another would be vacated at Whitsunday 1937, and two further renunciations were expected, so that at Whitsunday 1938 only half the settlement would be tenanted. An official of the Department commented, 'there is no cooperation, or harmony, in the township and on this account the management of the sheep stock suffers, and this combined with a general opposition to the "club" system makes fresh applicants rather chary of coming forward.'

In October 1936 Colin MacDonald—previously encountered as a senior sub-commissioner, now Divisional Land Officer—wrote that he considered the Claigan holdings amongst the best in Skye, and that the reason for the comparative failure of the scheme had more to do with the estate's attitude than with anything else. However, he admitted that things had come to such a pass that some kind of change in the scheme was necessary. He began his report of a meeting with Mrs MacLeod in August 1937, by setting out what he saw as the main causes for the comparative failure of the scheme. These were: (1) lack of mutual trust, (2) non-residence of holders (three had never resided on their holdings and often failed to do their share of the work, which had been a continuous source of complaint), (3) remoteness (there was no through road so the settlement was very isolated), (4) lack of educational facilities (this had deterred various applicants from taking holdings), (5) the club system, and (6) estate indifference.

Mrs MacLeod then proposed feuing the farm to the Department, but the Department did not think they could justify paying an annual feu duty on top of all the compensation already paid out to the estate. Colin MacDonald commented, 'The suggestion to purchase arose out of recognition that the Estate never seemed to have grasped the fact that the full responsibility of the scheme was theirs. ... This false position had so developed that whenever anything happened which called for ordinary estate management, the proprietor instead of functioning as an ordinary proprietor should, got into the habit of handing the trouble over to the Department.'

The estate took legal action to remove the non-resident holders, but by September 1938 there were nine vacant holdings, and Colin MacDonald was asked to submit a revised scheme. He analysed the situation thus.

> I have on several occasions recently in reports drawn attention to the slacking off of demand for holdings not only in Skye but in 'remote' districts throughout the Highlands and Islands. The truth is that present day applicants for holdings (bar perhaps in certain parts of Lewis, Harris and Barra) are not prepared to undergo the discomfort and hardships which their fathers readily accepted in order to establish themselves on holdings.

He went on, 'There is indeed a great contrast between the present demand and the clamant urge which characterised the demand for holdings in Skye before, and for some years after the War'. The Department at that moment actually had 30 vacant holdings on their Skye estates, with little hope of filling them. 'Provided there is on offer a good holding with a good house, steading, water supply and easy access to market, school and the outside world there is no lack of demand but where these conditions are lacking it is a very different matter.' He listed the chief factors which chilled demand for holdings.

(1) where houses are situated upwards of 2 or 3 miles from a town or considerable village or a bus route.
(2) where access roads to or within the settlement are in poor order.
(3) where the settlement is situated at a roadend i.e. where there is no through-going traffic. This is very important, as, in conjunction with long and bad roads it results in the women folk on the holdings being 'exiled' from shops and the outside world—'a terrible loneliness' as one woman so placed put it to me.
(4) where holders are expected themselves to erect with the aid of a limited loan, buildings which at contract prices would cost approximately twice that amount.
(5) where there is no water supply and sanitary accommodation in the house.
(6) where there is no school in the immediate locality.
(7) where there is a Sheep Stock Club and an obligation on ingoing holders to take over a share in same.

He concluded that all those factors applied to Claigan, but still thought 'the present deplorable situation' could have been avoided if the estate had shown less apathy during the initial years of the settlement.

A new scheme was planned, with only seven holdings, three self-contained and four sharing an area of common grazing. 'The existing scheme suffers from a bad reputation, and the intention is to present to applicants a scheme, new in form and character for the purpose of counteracting the general opposition to Claigan.' The Department began interviewing applicants, but in the summer of 1939 a serious misunderstanding arose with Mrs MacLeod concerning the estate's liability for the sheep stock at a holder's outgoing. In November 1939 the Department arranged to purchase the farm, and an era came to an end.

So much of Skye was taken over for land settlement purposes, encompassing such diverse areas and types of schemes, that an overall conclusion on the situation there is not be possible. It is ironic that the place where demand for land in the early 1920s was so clamant that all funds had to be diverted to it was also the place which in the late 1930s had more vacant holdings in it than the rest of the Hebrides put together. For many years it must have seemed that the land settlement programme in Skye had been a terrible waste of public money, but in recent decades the trend has, to a certain extent at least, reversed itself, and a Skye croft is once again seen as a desirable thing to have. Further discussion of this—since Skye in the 1980s cannot be discussed in isolation from the rest of the Highlands and Islands—must wait until Chapter 11.

CHAPTER 9

Schemes in the Eastern Lowlands

Although the Board of Agriculture received a number of applications for smallholdings in the Lowlands, the demand on paper was no guide to actual demand, because in the Lowlands most potential holders only applied once they knew that a scheme was definitely going ahead. Lowland schemes were rarely the result of applicants writing in to say they wanted land on a particular farm: they were proposed because the owner offered a farm or estate to the Board, because the Board's local officer learned that a lease was running out, or because the property was advertised for sale. The constant stream of letters from applicants demanding action which swell the files of most crofting estates are absent from the majority of files on estates in non-crofting counties. Another difference is that whereas a Highland applicant generally insisted on remaining in a specific area, Lowland applicants were much more flexible.

In 1921 H.M. Conacher summed up the situation in these areas thus

> The majority of the people in the rural districts acquiesce in the existing disposal and distribution of land. Indeed in many parts of Scotland the type of small holder corresponding to the crofter has died out, and the system with which he was associated has been so thoroughly superseded that, in the ranks of society which replaced him, nobody represents the succession and therefore nobody feels disinherited. Over great tracts in the south-east of Scotland there is nothing but arable farms, with large farmers and skilled workers. Such villages as exist are inhabited mainly by such tradesmen as are still required for a country-side, which has hardly any peasantry apart from the farm worker.[1]

Since the clamour from applicants did not exist, the main motive for land settlement in the Lowlands was to stem the tide of migration from rural areas into towns. However, the problems which beset schemes in the Lowlands were not necessarily different from those in the crofting counties, since landowner opposition or inefficiency by the Board could manifest itself on either side of the Highland line.

The North-East

Comparatively few holdings were created in this area. The reason may simply be that large numbers of small farms were already in existence there before the land settlement programme began.[2] However, one of the purchases which the Board carried out under the Small Holding Colonies Acts was an Aberdeenshire farm, Fortrie, which comprised 826 acres arable land, and 12 acres pasture.[3] The Board wrote to the Treasury in April 1919 requesting sanction to purchase the farm in spite of being unable to estimate of the costs of adapting and equipping the farm as a small holding colony. The K & LTR's response was

> A question of policy is involved, and it seems to me that you should insist on the Board presenting you with complete estimates of the total cost of carrying out the scheme, so that you can inform the Chancellor of the Exchequer of the amount of deadweight burden that will have to be carried, and he can then decide whether it should be gone on with or not.[4]

The Treasury sanctioned the purchase on this occasion but warned the Board that they would be unwilling to consider future proposals without some kind of estimate.

When the Board asked for sanction to purchase Old Whitemyres, another Aberdeenshire farm, in 1921, they provided all the estimates required but still ran into trouble with the Treasury.[5] The scheme was for twelve holders who had been trained in pig-rearing and poultry-keeping at Craibstone Training Centre (in Aberdeenshire). The K & LTR advised the Treasury he had been informed that 'some of the trained ex-service men in view for this settlement are disabled so I suppose criticism should be moderated'. However, the Treasury, while prepared to sanction the purchase, had plenty of criticisms to make. They wanted it to be limited to eight holdings as buildings already existed to accommodate that number, and they thought the proposed fair rental of £110 was unduly low for 70 acres of market gardens and six acres of pasture only three miles from Aberdeen.

The Board replied that the scheme was specifically designed to provide as many holdings as possible for specially trained ex-service men.

> It has so far been found very difficult to make provision for them and there is a good deal of public criticism regarding the non-provision of holdings for men who have been trained partly at the expense of the Government. The present scheme appears to the Board to offer a suitable opportunity of providing for these men. The holdings, besides being used for pig-rearing and poultry-keeping, will be developed into market gardens. In the meantime, however, they cannot be described as market gardens. They will only become such after heavy manuring and much labour on the part of the holders and the rents fixed in respect of the holdings cannot therefore be on a market garden basis.

The Treasury agreed to the Board's original scheme.[6] Prices of materials and labour then soared, and in 1923 further expenditure was sanctioned. This was still not enough, so in 1924 the Board had to ask for yet more money. The K & LTR wrote, 'The Board have spent all their money and most of the adaptation work is still to be done.' However, he went on, 'It seems impossible at this stage to refuse the sanction asked for. One reason for agreeing is that it is desirable to encourage as much as possible the disabled holders.' The Treasury wrote one of their stiff notes to the Board, bewailing the increased expenditure on so many items; however, because of the desirability of encouraging the disabled holders, they acquiesced.

Whitemyres is mentioned in one later file, entitled 'Reports on Successful Smallholders'.[7] The interest of this file lies in the honesty of the local officers' reports (the success stories were used for the Annual Reports; the remainder were buried in oblivion). The 1928 one on Whitemyres said

> The progress made by the holders here cannot be described as satisfactory. Those who have given their whole time to their holdings are in a more or less satisfactory financial position but a number of the others who depend on part time employment in the city have quite failed to give sufficient attention to the cultivation of their holdings with a result that the cultivation has been neglected and the rearing of stock has suffered, therefrom, considerably. Three of them are heavily in arrears and steps are being taken to have them removed. This policy should be continued and the holdings thus vacated, let to 'Bona Fide' residents with market garden qualifications.

A scheme in Kincardine which did not involve purchase shows how long it could take for such schemes to get under way even when there was no landowner opposition.[8] Crowhillock farm was offered by the proprietor, the Earl of Kerry, before the war and began to be seriously considered by the Board in 1917.[9] By March 1919 the proprietor had expressed agreement with the Board's provisional scheme under the 1911 Act; in August Secretary for Scotland sanction had been received for the required expenditure, and all that was needed was a formal Land Court Order. The tenant wished to relinquish his tenancy at Martinmas, and by agreement with the proprietor the four new holders were settled at that time.

Yet no application for an Order was lodged with the Land Court, and in April 1920 the Board advised the agent that since the Land Settlement Act had been passed, it was now necessary to proceed in accordance with that Act. The agent replied, 'In the circumstances our client has no course open to him but to assent to what is proposed'; he felt, however, 'that no adequate explanation has been given of the prolonged delay on the part of the Board in dealing with this matter but for which there would have been no occasion for the additional delay now necessitated by the Land Settlement (Scotland) Act. The delay has resulted in much inconvenience and, as you will understand, has been the occasion of much adverse comment in the district.'

The agents wrote again in August, still awaiting confirmation of the scheme and again in October:

> The lands were taken over by the Board at Martinmas 1919, nearly a year ago, when the price of the buildings and the compensation in respect of the loss of rental should have been paid. Not only has this not been done, but the Factor has even been unable to collect the half year's rents due at Whitsunday last, as

> the Landholders are without notification of the rents as finally fixed. Lord Kerry is not disposed to allow the matter to remain longer in its present position, and unless there is an immediate prospect of its being dealt with, he will have to seek for such redress as is open to him.

Secretary for Scotland approval was given later that month, but the Order confirming the scheme was not issued until July 1921, and Treasury sanction was not sought until February 1922. At that time the K & LTR wrote, 'This is undoubtedly an extravagant scheme but it is in effect completed and it is difficult to see that any useful criticism can be made now.'[10]

Perthshire and Angus

One of the properties acquired by the Board under the Small Holding Colonies Acts was part (about 690 acres) of the Castle Huntly estate in Perthshire, described by the Board's officer who inspected it in January 1919 as 'one of the finest agricultural properties I have been over'.[11] The transaction went through very smoothly.

At this time the Board were also enthusiastic about another property they wished to acquire under the Small Holding Colonies Acts, the 1624-acre farm of Gagie, Angus, just $4\frac{1}{2}$ miles from the centre of Dundee.[12] They were always keen to acquire farms near large towns and cities because of the ready market there would be for pigs, poultry and vegetable produce. (Such a consideration was never mentioned in connection with Highland schemes.) The Treasury wanted some idea of the cost of the provision and adaptation of buildings, and they were unhappy that about half of the arable land would not become available until 1923, which appeared to them 'to detract largely from the value of the estate for the purpose of the Small Holding Colonies Acts'. The Secretary of the Board replied

> In all cases of purchase under the Small Holding Colonies Acts it will be necessary to provide additional buildings since in all cases it is the intention of the Act to divide a small number of large holdings into a large number of small holdings. With regard to the possibility of furnishing estimates of cost of such adaptations and equipment they desire me to state that they have fully considered this question, and they are satisfied that it is not practicable to put forward comprehensive and reliable estimates of cost at the time of completion of a purchase.[13]

As for the availability of the arable land, the Treasury were reminded that 'it is practically impossible to find estates of sufficient size in Scotland where leases do not form a barrier to early entry to the lands.'

The K & LTR agreed with the Board on this point: 'it is perfectly true that every estate of any size must have farms which are let from varying dates, and it would be impossible to find any reasonably sized property where all the farm leases expired in a period of 3 or 4 years.' However, he thought it quite unacceptable that the Board could not produce estimates of future building costs at time of purchase. 'What business or commercial man would enter on a purchase of any kind of article from land to elephants without having some idea in his mind of what he was going to do with his purchase, and what sums he would require to develop and maintain the speculation he was embarking upon?' He thought that full figures concerning prospective costs should be given before sanction was granted to any purchase, 'or else you simply give them a blank cheque.'[14] The Treasury took a less hard line and sanctioned the purchase, though they added the 'hope' that in future the Board would give them some indication of future expenditure.

The delay in the acquisition of the 157-acre farm of East Pilmore, Perthshire was not caused by the Board, nor by the Treasury (though the latter did take their time about giving their sanction) but, very unusually, by the Secretary for Scotland.[15] In July 1921 a reasonable price was asked and the Board prepared a scheme for nine (ultimately seven) new holdings, but when the Secretary for Scotland was asked for his approval he wrote, 'Unless there is a strong demand for small holdings in this quarter I should much prefer to see this money expended in the Highlands where the demand is constant and ardent.' As was seen in the foregoing chapters, this statement was undoubtedly true, but the fact that Robert Munro, the Secretary for Scotland at that time, was a Highlander and in conflict with Lord Leverhulme over Lewis may help to explain his attitude. The Board replied that the demand was indeed strong: the number of unsettled applicants in East Perthshire and Forfarshire (as Angus was known at that time) was 186 ex-servicemen and 48 civilians, of whom 52 ex-service and six civilians specifically asked for holdings in this parish, and the acquisition of the farm was therefore justified. 'Account should also be taken', they continued, 'of the Board's objective, indicated to the Cabinet Committee that 300 ex-service men should be settled in the Lowlands during 18 months from January 1920.' The K & LTR advised the Treasury on 20 September he thought the scheme should go through ('Proximity to the large town of Dundee is a good feature for these small holders.'),[16] but it was 8 October before the Treasury gave their sanction—by which time a furious proprietor had complained to the Secretary for Scotland about the Board's dilatoriness in settling!

Lower Auchinlay farm, Perthshire, was discovered in October 1921 by one of the Board's officers who thought the 300 acres of arable land could provide for eight holdings.[17] The Director of Land Settlement met the proprietor and reported to the Board, 'The Estate would strenuously object to any proposal for small Holdings.' In July 1922 the Board intimated their intention to prepare a Part II scheme. The K & LTR advised the Treasury, 'The officers of the Board have been endeavouring to secure suitable land in this area for many months, and can find none other than the farm of Auchinlay.'[18]

The formal hearing was held in December. The proprietor had lodged objections but at the actual hearing backed down and offered to sell. The Board bought the farm in August/September 1923, though in November 1924 the escalating cost of building forced them to seek more money from the Treasury.

The Lothians

This was an area where large farms predominated, smallholdings 'being mostly confined to market gardens in Midlothian and East Lothian'.[19] The farm of Thorntonloch (about 670 acres), on the Dirleton estate in East Lothian, was inspected by a sub-commissioner in January 1919 and considered very suitable for smallholdings.[20] The proprietrix was unwilling to make it available under the 1911 Act but was prepared to sell. The Board decided to purchase it under the Small Holding Colonies Acts and, after some haggling over the price, agreement was reached in July and a submission sent to the Secretary for Scotland.

The Secretary for Scotland, however, refused to sanction the purchase until the new Land Settlement Bill was passed. The agents were not willing to suspend negotiations indefinitely, but the Scottish Office were adamant. The Board therefore arranged to lease the farm with an option to purchase (if the Bill was passed then the money would be available; if not then the farm could have been sub-let).

In 1920, after the Act was in force, there were constant protests by the estate at the Board's interminable delays in coming to a settlement. In August the Director of Land Settlement provided some provisional estimates and wrote to the Under Secretary for Scotland

> No building or other adaptation works have proceeded on this farm, but you will no doubt remember that this case was criticised in the Estimates Debate on the grounds that the Board was working the farm instead of carrying out the sub-division and was not working it to best advantage. The complete estimates for the scheme will in due course be submitted for the formal approval of the Secretary for Scotland and the Treasury, but, meantime, in order to avoid further criticism and to enable works on water supply, roads &c to proceed, I should be glad if the Secretary for Scotland can see his way to sanction such expenditure as may be incurred before the formal approval of the estimates.

The Secretary for Scotland felt he had to agree, although he was very alarmed at the cost.[21]

Broxburnhall, West Lothian, is unusual for the Lowlands in that pressure for holdings on the farm came from applicants.[22] In September 1917 the Scottish Smallholders Organisation sent fifteen applications for smallholdings in Broxburn to the Board. In August 1918 the Broxburn Smallholders Organisation advised the Board that the lease of Broxburnhall expired at Martinmas. The Board wrote to the agents, who replied that the owner, the Earl of Buchan, was in France, In October the Broxburn Agricultural Co-Operative Society urged the Board to 'take into immediate consideration the Applications forwarded to the Board some months ago from the Society, asking that land might be found for Smallholdings in this district. The need of providing land is imperative.'

It was November before the agents advised the Board of the proprietor's stance. The present tenant had been there for 19 years, had farmed the place well, and did not want to leave, and Lord Buchan felt himself bound to consider the man's wishes and allow him to stay. Other objections were fears of restrictions on further feuing and of the effects of smallholdings on the shale mines underneath. The Board felt a good scheme could be made if the estate acquiesced and if their claims were not prohibitive, but 'At present there are no signs that the Estate will assist.'

In the spring of 1920 the senior sub-commissioner now in charge of this scheme advised the Board that one of the tenant's sons was an ex-service man. He suggested that a large joint holding of about 100 acres, along with the dwelling house and steading, could be given to father and son, with the remainder of the farm divided up into two holdings and 50 to 60 allotments. This proposal—and the history of the case—were presented to Land Committee in May, with suggestions: that a meeting be held with a deputation from the Co-Operative Society to ascertain whether the provision of allotments would meet the main demand, and if so, to find out whether, if the tenant accepted the idea, the landlord would agree. A meeting was held with the deputation in June, but little came of it as few people would apply for an allotment without knowing its situation and rent first, so that assessing demand was not really feasible.

One unusual twist in this case was that while Lord Buchan was actively opposing a scheme, his heir-at-law, Lord Cardross, was on the side of the applicants and actively working on their behalf. (One would have to research more of the family history to understand the motives behind this conflict.) In August Lord Cardross too was pressing the Board for a decision. This was, however, 1920, when the Board's funds were nearly used up, and the Director of Land Settlement decided a scheme for this farm could not proceed until more money was available. When this decision became known floods of protests poured in from various organisations (e.g. Comrades of the Great War and the local branch of Discharged and Demobilised Sailors and Soldiers), as well as from Lord Cardross, whose letter criticising the Board was published in *The Scotsman* in December.

In 1921, when further funds were available, the Board prepared a new scheme for the 184-acre farm, providing for eight holdings ranging from 2 acres to 50 acres, with 2 acres reserved for allotments to be managed by the local parish council; the existing tenant was to be given one of the large holdings. Secretary for Scotland approval was given in October, and after some quibbling the Treasury gave their sanction in April 1922. The proprietor's agents presented objections,[23] and after further delays the formal hearing was held in November.

In July 1923 an assistant secretary of the Board wrote to the Chairman, 'Since the hearing unavailing efforts have been made to come to an amicable settlement with the proprietor and tenants in this case.' He recommended that a confirming Order be sent to the Secretary for Scotland with a request that settlement be carried out at Martinmas 1923, leaving compensation claims to be settled later. In September the Secretary for Scotland returned the Order with his consent and the authority to proceed in anticipation of assessment of compensation claims. Further complications ensued when it was discovered that one holding encroached on land previously feued, and the proprietor also got the Board's permission to feu an additional piece of land, so that the areas of several holdings had to be reduced in size. A new Order confirming the amended scheme had to be made, and it did not receive the Secretary for Scotland's consent until the end of 1925.

The farm of Parkhead, Linlithgow, West Lothian, was Crown property and was offered to the Board by the Office of Woods in September 1918 for the creation of smallholdings under the 1911 Act.[24] The Board took possession at Martinmas 1919 and 10 ex-servicemen were settled within the ensuing months.

In 1921 the Board purchased the property from the Office of Woods under Part I of the Land Settlement Act. In July of that year the Board realised that the cost of adaptation and erecting buildings was going to be much greater than anticipated; £8620 would be required for building loans compared to the £5690 sanctioned in April 1920. The Under Secretary for Scotland was puzzled by this, because building costs were certainly not above those of the previous spring; he wanted to know if the equipment now contemplated was more elaborate in some way.

The Board replied that apart from installing W.C.s in the houses, which was insisted on by the Local Authority, the equipment was not more elaborate.

> The increase is explained by the fact that while the estimates approved by the Secretary for Scotland on 23rd April, 1920 were actually prepared in December, 1919, the greater part of the work was carried out during 1920, when top prices were ruling for all building materials, and wages were advancing rapidly. For example, when the work commenced wages to tradesmen were only 1*s*.6*d*. per hour, while by July, 1920, they had increased to 2*s*.4*d*. per hour. The cost of bricks rose from 83*s*.6*d*. per 1000 in January, 1920, to 128*s*. per 1000 in September, 1920. Railway rates also rose 60% above pre-war levels on 15 January, 1920, and to 100% above the pre-war rate on 1st September, 1920. As a result of these increased costs the work has now been brought to a standstill owing to lack of funds.

Given the reaction of the Scottish Office to this request, the Treasury's response was predictable. The K & LTR's calculations showed that the cost per holder was £1931, and he added, 'The Board could surely use the money with more advantage elsewhere.' The Treasury considered the expenditure very extravagant and asked that the remaining work be carefully reviewed with the object of making economies. The Board replied

> The case is exceptional in the sense that the farm is Crown property and was offered to the Board in 1918 for Land Settlement purposes by the Office of Woods. The pressure exercised on the Board to project schemes of settlement to prepare for the position that would arise on demobilisation was at the time very great. There was difficulty in securing land at reasonable cost, and the Board could not reject an offer of Crown land which could be obtained without the need of resorting to the slow and expensive process of compulsory proceedings without leaving themselves open to legitimate criticism.

> The farm, moreover, while in some ways not an ideal subject for Land Settlement is situated in a district in which there was reason to anticipate a successful settlement. The Board made the most economical arrangements possible in their scheme of sub-division which as Their Lordships will know were undertaken before the recent Cabinet Enquiry at a time when the cost of works and equipment were at an abnormal figure, and they regret that no reduction in the figures is possible.

In August 1921 the holders wrote to the Board that they felt 'the time has arrived to make a remonstrance at the delay in getting various alterations and additions completed. Over a year has elapsed since we entered into occupation and many things are yet to finish.' There were gaps in march hedges and a number of gates had not yet been put up. The holders had been promised a road, which had failed to materialise, then recently they had been told by the Board's local officer that it was up to them to build the road, something they had not bargained for. They attempted to begin laying the road but the carts provided were unfit for the work; they also felt experienced supervision was essential and asked 'that the Board should take the matter over and complete the roads in a proper manner, as was promised.'

There were other complaints as well. The W.C.s had been erected some months earlier but were still not usable; the water supply was not yet secure, buildings on three holdings had been started and then left off very haphazardly, and it was now months since a workman had been on the job. The Board replied in September that they understood the holders had agreed to assist in laying the road and that tar was about to be delivered; the holders were also assured that all the works would soon be completed. An internal note of January 1922 commented, 'The bulk of the scheme is in an unfinished condition and if left any longer as it is the cost of finally completing the work may be greatly increased owing to damage by weather.' The urgency of the matter was stressed.

The senior sub-commissioner for the district remarked in February 1923, 'In my opinion the converted army huts will never be satisfactory as dwelling houses, since up to date they are neither wind nor water right.' In April the holders were 'making the state of the road an excuse for non-payment of rent.' In July questions were asked in parliament about the water supply and roads at Parkhead, and the chief surveyor was asked for the estimated cost of works 'necessary to remedy the complaints.' In September the Board asked the Scottish Office to authorise increased expenditure on both the water supply and roads. The Under Secretary for Scotland queried the cost of roads since he had understood that the Board would only supply the materials if the holders would lay them. 'Do the Board now propose to do the *work* necessary to put the roads in order?', he asked, 'If so, what about future upkeep?' The Board replied that they now proposed to do the work on the roads provided that the holders would then maintain them.

Mrs Waugh, who was 12 years old when her father got one of the Parkhead holdings, remembered clearly the problems they had in obtaining an adequate water supply.[25] They got their water for washing from Linlithgow loch and their drinking water from a spring running into it.

> Aye, we used to carry the water along, and I used to hate having to go down to the loch for water or to the wee spring, be coming home with a pail of water—you'd pass people on the path going for a walk from the town and you'd be carrying pails of water.

Then 'they discovered there was water at the top of the hill and they put up a windmill, and they drew the water and the water went along into two tanks and then from the tanks we got it.' (Later they got a proper water supply from Bo'ness.)

Nothing more was heard about buildings for a long time, and indeed Mrs Waugh remembered how cosy and comfortable their corrugated iron house was. But in August 1935 one holder asked the Department if he could have a loan for a new house, as there was really no way any alterations could make the corrugated iron houses comparable to the houses now being built by the Department. A report on the conditions of the older Parkhead houses concluded, 'Generally speaking these Army Hut dwelling houses and steadings can be said to have completed their normal life and from now onwards are bound to deteriorate at an accelerating rate.'

However, it took a long time for anything to happen. A holder appealed for assistance in getting a new house in April 1938, as the family had had to continually patch the existing house against high winds and rain during the previous winter. In July of that year the Department asked for money to replace the old army huts with new houses, but in December they learned that the Ministry of Transport planned to construct a new road on the north side of Linlithgow Loch across the site for the new houses. It was May 1939 before the compensation payable by the Ministry of Transport was established, though in the end the road was never built. New houses were finally erected after the Second World War, but in the 1970s the M9 motorway cut a swathe through the holdings, and that was the end of the settlement.

Fife

In this county smallholdings were common around the small towns, and there was a ready demand.[26] One of the properties acquired by the Board under the Small Holding Colonies Acts was Dysart.[27] A block of about 1200 acres of the 2000-acre estate was offered by the owners in the summer of 1917. The Board decided against acquiring the northern portion of the block because of the poor quality of the land and subsidence from underground workings and eventually purchased 650 acres of good land. Negotiations were protracted because, as the Chairman noted, the trustees were reluctant

> to consider the sale of a portion of the estate which in their opinion cannot fail to increase considerably in capital value in the near future. The feuing value of the subject was a difficult obstacle to overcome, seeing I had to justify any purchase on a commercial basis. After two meetings with Lord Rosslyn (who was sympathetic to the purpose for which the Board desired the land) I was able

to get from him an option to purchase in favour of the Board up till the 30th June.

He considered the asking price of £23,529 well justified: best quality land; the situation was excellent; a large and increasing industrial community, forming a market for produce, adjoining the land; very good transport facilities; industrial employment to meet the varied requirements of families within easy reach, and so on. Some 332 acres would be available at Martinmas 1919 (and the tenants had been given notice), 216 acres in 1921, and 102 acres in 1927 (which might be brought forward as this latter tenant had another farm).

The Secretary for Scotland approved the submission which was then passed to the Treasury. The K & LTR wrote, 'The ground lies between populous areas, and is suitable for this purpose, which none of the other properties which have so far been acquired by the Board are in any way fitted for.' However, he thought the price 'very much too high for the value of the subjects that are to be acquired.' The Treasury were also unhappy that so much of the arable land would not become available before 1921; however, sanction was given to purchase. In the spring of 1919, when a group of ex-servicemen petitioned Kirkcaldy Town Council for assistance in obtaining holdings on Dysart estate, the Board had to explain yet again that because of the leases only a limited area of the estate would be available at Martinmas of that year.

In November 1930 the local officer reported: 'The efficiency of this Scheme has steadily improved within recent years and nearly all the men are doing well considering the times.' He added, 'The only serious trouble on the Scheme is the risk of continual subsidence.'[28] Subsidence does indeed appear to have been the only problem with this scheme. However, the headache proved to be the Department's rather than the holders'; a long drawn-out legal battle for compensation ensued (which does not appear to have been finally settled until 1969), but fortunately for the holders in August 1934 the District Surveyor found no evidence of further significant subsidence.

A second Fife estate was also purchased under the Small Holding Colonies Acts, Thirdpart & Barns, near Anstruther.[29] It consisted of five large farms, about 1440 acres (1373 arable), and was advertised for sale in March 1919. Agreement was quickly reached between the Board and agents, but long delays occurred before Treasury sanction was given. When writing to the K & LTR to ask his opinion of the scheme, the Treasury made it clear that it did not look promising to them. Once again the main reason was the fact that access to about half the land could not be got for some years; also, the adaptation work was going to be expensive. After sounding off on his views in general concerning land settlement policy—'What, I think, you have to recognise is that, in all these cases, you are going to saddle the Country with a perpetual loss so as to carry out a policy the Government is pledged to undertake on behalf of the men who have fought'—Sir Kenneth Mackenzie got down to specifics. As far as he was concerned, there was a positive side to the fact that the Board could not immediately get access to all the land, since he foresaw building costs falling in the future.[30]

The Treasury were, of course, at perfect liberty to ignore the K & LTR's comments, and they asked the Board whether, since entry to two of the farms could not be had until 1925 and 1927, it might be possible either to purchase only part of the estate or alternatively to resell the part not immediately available. The Board had again to stress the impossibility in Scotland of finding suitable properties where immediate entry could be given to all the farms (two of the Thirdpart farms were immediately available). The estate had received offers for individual farms but insisted on selling it as a whole. The Board had no objections to reselling any farms 'where it is found impossible to come to a satisfactory agreement with the tenants for the surrender of their leases.' The K & LTR, while admitting a single instance of this practice might be acceptable, thought it 'undesirable for a Government Department to buy land, portions of which may have to be sold in the future. It puts a public Department into a sort of speculating position, which it ought not to occupy.'

In September 1921 the *Dundee Advertiser* ran a series of articles about the deficiencies at Thirdpart. The first one (on the 5th) began, 'The land raiders of the Western Highlands are giving active expression to their impatience with the delays of the Board of Agriculture for Scotland in settling men on the land. The experiences of some of those already settled gives reason to question whether the landless men of Skye and Raasay have not, after all, the happier lot.' The delays in providing housing and the dirty state of the land (an agricultural term meaning it was infested with weeds) were particularly stressed. Further pieces appeared on the 6th, 12th, 13th and 14th, concentrating on the negative experiences of individual smallholders and concluding by calling for a review of the whole situation.

In anticipation of the promised visit to the farm by the local M.P., a memo was prepared, detailing the position of each of the individual holders. It shows the Board attempting to deal with what they considered legitimate complaints, but also that they were not always responsible for the problem. For example, a house and steading had been erected on Holding No.14, but the holder now wished to sell milk and was complaining

> that his steading does not comply with the requirements of the Local Authority. He made no mention of this until the building works were well advanced, and it was then too late to make the necessary alterations, which would also involve further expenditure. It is understood that he has no real intention of establishing a dairy, but simply to sell milk to callers, and he has therefore been informed that any alterations such as he desires must be carried out at his own expense.

At the beginning of October the local M.P. visited Thirdpart; afterwards he had an interview with the Director of Land Settlement. He explained that his visit had been made because of the criticisms which appeared in the *Dundee Advertiser*. After seeing the settlement and speaking to many of the holders he had informed the editor that he considered the articles 'considerably exaggerated'. He appreciated the Board's difficulties in erecting buildings and did not think a delay of one or even two years was unreasonable. 'He also quite understood that the dirty condition of the land could not be avoided and apparently he was of opinion that some of the holders had made little effort to improve matters in that respect.' In conclusion, he 'thought that the holders had no real ground for complaint and that the Board had done everything reasonable for their settlement.' It was not often that an M.P. was more sympathetic to the Board's point of view than to that of his constituents!

In November 1930 the local officer advised the Department, 'This scheme continues to show steady improvement both as regards management of holdings and stock rearing. ... The introduction of Mr. Phimister, Bank Agent, Crail, as Secretary of the Smallholders' Society has been a distinct gain to the holders. He has run their various activities on business lines and there is a minimum of grousing.'[31] However, in August 1931 the Thirdpart holders wrote to their M.P., appealing for a reduction in their financial burdens; they had done their best to make their holdings pay, 'but in common with agricultural effort throughout the country the struggle is too severe, and fighting for bare existence appears to be all the future promises.' The M.P. forwarded the letter to the Secretary of State, claiming to have personal knowledge of the hardships which the holders had suffered and the difficulty they had in making ends meet.

In response to the Secretary of State's request for information, the Department advised that 'with few exceptions the holders are working their holdings satisfactorily and two of them are leaving to take up two-pair farms.' Some thirteen of the holders were now eligible to have their rents revised by the Land Court. The Department did not doubt that the Thirdpart holders, like farmers throughout the country, were suffering from the Depression, but the Landholders Acts did allow for a periodic revision of rents, which none of the eligible holders had taken advantage of. In May 1933 a question was asked in parliament about the high rents charged on this estate. The Department advised the Under Secretary that the three holders who had applied to the Land Court had had their rents reduced (from £31 to £27, £38.10*s*. to £32, and £36 to £30), and that the other eleven holders now eligible were preparing to make similar applications.

Shortly after World War I there was also a Fife scheme which did not involve purchase. Only three holdings were formed, but the case is a good illustration of how much time and trouble could be expended on such schemes. The farm was Kinshaldy, part of Tentsmuir forest.[32] It had originally been suggested in 1919, at which time the sub-commissioner's report had been very unfavourable. In 1922 the Forestry Commission offered the land to the Board and another inspection was commissioned. A different sub-commissioner was equally negative. He found three main objections to land settlement on the farm: the distance from a station and other facilities, the poor land, and the infestation of rabbits. The only points he could find in its favour were the low land rent and the possibility of forestry as a subsidiary occupation, 'but even the value of the existing buildings is more than the land is able to bear, and adaptation costs would add to this considerably.' The only possible economic scheme, he thought, would be to create three large holdings, of about 40 acres arable and as much pasture as possible, but he foresaw great difficulty in getting men to take such holdings and he did not recommend any scheme.

One would have expected the Board to forget about Kinshaldy, but not a bit of it. In July 1923 a third sub-commissioner was sent to inspect and report, and he wrote just what the Board wanted to read—a list of reasons why a scheme could succeed. He suggested two holdings for the sons of the present grieve (they were ex-servicemen, but as they had not applied by the deadline they were considered only second preference applicants). The Forestry Commission pressed the Board hard, but why did the Board bend over backwards to accommodate them? The explanation may partly lie in the fact that the Commissioner with whom they dealt was John Sutherland, who had previously been the Board's own Small Holdings Commissioner.

The Board sent their submission to the Under Secretary for Scotland in December 1923. The proposal was to let the third holding to the other two holders for a year while they sought a suitable tenant; there were no first preference candidates available for this type of holding. The Under Secretary wrote to the Board in June, 'It seems difficult to justify a scheme on which no first preference ex-service men are to be settled and I expect Treasury may kick. Suppose Board do not agree to the conditions laid down by Forestry Commission what will be the position? Will the Commission carry out a scheme of their own or will they allow the buildings to become derelict?' The Board replied

> The Forestry Commission, anticipating that the Board would have little or no difficulty in connection with the proposed scheme, have displenished the farm and allowed entry to two of the prospective holders...who purchased most of the implements at the sale. If the Board are not permitted to cooperate with the Forestry Commission in the constitution of new holdings, the Commission would be obliged to consider the position afresh and would be involved in considerable expense and loss by having to restart farming operations or by having to let the farm on lease. It is unlikely that the Commission would carry out a small holding scheme themselves, the best that could be expected is that they would endeavour to let the land and buildings to a single tenant.

In response the Under Secretary wrote to the Secretary for Scotland, 'It would be rather awkward to go back on this scheme now looking to the fact that two of the holders have already obtained entry, so I suggest that it should go forward to the Treasury.' The K & LTR advised the Treasury he was somewhat doubtful about the scheme: 'The probability is that the Board would not have put it forward if it had not been the case that the Secretary for Scotland personally inspected the place last autumn and took the view that it was desirable to work in sympathy with the plans of the Forestry Commission.' (No explanation of this unusual action appears in the Board's files; considerable pressure was clearly being put on the Scottish Office by the

Forestry Commission.) The Treasury had strong objections but, in view of the special circumstances, gave their sanction.

In May Sutherland advised the Board that the third holding should be given to the father, as the scheme would otherwise fall through. The Board then had to write to the Scottish Office. They began by denying that they were already committed to the scheme, 'but the Forestry Commission by displenishing the farm and giving entry to the two sons of the grieve...had anticipated approval, and so, as it were, compelled both the Board and the Treasury to follow the Commission's lead.' It had been the Board's understanding that the settlement of the grieve's sons would satisfy the grieve, who would work with them and provide them with capital. The Board had not yet found a suitable ex-service applicant for the third holding and now had to pass on the Forestry Commission's request.

> The Board feel a degree of disappointment at 'co-operation' of this kind; they are aware that the settlement of this family is open to criticism, but in the circumstances and with the object of examining the results of small holdings established on land of this class, they feel they would not be justified in recommending the abandonment of the scheme.

The Secretary for Scotland and Treasury had little option but to let the father have the third holding. But in December 1929 the Board noted: 'The poor price for potatoes has practically forced the holders to give up and they have given notice to quit at Martinmas 1930. ... It will be difficult to get suitable holders for this type of land to replace the present family.[33]

The file on a Fife scheme which was abandoned provides revealing insights into the whole subject of the acquisition of land for settlement purposes. Dundee Town Council wrote to the Board in April 1924, offering to let the farm of Scotscraig (Tayport) for smallholdings.[34] There were no suitable first preference applicants in the area but plenty of second preference men and civilians. A scheme was drawn up for 15 holdings, but there was a hitch. The Board had understood that a Part II scheme would be acceptable to the Town Council and on that basis everything had been prepared and the submission was about to be sent. Then an officer of the Board discovered that the Lord Provost was under the misapprehension that under a Part II scheme the Board would guarantee the fair rents payable by the holders. When he had explained that it was not so the Lord Provost refused to consider a Part II scheme.

> As the discussion proceeded I found that they were not so altruistic in the matter as we had supposed. As a matter of fact I gather that having bought Scotscraig years ago at a high price they now find the Estate a colossal white elephant and it seems to me that they have an idea at the back of their minds that it would be a stroke of good business to get the Board to take over for small holdings the farm of Scotscraig which becomes vacant at Martinmas.

By August the Council had decided to sell the estate, and in September the Board sent a submission to the Under Secretary for Scotland for a scheme on this basis. The Secretary for Scotland approved it, but there followed a good deal of discussion within the Treasury. It was going to be extremely expensive, and both K & LTR and Treasury agreed that the decision was really one of policy. At the end of September the Treasury advised the Board that a scheme providing 15 holdings for second preference ex-servicemen and civilians for whom initial expenditure would amount to £2240 each was 'not justifiable at the present time', and they therefore refused their sanction. The farm was sold to a private purchaser. Clearly the situation of the immediate post-war period, when pressure to be seen to be doing something was so great that the Treasury almost invariably ended up sanctioning every scheme put before them, was no longer the same in 1924; some genuine discretion could be used.

A general conclusion to this chapter, in which such diverse schemes have been discussed, would be difficult. There is no denying that—particularly before the reconstitution of 1921—the Board of Agriculture were slow and inefficient, but they had much to contend with: the unforeseen dramatic rise in prices, the obstructiveness of the Treasury, the opposition of landowners. The chapter has concentrated on the immediate post-war period because that was when the teething troubles were at their greatest. By the late 1920s—when the worst of the pressure was off and the Department of Agriculture had developed a certain expertise—most settlements in the eastern Lowlands had worked out quite satisfactorily, and holdings created at that time and in the 1930s were put into operation smoothly and efficiently.

CHAPTER 10

Schemes in the South-West

Arran

Although geographically Highland, the island of Arran was not amongst the crofting counties and was treated administratively as 'Lowland'. But though the Board tried to to purchase Lowland properties whenever possible they certainly never contemplated buying any Arran farms.[1]

The earliest farm in which the Board took an interest—after receiving a number of applications—was Bennicarrigan in 1912.[2] This 511-acre farm was held nominally by one tenant but was actually farmed by two brothers; the proprietor was the Marquis of Graham.[3] The Board's scheme was for six new holdings and two enlargements, with the larger holdings (along with the buildings) being granted to the brothers. The case went before the Land Court in April 1913; after hearing representations the Board prepared an amended scheme, and the Land Court Order was issued in March 1914. The Board were not, however, prepared to commit themselves to a scheme until the amount of compensation was known, while the proprietor refused to provide any further assistance in dealing with the tenant's claim until he was assured that the Board would proceed with a scheme. By the spring of 1915 matters had thus reached an impasse, and in view of wartime conditions and 'the heavy cost of this scheme as foreshadowed by the claims made by the Landlord and outgoing tenants', the scheme was dropped.

In 1919 the Board were advised that the two brothers, who were old men between 70 and 80, were 'making a poor job of the Farm', and the estate factor would have liked the Board to take it over, but nothing was done at that time. It was only in 1928, when the tenant died, that a scheme for four new holdings and five enlargements was amicably arranged.[4]

Immediately after the war, however, the Board were negotiating with the Marquis of Graham over two other Arran farms: Balnacoole and Shedog.[5] Toward the end of 1918 the proprietor offered part of both farms, and negotiations went ahead for Balnacoole. In the spring of 1919, however, he claimed compensation for the buildings on the farm, which as far as the Board were concerned had never been part of the bargain, and which would have added enormously to the cost of the project. After months of discussions, a compromise was reached. In view of the keen demand for the farm and 'the criticism that would be directed against the Board in the event of failure to adjust a scheme for ex-service men with a landlord who had *ostensibly* offered generous terms', the Board went further toward meeting the proprietor's demands than they would have liked. The letter of 17 December 1920 which the Board wrote to Lord Graham accepting his terms crossed one which he wrote to his M.P., expressing his opinion of the Board, an opinion which he was later to make more public.

> The Board of Agriculture have now refused Balnacoole, and also 'refuse to abandon the scheme'; the result is—the old tenant, Mr. Allan, has gone: no one else will take it—and the finest farm in Arran is lying *derelict* and *empty*. They have had the offer before them for 12 months, and *nothing whatever has been done*. I call it downright scandalous.
>
> I have given the Board now another offer, for definite answer 'Yes' or 'No' within 14 days, failing this achieving results, I am going to call a meeting of the ex-soldiers, and arrange for a big deputation to Edinburgh. We will take Press Reporters with us, and we will fairly 'go for' the Board. It will be the liveliest experience they have ever had!! I am about 'fed up' with this dawdling and powerlessness of people. They *must* get a move on.

The scheme went ahead and by February 1920 new holders were settled, although bickering over details continued for many months afterwards.

The delay in settling Shedog was for different reasons. There were no major disagreements with the proprietor, but this scheme was not seriously considered until after Balnacoole was settled, and that was 1920, when the Board were in financial straits and in no position to commit themselves to new schemes. In June 1920 the estate advised the Board they had made arrangements for entry at Martinmas. The Director of Land Settlement advised the agent privately of the financial position, informing him he could convey this information to Lord Graham strictly confidentially. But shortly afterwards 'the Board's officer had it repeated to him in the market at Brodick that it was understood in Arran that "the Board had no money to proceed with Shedog unless it were put in an urgent category".'

The local M.P., General Hunter-Weston, seems to have exerted considerable pressure, for in September 1920 the Board did decide to treat the scheme as 'urgent' and proceed with it before they knew they would have extra funds. But although he had been advised of this decision, Lord Graham heard nothing more for the next two months, and on 9 November he wrote

> I beg to remind you that it is now nearly two years since this scheme was first put before you, and not unnaturally all the soldiers concerned are most anxious to know their position, so that they may formulate plans for starting work at the Martinmas term. I consider the Arran soldiers have been exemplary in their patience during this long wait; and, as we (in the position of landlords) have been willing to assist in every reasonable way, I cannot understand why things proceed so slowly, and why the whole business cannot be completed at once.

The Board acknowledged receipt but did not reply until mid-December (they later claimed to be waiting for their next Board meeting to finalise the scheme), by which time Lord Graham had sent a letter to *The Scotsman* bitterly attacking them. The Board had to justify their actions to the Secretary for Scotland; they insisted that Lord Graham had 'maintained an attitude of querulous criticism throughout' and that no blame attached to the Board for any of the delays. The Marquis of Graham was no saint, but the length of time which the Board were taking even to respond to a letter would have tried anyone's patience.

Fortunately, the approval of the Shedog scheme in December 1920 restored good relations with the estate, and in the same month they offered the Board the farm of Springbank, $77\frac{1}{2}$ acres at Brodick considered suitable for the settlement of two ex-soldiers.[6] In view of the cost of equipment (£1160 per holder) and the anticipated annual deficit of £116, the Treasury deprecated the fact that only two new holdings would be formed, but the Sir Kenneth Mackenzie advised them, 'In view of the nature of the soil and the difficulty of splitting the area into more than two portions, I do not think you can do anything but accept the scheme as put forward.' His closing remark aptly illustrates the K & LTR's views on land settlement policy: 'If we were only allowed, it would be far cheaper for the Country to give this class of applicant a life pension of £50 and no land!'[7]

Dumfries & Galloway

The earliest scheme in this part of the country was carried out under the Small Holdings Colonies Acts, whereby the Dumfriesshire farms of Midlocharwoods and Netherlocharwoods were purchased.[8] Midlocharwoods, seven miles south of Dumfries, was offered to the Board by the proprietors, the Scottish Labour Colony Association, who had bought it in 1900 'for the purpose of providing food and shelter, in exchange for labour, to able-bodied men out of employment'. As 'no able-bodied unemployment now exists', they wished to sell the property. The whole farm comprised about 150-200 acres of arable land and about 300 acres mossland (the amount of mossland in the area eventually sold to the Board was only 65 acres). The sub-commissioner who reported on the farm in September 1916 did not think much of it and advised against considering the farm for a small holdings colony.

In December 1917 the farm was offered again, and by then the Board knew they would also be able to acquire the adjoining farm of Netherlocharwoods, extending to 217 acres arable, 30 acres rough pasture, and about 17 acres woodland. In March 1918 the Secretary for Scotland's approval was sought for the purchase of both farms. At this stage the Dumfriesshire branch of the Naval & Military War Pensions Committee stepped in and protested. The sub-commissioner responsible for the district reported on his meeting with them to the Chairman of the Board: 'They felt that owing to the distance from a Railway Station (3 miles) and the lack of any village social life near at hand the scheme was foredoomed to failure.' He went on, 'Their idea of small holdings was a market garden of an acre or so and it never seemed to have entered their minds that if a soldier had sufficient capital his building might extend to 20, 30, 50, acres or over.' He had further pointed out—and, as will be seen, this really was the crux of the matter—'that in any case the Board had been seeking for land for a soldiers' colony for the last two years and for which they had advertised repeatedly in the daily press and that the land on Mid Locharwood was the best and most suitable for a settlement as far as I knew that had been offered to them.'

The committee were far from convinced, but by this time the submission had been approved by the Secretary for Scotland and passed on to the Treasury. The Chairman of the Board wrote personally to the K & LTR asking as a special favour that the scheme be processed without delay. The reasons he gave were '(1) that several such Colonies have already been taken in England under the same Act, and it creates a bad impression that we are so far behind them in taking definite action. (2) we cannot obtain immediate admission into any other property.' It is very clear that the overriding reason for the Board's keenness to acquire this property, considered unsuitable by so many people, was simply to demonstrate that the Scottish Board of Agriculture were not lagging behind their English counterparts in the provision of land for demobilised soldiers.

The K & LTR was undoubtedly swayed by the Chairman's appeal. He began his report to the Treasury by stating, 'I have doubts as to the advisability of this scheme', and he thought it expensive, but

> On the other hand I have interviewed Sir Robert Wright on the subject and find he is strongly in favour of it. One of his reasons is the great difficulty (which I venture to doubt) of obtaining any place in the South of Scotland to which immediate entry can be got without paying compensation to a tenant whose lease has to be broken, and the Board can get possession of those two places next May with no cost of this nature. He considers the dormitory accommodation a great advantage, as he thinks that many men will have to be taught agriculture before they can be settled in small holdings, and proposes to use this farm to a certain extent for instructional purposes.

'It is necessary to get land somewhere', he continued, 'and as they have bought Arabella in the North, they must have another place in the South. On balance, and with some doubt, I suggest that you should consent.' The Treasury sanctioned the purchase of both farms in April, which did not stop the War Pensions Committee's protests. They insisted that the farm was 'most unsuitable for the contemplated purpose, in regard, not only to its situation, but to the character of the land, and the impossibility of any subsidiary scheme, such as Forestry, being carried out in connection with the farm'.

Nevertheless, the Board went ahead with the purchase and took over management of the farm in May, although the dormitories had to be cleaned and plumbing seen to before discharged soldiers could be taken. In August the Board was sent a copy of a letter from the Dumfriesshire War Pensions Committee to the Director of Training at the Ministry of Pensions, advising they did not consider the farm a suitable place to send disabled men for training: 'The farm house contains three dormitories accommodating about 20 or 30 men but the conditions under which they would have to live would be so reminiscent of army life that it is feared they would discourage any who might be thinking of adopting agriculture as a profession, more especially as it is in a particularly lonely district'. However, from 1919 to 1921 disabled men were trained at Midlocharwoods (also two fit ex-servicemen who worked for wages while being trained and then got holdings at Netherlocharwoods). Subsequently an ordinary scheme for seven new holdings was effected at Midlocharwoods. The Locharwoods schemes proved highly successful, and the lack of 'village social life', far from being a deterrent, actually led to greater social cohesion (see Chapter 11).

Another estate purchased by the Board in this area was Gretna.[9] Some 6000 acres were owned by the War Office who, in the spring of 1919, offered to sell about 1600 acres to the Board. There were two bones of contention. The first was that the War Office intended to sell tenanted farms instead of the land in their own hands; both Annan and Dumfries branches of the National Farmers Union protested and demanded that all the land in the government's hands should be utilised for land settlement before farmers in the area were dispossessed. Protests along those lines continued to pour in during the rest of the year.[10]

The second problem was a familiar one in transactions of this kind but rather unexpected between two government departments: price. The Board were offering under £35,000 while the Ministry of Munitions wanted £41,000. The Treasury were willing to agree to this, but the Board were not. In February 1920 the Chairman wrote internally

> With reference to Gretna the only reply we can send to the Scottish Office is that we cannot purchase the property at £41,000. The concurrence of the Treasury is easily understood as an additional price obtained for the property would reduce their loss in the Department of Munitions, while, on the other hand, as the £7,000 extra that we are asked to pay would come out of the 2 millions voted to us, and not out of the Treasury, the advantage to them is to support Sir Howard Frank's position. By paying the extra £7,000 we reduce by so much our capacity for purchasing suitable land, and the total number of soldiers we can settle.

There was stalemate at this point, and shortly afterwards a new element complicated the situation, as a syndicate were interested in purchasing the estate in order to erect a sugar beet factory, with smallholdings created for the workers. The Board were unanimously in favour of this idea because it would have created many smallholdings whilst sparing the Board the cost of purchase. The applicants for holdings, however, objected vigorously to the proposal and enlisted their M.P.'s support. By the end of 1920 the project had fallen through.

Finally, in 1921, agreement was reached: the Board purchased the whole of the estate (some 24 farms) with £90,000 fixed as the value of the lands for the purpose of determining a perpetual annuity to be paid by the Board. It

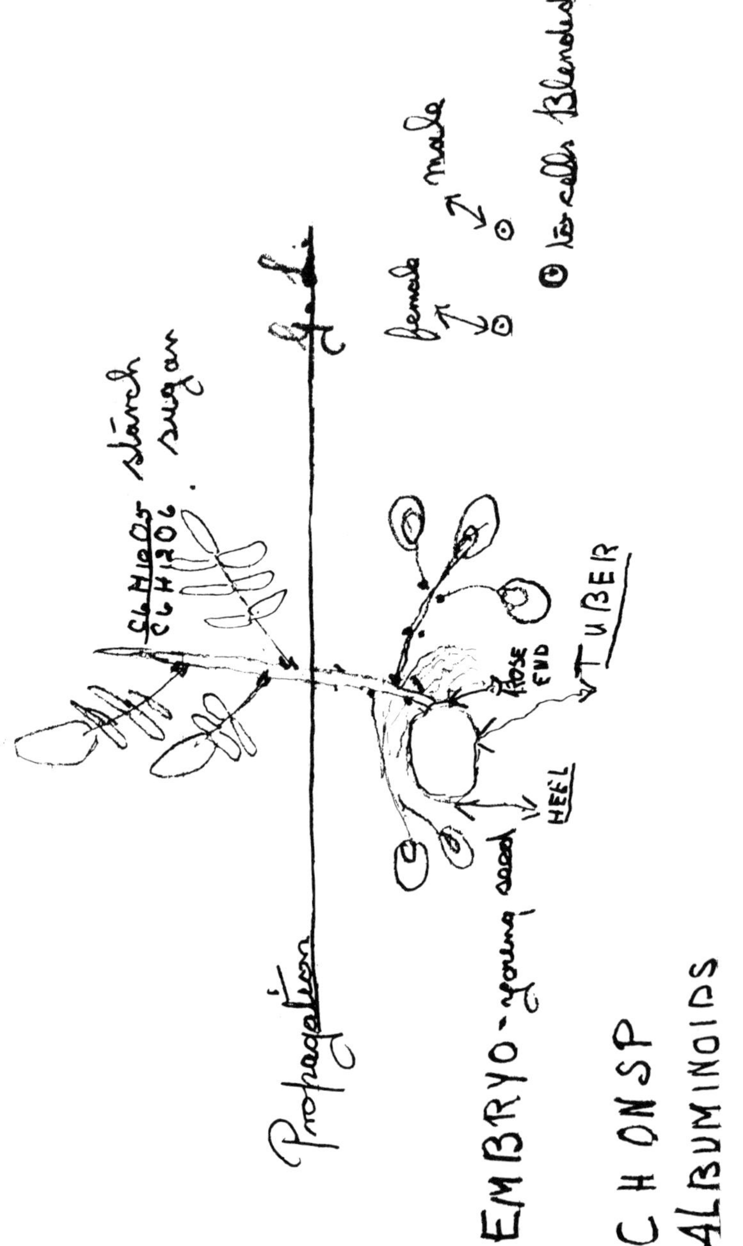

9 Page of James Baird's Notebook, Midlocharwoods Training Centre, 27 October 1919.

10 The Bairds at Netherlocharwoods.

was planned to create 120 new holdings, although this meant the dispossession of some tenant farmers.[11] In March the K & LTR commented: 'There are a large number of ex-service men in the district who are getting a bit out of hand, and some scheme in that area is essential for the preservation of order.'[12] This is one of the very few such comments to be made about anywhere in the Lowlands.

In October 1930 the Board's local officer reported very positively on the way the Gretna scheme had turned out.[13] In the 115 original holdings there had been 40 changes of tenancy. Some holders had emigrated, some moved to larger holdings or to farms elsewhere, some returned to other lines of business; there were only six recorded cases of complete failure. 'This is surely a remarkable fact', he commented, 'that the failures in this scheme are less than 1%, when one realises that in January 1921, the agricultural index number was 180, i.e. prices were 180% above pre-war, and that in August of this year it was 35, prices of produce being less than half of those reigning in 1921.' He was aware that some holders had had a struggle in recent years, but he insisted that the vast majority were doing well. He found two main reasons for success. The first was that most of the large holdings were equipped for dairying and the holders had a market for their milk with Nestles, and the second was the large increase in the number of poultry kept. He went on to estimate that the population increase was roughly 200%, and added that he knew of no scheme in which the average of housing and steading equipment was so high, and that that had an important effect on the morale of the holders.

The third scheme in this area was Terregles near Dumfries.[14] Initially the Board wished to purchase only one farm, to be used for the establishment of an intermediate agricultural school, but then they decided to acquire the whole estate, which comprised ten farms, about 2313 acres. Everyone agreed about the suitability of the estate, there was no difficulty about the price, and the transaction was carried through smoothly, with the Board coming into possession early in 1920. The interest of this scheme is the effect that the change in conditions after the war had on it.

In August 1920 the sub-commissioner reporting on the estate suggested a scheme of some 76 very small holdings, of about five acres each, with a large central farm (as had been established at Arabella). However, by February 1921 it looked as if food prices would slump, and he was having considerable difficulty in getting applicants to look at the smaller holdings. A year later a number of holders had been settled, but a final scheme still had not been agreed, and in view of the escalating building costs, there was discussion about dropping the idea of a central farm. The sub-commissioner responsible was very much opposed to this, for

> the proposal for a Central Farm at Terregles is a matter of grave moment not only to the holders to be settled later but to holders who have already received entry to the land. This year the latter have been able to avail themselves of the extra horse labour and assistance which the temporary management by the Board of certain portions of the Estate have rendered necessary but thereafter these small holders, should there be no central organisation for the purpose, will be bereft of such assistance and will not be able to get it easily from surrounding farmers. Indeed the estate is of such magnitude and the settlement so dense that such extraneous aid cannot be expected.

When he submitted his scheme in September 1921 he noted, 'I appreciate the difficulties of dealing with Treasury in view of former estimates, but agriculture has now entered a most critical time, a time which has overtaken us with exceptional rapidity.'

In May 1922 the scheme was revised yet again, as the Chairman had ruled that the central farm was to be abolished and offered to smallholders. The sub-commissioner stated, 'As a number of the holders were already in it was impossible to disturb these, and the scheme now submitted is pretty much a patched up arrangement.'

From the Board's Annual Report for 1924, one would have thought that the Terregles settlement was a trouble-free, model example,[15] but in fact the preceding years had been marked by enormous discontent. In July 1921 the local officer, T.B. Manson, drew the senior sub-commissioner's attention 'to the fact once again that dissatisfaction is becoming very acute amongst the holders that no progress is being made with the erection of the dwelling houses, or with the water supply.' He also advised that the steadings so far erected at Terregles had been condemned by the sanitary inspector.

After various meetings between the Board of Agriculture and the Scottish Board of Health, a joint submission about these steadings was sent to the Secretary for Scotland in March 1922. The Board of Health adhered to the model dairy guidelines of 1906 which set a minimum of 600 cubic feet and 50 square feet per cow. The Board of Agriculture's byres provided 400 cubic feet and 30 square feet per cow, which they considered ample as long as sufficient ventilation was provided, insisting that to increase the space would be to spend money unnecessarily.

The joint submission presented the Secretary for Scotland with two alternatives. The first was that special provision be made to exempt smallholders from the regulations; the Board of Health objected to this because they felt the space was inadequate from a public health point of view and because it would be impossible to make others conform to requirements which were not enforced in the case of smallholders. The second alternative was that the Board of Agriculture conformed to existing requirements; they objected that the extra cost would be more than the holders could bear. The Secretary for Scotland wrote, 'I regard the first alternative as impossible of adoption—for obvious reasons. I think the two Boards should confer regarding the second proposal, and endeavour to reach agreement.' At an ensuing meeting the Board of Health decided to allow the Board of Agriculture to build the remaining Terregles steadings along their own lines, with future minimum standards to be agreed between the two Boards.

In the meantime the tenants were no happier. On 1 January 1923 Manson advised, 'I have been informed that the holders on Terregles are massing themselves to express discontent with the regime of the Board.' They had arranged for a public meeting to be held with their M.P., Major Dudgeon, on the 15th. Manson also advised that the holders wanted a member of the Board to be present—'They do not want a mere Sub-Commissioner. His status is not sufficiently high.' However, the Board decided not to be represented at the meeting.

Press coverage of the meeting, and of the holders' complaints against the Board, was extensive.[16] Along with the cuttings, Manson also sent his own comments to the senior sub-commissioner, James Dunlop, and coming from an employee those comments are far more damning to the Board than anything the press had to say. He emphasised that the meeting was not the result of just a few agitators: 'the greater number of the holders are decent fellows but they all have a bone to pick and widespread dissatisfaction is prevalent.' He went on to list their grievances. The first was that the land rents were considered too high. The second concerned buildings: 'The new houses almost invariably let in water at the window sashes. I do not think there is a single new house which is not liable to this defect.' As for the byres, most had not stood up to expectations. 'The weather boarding is a failure in practice. Attention was drawn on numerous occasions to several of these, but the delay in correcting these deficiencies has soured all the occupants.'[17]

In addition, dissatisfaction was expressed over fences, ditches and roads; also sewage tanks ('These are almost universally unsatisfactory. In most cases they cannot cope with the volume of water for which they were designed. A year has passed in many cases since complaint was first made.'), and the delay in starting new works as well as the inadequate water supply. Manson summed up the problem by stating that the holders

> feel they are dealing with a body which is absolutely intangible. There is no individual which they can fasten on and hold responsible for work ill-done. They come to me and I promise to communicate with the Board. I seldom receive nor does the holder receive a prompt and satisfactory response. The holders are further told that no local official is a responsible person i.e. that he has no mandate to act. They write to the Secretary hoping for quicker action—they get a post card.

The final grievance was that the holders still did not know the exact cost of their houses, although some had been in occupation for nearly two years.

Dunlop sent the press cutting with Manson's comments on to Land Division, stating he thought it a great pity the Board had not been represented at the meeting, as there were many facts which a representative could have explained satisfactorily, and 'nipped in the bud the false impression regarding the Board and its works which the press have published broadcast uncontradicted.' He added, however, that he agreed generally with Manson's statement of the position.

The Board conferred internally about what action to take. At the end of February they asked their solicitor how much of the Board's intentions should be divulged to the holders, a pointless thing to do since he reacted in the predictable manner of legal advisers by saying that the Land Court should take care of most of the difficulties, 'and undertakings to spend money should be avoided. It would be best to take a note of the Complaint & offer a report & recommendation on the subject without indicating to the Complainer that his is a deserving case for future expenditure. The Board should not be committed in any way.'

At the end of March Dunlop and another senior officer met with the holders and inspected the settlement. They made a number of recommendations, the first and foremost being that the buildings be put in order. Dunlop pointed out that if the buildings were to be revalued by the Land Court their defects would seriously lower the Court's valuation. Aside from that, he felt the Board were morally obliged to leave the buildings in good order before placing the burden of maintenance on the holders. An internal minute of 24 May agreed 'that the holders have a genuine grievance and that the Board who have been acting as contractors, are bound in equity to make good defects in the new buildings erected by them before handing them over to the new holders to maintain.'

The grievances persisted. In March 1924 the Under Secretary advised the Board that the Terregles holders had asked the Secretary for Scotland to visit the holdings or to receive a deputation. The Board did not think this was a good idea and insisted that once the works in hand were completed and the burdens adjusted by the Land Court, the holders would settle down quietly. To a certain extent this proved true, but after the Land Court revaluation

11 James McNay, Terregles Holder, in Dumfries.

was made known and rents were lowered a number of tenants fell into arrears because when refusing to pay rent they had not put aside money ('though...any prudent holder would have made provision of a sum to be in a position to pay his revised indebtedness so soon as the Court gave their decision'). As a result of this, the Board ended up taking legal action for recovery of these arrears, and all this dragged on through 1925.

In November 1928 James Dunlop wrote: 'On the Terregles scheme where four hopelessly inefficient ex-service men have been removed, the new holders, if less deserving of a holding from an Army service point of view, are proving themselves efficient holders. The older settled holders in Terregles are developing well, a number of them branching out in new lines, such as market gardening.' A year later T.B. Manson was able to provide the Department with a positive report: 'On the estate there are now 76 holders with statutory rights. The population can now be placed at not less than 300, an increase of almost 400%. This population is housed in sound buildings, of adequate accommodation all supplied with gravitation water of good analysis and equipped with modern sanitary conveniences.'[18]

There is one final aspect of the Terregles scheme worth mentioning, and that is the co-operative society. In November 1922 Manson requested to be allowed to act as Honorary Secretary and Treasury of the Terregles Small Holders Co-Operative Society. Dunlop commented that this would entail an immense amount of work; 'I hope he does not break down with this addition to the overwork with which he is already burdened.' The Board gave Manson permission.

In June 1933 Manson was asked to report on the Terregles Association. He wrote that after a shaky beginning when the Association nearly collapsed, it had performed a useful function in the community. It had received no assistance whatsoever from the Department, and indeed an admirably adapted store had been lost because the Department refused to accept deferred terms of payment ('This store was subsequently sold for a trifle of what the holders offered.'[19]). He went on

> The failure in co-operation is almost always due to lack of initial capital which precludes forward buying, means inadequate storage accommodation and lack of transport. Initially the Terregles Association was financed by myself. I furnished the funds free of interest to purchase the original store and also for their first purchases. These loans were paid back promptly and in full. Another essential condition of success is an executive officer of enthusiasm, a believer in the principles of co-operation who possesses a good buying instinct. I acted as Secretary and Treasurer for the first three years and was succeeded by a capable holder who has remained at his post since.

Manson's name was mentioned spontaneously by two of the Terregles people whom I spoke with (both had been children when their fathers obtained holdings[20]). Alfie Smith said Manson had been 'absolutely hated. ... He got blamed for everything that went wrong.' (Smith was also fairly scathing about the co-operative society.) However, Mary Brunton remembered her parents speaking of Manson as 'an exceptionally good man', which seems a more appropriate epitaph for someone who went so far beyond the call of duty to assist the holders.

Ayrshire

Whereas in Dumfriesshire three estates—of which two provided for a large number of holders—were purchased, in Ayrshire there were various small-scale settlements on a mixture of state-bought and privately-owned lands. The earliest proposal was made in 1914, concerning the farm of Downan.[21] The difference in outcome at that time and in 1930 demonstrates the changes in attitudes between those periods. After a good deal of correspondence between the Board and the estate, the agents wrote in the spring of 1915, 'our Clients will strenuously oppose any attempt to establish Small Holdings on the farm of Downan, and if it should happen that in spite of their opposition these Holdings are compulsorily established, they will claim the fullest compensation that the law allows them.' The farm was let at that time, and the sub-commissioner, noting that 'a scheme in this district is much needed', suggested waiting to see if there was a change in the tenancy. There was, but the farm had been re-let before the Board were able to take action, and in August 1915 the scheme was dropped. In February 1930, when the tenant gave notice to quit at Martinmas, agreement was easily reached with the estate for a Part II scheme. The 680-acre farm was formed into seven new holdings.

The first farm which the Board purchased in Ayrshire was Maxwood.[22] In January 1919, having discussed land settlement for soldiers and sailors with the Secretary for Scotland, the Duke of Portland (described by the K & LTR as 'one of the most liberal land lords in the country') offered to sell this farm to the Board under the Small Holdings Colonies Acts. The 288 acres offered was a much smaller area than the Board usually chose for colony settlements, and several places of about that size had been passed over as being too small; however, because of the favourableness of the offer and the suitability of the land otherwise, the Board considered themselves 'justified in departing from their attitude with regard to the size of colony settlements.' Purchase was sanctioned by the Treasury in February.

In May 1919 another farm belonging to the Duke of Portland—Collenan—came on the market. The Board put in a bid which proved to be the highest. The estate then began to fear that the creation of smallholdings on the farm might have a detrimental effect on the Duke of Portland's grandiose plans for Troon and environs. However, when agreement could not be reached with the next highest bidder, the estate made the Board a new offer: the Duke would gift the Board 166 acres if they would also purchase an area of 89 acres. A follow-up telegram emphasised that both gift and sale were for placing ex-servicemen on the land.[23]

The sub-commissioner, James Dunlop, met the Duke's agent and took exception to 'the changed "conditions" he lays down in his letter compared with the conditions of sale which he issued when the farm was exposed to sale, he takes up the attitude that he is giving us a present of £5000 and that we should not be too fastidious about trifles. I think his attitude somewhat detracts from the generosity of the gift, but it seems to me that it is not a case you can press what he calls "trifles" unduly.'

The Board intended to adapt the land for ten smallholdings, from six to twelve acres, and to use the remainder (130-150 acres) as a central demonstration and depot farm for the holders here and at Maxwood. The Secretary for Scotland had no difficulty in approving the purchase, and the Treasury sanctioned the scheme in January 1920. By October 1922 the Board considered the demand for assistance by holders in the district no longer sufficient to warrant the continuation of the central farm, so it was subdivided into six new holdings of the 'dairying, market gardening, pig and poultry types ranging in area from 5 to 53 acres' as well as two enlargements to holdings on the adjoining settlement.

The Board had a rough time with the Treasury over their proposed purchase of the 190-acre farm of Auchenwynd. The Board pressed this as a matter of some urgency in their submission to the Secretary for Scotland in April 1920, because the proprietor needed to sell the farm by Whitsunday and failing purchase by the Board he would close with one of the other offerers. The Secretary for Scotland approved, but when the Treasury asked the K & LTR his opinion, he wrote: 'I think you should absolutely refuse this proposal. The present rent of the farm is £321.8*s*. less Burdens of

£60.15*s*.9*d*. (which does not include upkeep and repair)—a net rent of £261. The proposal to pay £7500 for this is, I think, absurd.'[24]

The Treasury advised the Board of these views. They asked the Chairman whether the purchase of such a small estate was really vital; whether it was to be worked in conjunction with other schemes, thereby reducing costs or at least assisting administration; whether the price did not appear too high, and so on. The Chairman replied that other schemes in the same area would indeed reduce costs and facilitate administration, and that the farm would undoubtedly sell in the open market at the price they proposed to pay. 'It is specially suitable for the constitution of holdings under the Land Acts and, although small in area, would accommodate thirteen holders in a district where it is difficult to get land for our purposes, where there is a great demand for holdings and where there is every opportunity for a holder making a success of his venture.'

Those arguments were not enough to sway the Treasury, and on 12 May sanction was refused. The next day an official of the Board called on the Treasury and explained circumstances which had not been set out in their letters. The Board had originally planned to constitute holdings under Part II of the Act and issued a Section 9 notice to the proprietor. They then discovered that negotiations for the sale of the property were already under way; if a private purchaser had bought a farm of that size he would probably have wanted it for his own accommodation which would have put it out of the Board's reach. They therefore made a provisional arrangement to purchase the farm; that, plus the Section 9 notice, had scared off private purchasers, so the proprietor was really counting on the Board. The Treasury memo noted

> We could still leave the Board, and the owner, to bear the consequences (though the Board has some excuse, in this sort of case, for acting quickly). In practice however it appears *now* that the bargain itself is not so bad. There is nothing wrong on the equipment side, and the other considerations now mentioned by the Board all count for something. And we have already admitted that the Board has to be left with a fairly free hand in spending the fixed amount allotted to it for Land Settlement, within reason.

There was no time to get the K & LTR's views, and, as the Board considered that 'public faith has already been pledged in the matter', the purchase was sanctioned.

The story of Grassmillees illustrates graphically the kind of long drawn out squabbles that so often accompanied schemes on privately-owned lands, even when the proprietor was not in principle opposed.[25] The sub-commissioner for the district, James Dunlop, reported on the farm in March 1920. It was about 189 acres and considered suitable for the settlement of 15 soldiers on holdings ranging from 3-4 acres up to 40 acres. The lease expired at Martinmas 1920, but the proprietors (trustees of the late owner) had re-let the farm to the tenant on a new 14-year lease. Dunlop advised the Board that the tenant was willing to accept £2000, plus £150 for expenses, as compensation. Not all the Board members were happy about this. One of them wrote

> (1) The proposed payment to Mr Paton must be regarded more or less as 'hush money'. He has plenty of time to get another farm and will in fact be in no worse position than if he got Grassmillees.
> (2) Accordingly I think we should only proceed if (a) There is an urgent demand for land in Ayrshire (b) No other farm is available to meet this demand or (c) Any other scheme would be more expensive than Grassmillees including the payment of £2150 to Mr Paton.

Dunlop replied that there was certainly an urgent demand in Mauchline parish; no other suitable farm was available; and any other scheme *would* be more expensive. In July the Board submitted this to the Scottish Office. The Under Secretary considered the compensation excessive for a tenant who had not yet entered into possession and had had ample time to find another farm, and the Secretary for Scotland refused his sanction. The Board wrote back stating that the Land Court would be likely to assess the compensation figure as even higher. This argument alone did not sway the Secretary for Scotland, but the fact that Dunlop on behalf of the Board had agreed this amount as a fair one with the tenant made it difficult for the Scottish Office to refuse, and in September the Secretary for Scotland approved the scheme.

Negotiations then opened between the Board and the proprietor's agents, who claimed compensation against possible future claims for damage for subsidence due to mining operations.[26] A meeting was held between Dunlop and the agents toward the end of November, at which the agents contested the scheme only over the compensation issue. However, when the Board wrote to them a month later, they replied that the conditions set out were so different from those agreed at the meeting with Dunlop that they now opposed the scheme *in toto*.

A further meeting and correspondence followed. In March 1921 the agents wrote that if they agreed to the scheme they felt the Board should be prepared to agree a compensation figure. 'We feel that the two matters must go together. Our endeavours to meet the Board upon the Scheme are made in reliance upon the Board endeavouring to meet the proprietors upon the amount of compensation.' If agreement could not be reached on the latter then the agents would oppose the whole scheme. They also expressed their regret at the farm being unoccupied so late in the season and insisted that 'if the condition of the farm is deteriorated owing to the enforced absence of an agricultural tenant resulting from the operations of the Board', damages would be claimed. The Board did not reply to the agents by the date requested, and the agents therefore prepared for a formal hearing opposing the scheme *in toto*.

At the end of March there was still stalemate: the lowest compensation figure which the agents could accept was £2500 while the Director of Land Settlement would not go above £1800. The Board asked if the estate was prepared to work the farm for a year; the answer was no. They then asked if the estate would allow them to work the farm for a year; the reply was that the tenant's lease was still in force and the Board would therefore have to come to an arrangement with him. (The Board were subsequently able to obtain a formal assignation of the lease from the tenant). Later the agents wrote

> The obstructive action of the Board is solely responsible for the present position of this valuable farm. May we remind you that the Board took over six months, from the date of their notice preventing us putting our tenant on the farm, to prepare their Scheme most of the clauses of which are, we presume, stereotyped. This inexplicable delay has consequently resulted in the present danger of damage to the farm of which the skilled agriculturalists of the Board are just now apparently becoming sensible. These and a number of other points in connection with the Scheme would not, we believe, bear public scrutiny with any favourable result to the Board.

In April the Board asked the Secretary for Scotland to sanction the expenditure required to manage the farm for a year. According to their version of events, it was the agents who had caused the delay by linking negotiations on the scheme to agreement on compensation.

The formal hearing was finally held in August. The Board then sent the Order confirming the scheme to the Secretary for Scotland. The agents made representations, which were chiefly concerned with the coal deposits, and which the Board felt were 'mainly put forward for the purpose of establishing a basis for compensation claims'. At the end of September the Secretary for Scotland gave his consent to the confirming Order, and the scheme went ahead.[27]

The cases of Harperland and Ploughland illustrate two things: first, that the passage of years did not automatically make landlords amenable to schemes on their farms and second, the attitude of individual proprietors could differ greatly, even on neighbouring farms.[28] In July 1927 Harperland was being advertised to let. As the outstanding demand in the surrounding four parishes was 36 ex-service men and 30 civilians, the Board immediately issued a Section 9 notice. The proprietor objected and contacted his M.P., Lieutenant-General Sir Aylmer Hunter-Weston, who wrote to the Secretary of State insisting that the farm was not suitable for smallholdings. The Board's response was that the farm (of about 314 acres) 'would, in view of the nature of its soil, the presence of public roads and a water supply, its proximity to a railway station and to the Kilmarnock markets, prove a good subject for small holdings.'

The Board commissioned a report on the coalfield underlying the farm. Fairlie colliery had closed, but further working of the coalfield was expected. Suggestions were made for reinforcing the foundations of the mines to prevent subsidence of farm buildings if old pits were reopened or new ones sunk.

In October a scheme was prepared for 15 new holdings. There was disagreement within the Board about the scheme, as Land Committee thought there were too many very small holdings. The senior sub-commissioner,

James Dunlop, was indignant that the committee, none of whom had even seen the land, should criticise his scheme in his absence. As for the doubts about the holdings under four acres, he insisted he could 'show holdings of even one acre and 2 acres on which the holders employ each a number of hands and have made plenty of money.' His revised scheme was for 16 holdings instead of 15! A member of the Board noted, 'while giving full weight to Mr Dunlop's enthusiasm for small holdings & more of them', it nevertheless seemed expedient to limit the scheme to 13 holdings.

The formal hearing was held in November. After modifying the scheme somewhat in light of the proprietor's representations, the Board sent the confirming Order for the Secretary of State's consent on 17 December. On 10 January 1928 the proprietor's agents objected about the coal, but the Board pointed out that no such objections had been raised on Ploughland, which overlay the same coalfield. The Secretary of State consented to the confirming Order in February. Subsequently a problem developed with the water supply which, it was discovered, would have to come from Ploughland, so as late as 1930 no holders had been settled on the farm (the Board kept the existing tenants on as their sub-tenants during this period).

The case of Ploughland certainly presents a contrast. In July 1927 Dunlop learned that the tenant of this farm, which was 'sandwiched into Harperland', was giving up his tenancy. The proprietors had no objection to a Part II scheme, and agreement was reached on a scheme of 12 holdings (two dairy holdings of 46 and 48 acres and ten market gardening, pig and poultry holdings from 4-11 acres). By the beginning of 1928 formal consent had been given by the Secretary of State, and the holders were settled that same year.[29]

Glasgow Area

As was indicated in the previous chapter, in the Lowlands the Board of Agriculture were always keen to acquire land for smallholdings in the vicinity of cities, because of the ready-made market which a city provided. (Over the last two decades most schemes of this nature have been swallowed up by the relentless spread of these cities.) West Millichen farm was only $5\frac{1}{2}$ miles from the centre of Glasgow and was considered extremely suitable for smallholdings.[30] In June 1921, when the Board's sub-commissioner initially reported on the 176-acre farm (held on a yearly tenancy) he found the factor not inclined to oppose the scheme; the tenant, who was about 74 years old and whose father had occupied the farm before him, 'although not favourably disposed towards giving up the farm, appears to be somewhat indifferent'. At the end of September the sub-commissioner advised that the factor had thought the Board meant to purchase the farm; he was opposed to a Part II scheme.

The Board sent the prepared scheme to the proprietor's agent in January 1922; representations were lodged, and the formal hearing was held in March. The proprietor offered the Board a choice of two other farms on his estate in place of West Millichen, but both were unsuitable for smallholdings, so the Board stuck to their original scheme. Their submission in July to the Secretary for Scotland was approved and sent on to the Treasury. The K & LTR wrote: 'This scheme is, I think, a good one and not too costly.' Treasury sanction was given in August, and the confirming Order (with amendments to meet the proprietor's objections) sent to the Secretary for Scotland for consent that same month.

As anticipated, the proprietor lodged representations with the Secretary for Scotland. One of them was that he would be prepared to feu the property rather than have a Part II scheme constituted on it; another was the unfairness of evicting the existing tenant. The proprietor's concern for the tenant was rather vitiated by his willingness to sell, as the Board were not slow to point out. The representations engendered some discussion within the Scottish Office. The Under Secretary wrote to the Secretary for Scotland: 'The one objection which weighs with me is the dispossession of the sitting tenant, and I am unable to agree with the Board that the hardship on him is mitigated owing to his age. To me it seems to be the other way. However, this is an element of hardship which has to be faced in many if not most of these schemes and I suggest approval.'

Before consenting to the Order, the Secretary for Scotland asked the Board to try proceeding by feu, but the agents were against this, and the confirming Order was granted. However, by April 1923, when negotiations on compensation were bogged down, the agents changed their minds, and negotiations to feu commenced. As the confirming Order had stated that holdings were to be constituted by May 1923, the Board had to get the time limit extended by a year. By the end of 1923 it was obvious that no agreement would be reached on feu terms, although it was not until April 1924, after the death of the tenant, that the Board finally initiated a Part II scheme.

In May of that year James Dunlop reported on the neglect that had overtaken the farm since his last visit three years before. Forty acres of land were flooded, the buildings had deteriorated, and the farm had got out of rotation. He had also been informed that as water pressure was insufficient to rise to the original holdings proposed new buildings were to be re-sited along the edge of the marshy land. Dunlop could not agree to the erection of houses 'on so close proximity to what seems inevitably and surely becoming a swamp.' Unless the surveyors were able to devise a way of getting the water to a higher level he recommended the Board abandon the scheme.

But the Board decided to go ahead, whereupon further complications arose concerning fair rents, landlord's compensation, and the cost of buildings. In December the Board decided that until the buildings were adapted and new ones built, they would have to manage the farm themselves. Their plan was not to buy stock and employ a ploughman to work the farm 'but to let it to prospective holders who will cultivate it according to the Board's directions'. Sanction was received for the additional expenditure required, and holders obtained entry at Martinmas 1925.

The case of a scheme in this area which had to be abandoned is also revealing.[31] Early in November 1925 the Board learned from the outgoing tenant that the farm of Windlaw, Lanarkshire would become vacant at

Martinmas. In view of its proximity to Glasgow and the demand in the district, they issued a Section 9 notice. The agents advised the Board that the farm had been relet for another 14 years, and that both the proprietor and incoming tenant, who had given up another farm for this one, would oppose the Board's scheme 'in every way that may be competent to them'.

After further correspondence and consideration by the Board, in February 1926 the Chairman advised the Under Secretary for Scotland of the story behind this. Apparently the outgoing tenant had threatened the landlord that unless his lease was renewed he would inform the Board that the farm would be vacant. It was not unusual for a tenant to inform the Board that he was leaving a farm if he knew there was a demand for smallholdings in the district and the Board naturally did not realise the rancour that existed between the landlord and outgoing tenant. It was because of this hostility that the proprietor was so determined to oppose the formation of smallholdings on the farm.

> The proprietor is doubtless known to Sir John Gilmour [Secretary for Scotland] and the former and his friends will probably make strong objections to the Board's proposals. There are 21 suitable ex-service applicants in the district and 136 civilian applicants, many of whom are suitable. As Windlaw is near to Sir John's constituency he will probably have to face some local pressure, and if the scheme is abandoned, some local discontent.

Had this been a Highland district the pressure for holdings would have been irresistible, but in the Lowlands landowner influence was the stronger, and the Secretary for Scotland advised the Board to proceed no further with the scheme.

In 1921 a member of the Board had pointed out that Lowland demand was highest in the south-west. He did not find this surprising because of the long tradition of small dairy farms and the proximity of good markets.[32] No doubt this explains why there was such a concentration of schemes in this area. Although some market garden holdings did well, it was the larger dairy holdings—i.e. those which fitted into the existing tradition—which provided most of the success stories. The chapter has once again illustrated how dilatory and inefficient the Board could be in the early days, but their choice of farms on which to settle new holders was vindicated in the long term.

CHAPTER 11

The Experience of Holders

The previous chapters have all looked at land settlement from the viewpoint of those doing the settling rather than from those who were settled. The second perspective is, naturally, a very different one, and this book would be incomplete without it. In order to obtain this perspective I wrote to local newspapers in various parts of Scotland, inviting anyone who had been settled on a government-created holding after World War I—even as a child—and who would be willing to talk to me, to get in touch. This approach helped me locate fourteen Lowlanders who were willing to be interviewed (one, Mr. R. McClumpha, by letter, as he was in New Zealand). The schemes represented were Parkhead in West Lothian; Grassmillees and Ploughland in Ayrshire; Locharwoods, Terregles, and Gretna in Dumfriesshire. One reason for the greater number from the south-west was because the local DAFS officer in Dumfries was interested enough in my research to supply the names and addresses of some of the older tenants on the Department's holdings. Those who contacted me obviously typified the keener holders; absentees and the apathetic would not bother to write. In theory, men or women who had failed to make a success of their holdings might have contacted me to air their grievances, but in practice this did not happen, so there is a bias in the sample toward success stories. Only one of the fourteen was first-generation (Daniel Mackay at Parkhead, who was 19 when he got a holding in 1920); the rest were either children when their fathers got the holding or else they were born on the holding.

My letter was published in very few Highland newspapers and produced only one interviewee. The *Stornoway Gazette* carried two articles by me, presenting the story from the Board's viewpoint and inviting readers to tell me their side of it, but the articles produced only one letter in response. The areas I visited (chosen because they dominated so much of this book) were Sutherland, North and South Uist, Lewis, Harris and Skye. Initially I thought I would have to do so 'on spec', and that would probably have worked, as a number of those I interviewed were people about whom I was told only after arriving in a particular locality. However, I was grateful to be given a few names to start off with.[1] Not all of the 18 Highlanders I spoke to were descendants of post-World War I settlers; those who were not had other kinds of information to impart, being very knowledgeable about their particular area. Of the descendants I met, only one had remained *in situ* throughout (James Macaskill, Skye); the remainder had followed the traditional pattern of leaving to work elsewhere for a number of years, returning only when their parents died or became too old and infirm to work the croft.

In view of the cultural and geographical differences between the Lowlands and Highlands, it is not surprising that the experiences of holders in the two areas were quite distinct and that the later development of settlements diverged widely. Admittedly, this division into 'Lowlands' and 'Highlands' is simplistic and fails to take into account the experience of holders in crofting counties such as Caithness and Easter Ross where the pattern was very different.

One thing which must be emphasised at the outset is that the experiences of smallholders on government-created settlements were in no way unique. Although, as will be seen, having the Department of Agriculture as landlords was different from having a private landlord, both the positive and negative aspects of the lives of these people were similar to those of many other crofters, smallholders and small farmers during the Depression.

The Lowlands

The original Lowland holders all had a rural background, and most had had agricultural experience, even those who worked in towns. (For example, one Parkhead holder was a messenger clerk in Edinburgh, but he had been brought up on a croft.[2]) Those who had succeeded without previous agricultural experience emerged as characters of enormous grit and determination. Three of the original holders at Nether Locharwoods (Alexander and James Baird and David Ross), who had a country background but no previous farming experience, were trained at the Midlocharwoods training centre.

The question of what had prompted the application for a holding was one on which second-generation holders could usually only speculate. One woman, whose father had had a job in Ayr, thought 'it was just being born in the country and reared in the country, he maybe wanted to go back'. Both the West Lothian people said it was simply because of the difficulty in finding accommodation. Daniel Mackay, who had a job on the railway, wanted a home for his parents, while Mrs Waugh, who had been twelve at the time, said it was because her father 'couldn't get a house.' Nevertheless, although both men held down a full-time job, neither neglected the holding, and Mrs Waugh admitted that they probably could have got a house in Edinburgh if they had waited, but that her father really was quite keen on having the land.[3]

One of the most strongly felt issues proved to be the size of holdings necessary for viability. This was, of course, tied in with the question of ancillary employment. All sizes of holdings, from 5 acres to double holdings of 100 acres, were represented in the sample, and strong views were held by nearly everyone.

The two who expressed themselves with most force on the subject were

Ploughland holders, Robert Kirk and Bob Fraser. Their own families had in fact done very well out of their holdings; indeed, the Fraser holding of $5\frac{3}{4}$ acres was now supporting a third generation. But the reason for their success was that the first Fraser holder had been a nurseryman, and he grew 30,000 roses per annum on his holding. This intensive horticulture provided a good living, but all around them the family saw holders trying to survive on holdings of similar size with poultry or pigs and failing to do so. To the two men the claim after World War I that ex-servicemen would be able to stand on their own two feet with just 'five acres and a cow' was a terrible con. Not that they thought that those who formulated the policy had been insincere, but rather that it had been lunacy from the start although the ex-servicemen had believed what the government told them.[4]

This was echoed by Alfie Smith, whose father had got one of the larger holdings at Terregles. When I remarked that the myriad very small holdings there had been created to give ex-servicemen a chance, he responded, 'It will be civil servants who dreamt that up, because they couldnae have been practical men or they would never have gave anybody a holding of four acres say to make a living out of.'[5] Of the Terregles people on the really small holdings, only those who found jobs of some kind managed to keep going. It was the same at Parkhead. Although none of the other holders commuted to Edinburgh as did Mrs Waugh's father, only the two larger holdings (25 acres and 35 acres), which went in for dairying, were self-supporting; the rest of the holders had to find jobs locally. Daniel Mackay, who had 10 acres, worked as a guard on the railways. One holder with only six acres was a stamp dealer and did well out of that. Mrs Waugh remarked that another with a holding of that size was so hard up 'he had to go on the parish even' until the mill gave him a job.[6] A Terregles woman felt that it was actually harder having a slightly bigger holding. Theirs had been 12 acres, which could not support the family—her father worked at a nearby farm—but was a lot of acreage to work on top of a job.[7]

In the light of the numerous comments about the impossibility of making a living out of the smaller-sized holdings without ancillary employment, it is worth recording that Bob Fraser's father was not the only one to prosper, although in some cases it took years to do so. When Mrs Gibb's father got a holding at Grassmillees, Mauchline in 1923 he initially kept on his job as a telephone linesman in Ayr, but as this entailed *walking* between Mauchline and Ayr (trains and buses did not leave early enough) it became too much and he gave it up and tried to making a living from the holding. At that time it proved impossible to do so, and he was all set to emigrate to Australia when a job with the Ayrshire Electricity Board came up in Mauchline. However, by the time he reached his fifties (he was born in 1885, so this would have been in the years leading up to World War II) he was able to give up the job and make a full-time living from the holding.

The family grew vegetables and all the soft fruits, kept 500 hens, two or three pigs, a cow for themselves, and three greenhouses for tomatoes. When I enquired how they transported their goods, Mrs Gibb told me that 'people came and bought': 'They came and bought tuppence worth of vegetables.

For that they got turnip, carrot, leek and parsley. If they came for threepence worth they got a cabbage in, and if they came for a pound of tomatoes they got a lettuce.'[8]

The Martins' holding at Nether Locharwoods provided another example of a small acreage made to pay. David Martin's mother got a vacated holding of 17 acres there in 1932. She was a widow whose husband, a farmer, had been killed by a bull. On that holding—with pigs and poultry—Mrs Martin brought up four children, the youngest only three years old at the time. And David Martin remembers that their neighbours had only 15 or 16 acres to support them: 'They kept pigs and a few cattle. And that was their lot. I mean, you often used to think, they've only got that, at least we've got a few hundred poultry and a lot of pigs and two or three cattle, how do they manage?'.[9]

How indeed did they manage? There were two answers which applied to all the holdings, of whatever size. Firstly, they managed by unremitting, back-breaking work. The second answer was the crucial participation of the women and children. More than one holder said that it was only through the family that survival had been possible. The three men who got the double holding at Nether Locharwoods had no children, but their parents joined them along with two unmarried sisters. As their niece put it, 'My Uncle Jimmy made the butter with my grandmother and Sandy he did the ploughing and Davy did the work in the fields and of course my two aunties were down there and did the cooking.' But then her grandparents died, and 'my uncles got old and my aunties got old. And the work, quite frankly speaking, killed them.'[10]

By the age of 50 Mrs Gibb's mother was so crippled with arthritis she could hardly walk: 'I always say it was the holding that did it because she had strawberries, thousands of plants of strawberries, and she had to be on her knees to weed them, and if the rain came on and if she had that job to finish she would finish it.' Mrs Gibb herself continued to work on the holding even after she was married with three children.[11]

All of the second-generation holders remember the work they had to do as children and young adults. At nine years old William McNay at Terregles was 'in the byre every morning and at night when I come back from school.' Later he served his time as an apprentice joiner, 'and I milked cows before I went in the mornin' and when I came back at night. The weekends we were muckin' in, whatever was to be done, whatever croppin' was going on, the hay harvest or whatever.'[12] Another Terregles holder, Alfie Smith recalled: 'you started workin' the day you started walkin'.' Smith worked on at the holding until he married in his mid-twenties; his father gave him only pocket money, so if he needed a new suit of clothes he would have to go off and find casual work elsewhere.[13]

As for the role of women, this was perhaps best articulated by a Gretna holder who commented on the requirements for running a successful smallholding: 'I think that the most important thing was you had to have a good wife—I think it was the most important thing about the smallholding life.'[14]

A smallholder did not, however, depend *entirely* on his family, for on any settlement the holders all helped one another. As William McNay put it: 'It was great how they all worked together when you think back on it, like, say at millin' times and everything ... a sort of "I'll help you and you'll help me"—there werena any money come into it.'[15]

The strong sense of community which holders felt was not, of course, confined to work; 'they made their own entertainment' was a phrase more than one person used in this connection. Another factor which sometimes contributed to the holders' sense of community was their non-acceptance in the local neighbourhoods where their holdings had been created. Mrs Gibb remembered vividly from her schooldays what a terribly clannish place Mauchline was at that time: 'unless you were born in Mauchline you weren't accepted.' On one occasion all the girls in her class had been invited to a party by a girl she was friendly with, but the girl had told her, 'you can't come to my party because my mum doesn't know your mum.'[16]

Nor was Mauchline unique, for Robert Kirk and Bob Fraser had similar experiences in Dundonald. Bob Fraser said

> When Robert's father and my father came to the village we were looked upon as real outsiders. ... We were classed as the poor people who moved into the crossroads. When I went to school in Dundonald Alex [his brother] and I were looked on as the sons of the poor people who had moved—and there we were in the thirties with five and three quarter acres of ground supporting a family of four—we had a couple of pigs and everything—and there were folk up in Dundonald who were unemployed, living on literally soup kitchens, and they referred to us as poor people.

Robert Kirk remembered that in about 1950—20-odd years after the holders moved in—someone in the village had made a remark about 'these new folk at the crossroads'. However, if the Ploughland smallholders felt themselves 'a group of people who were set apart from Dundonald', the positive side was the tremendous loyalty they felt toward each other, a feeling which has extended into the second generation.[17]

Of all the Lowland settlements where I interviewed holders, the one where the sense of community came across most strongly was Locharwoods. This was exemplified by the letters from Robin McClumpha, who had emigrated to New Zealand in 1966 (the holders I spoke to reckoned he had gone there only because his son was so keen). He remembered every holder and every holding in the most amazing detail.[18] At Locharwoods it was perhaps their relative isolation that created such a strong community spirit. This was the scheme which had been so vigorously opposed by the War Pensions Committee and others because they could not believe men would settle happily where there was no village social life. I asked Mrs Mason, who spent her school holidays on her uncles' double holding, if there had been any complaints about this. She described how the holders

> would come along and they would stand at the road end and some of them would bring their penny whistles and their melodeons...Jimmy Jackson used to play the melodeon and they'd stand at the road end, all the ones that played the

12 The Bairds at Locharwoods.

> different things, and the different ones would come and have a sing-song and a dance at the road end. There was no discontent.[19]

Her sister, who was 13 years younger, remembered the entertainment there in a slightly later era

> The families used to travel around with the big gramophone, you know with the big horn, and on a Sunday they would go across the water and visit relatives from across the water down the loaning where there's a little bridge, they'd sit the gramophone on the bridge and then we'd all have a dance.[20]

In view of the source material used for so much of this book, it was of interest to learn how the holders felt about the Department of Agriculture. The only one who remembered the days when it was still the Board of Agriculture was Alfie Smith at Terregles. Initially Terregles was one of the most ineptly managed schemes of them all (see Chapter 9), and the holders had a very real grievance against the Board. As Smith put it, 'the originals were always at war wi' the Board as it was called then, they were always at war wi' them.' He recalled his father putting some of the officers out of the gate—'I can remember him showing them through the gate and down the road—in no uncertain manner either.' However, he felt this had as much to do with the psychological state of the men as with the Board. He described his father as a 'wild man', and went on

> Of course a lot of them were wild men. They men they had had up to four years of a war, ye ken, and the conditions—to be quite frank there were some of them

> werenae just a hundred per cent, ye know they were damaged, war damage, and that's how they hated the Board officials so much.[21]

In his own era Smith had a very good relationship with the Department of Agriculture's officers ('We fell out, had a good row, but we could always come back and go, aye, we understood each other.'). This was echoed by the majority of holders, many of them speaking of the Department as 'good landlords'. Locharwoods holder Robin McClumpha wrote: 'I remember around the 1950's we used to get a team of holders (Mid & Nether) and challenge a team of Dept officials to a game of carpet bowls. They would challenge us in return to a game of skittles.'[22]

One holder (Janet Tarbin) felt, however, that the holders were over dependent on the Department, calling on them for the slightest little thing in a way that would never have been tolerated by a private landlord. She believed that the Department encouraged this attitude, which she termed 'parental'.[23] One example she cited occurred at Gretna.

> A bullock went into a neighbour's field so he thought all right he would go in and get it—but they weren't friends at all...[and] at the field the man that owned [sic] it says 'Where are you going?'. He says 'I'm going to get my bullock.' He says, 'No, you'll no.' And he wouldn't let him take the bullock out. And they had to send for the Department of Agriculture.[24]

William McNay confirmed that if ever there was a problem with fences or bridges, or a dispute among tenants, the first thing one would do would be to phone the Lands Officer: 'That was quite normal, yes. The Department was the first place you thought of ringing.' However, not all the Department's tenants were so dependent. Gretna holder Douglas Ritchie was grateful for advice given by the Department, but his family made (and paid for) all the improvements to the holding, and it clearly never occurred to him to call on the Department for help.[25]

One thing which became very clear in the course of the interviews was that virtually all of the holders on the Department's own estates had, over the course of time, substantially extended their holdings. Once the 50-acre limit was abolished after World War II, the Department were very happy to let existing holders take over lands which were not being used or had been vacated. At Terregles Alfie Smith's father started out with 40 acres while Smith ended up with 80, and whereas the original McNay holding was only 21 acres, the present one is 118. At Gretna the Ritchie holding started as 40 acres and is now 70. And the 17-acre Locharwoods holding on which David Martin's mother reared her family is now 100 acres.[26]

It is worth harking back for a moment to the original idea that smallholdings would supply a ladder of opportunity, with holders in due course moving on to bigger farms. This did happen from time to time—several holders were able to recall isolated examples—but the majority of successful holders stayed in one place and enlarged their original holdings. This meant that they were able to carry on with what they themselves had built up.

Holders on privately-owned estates—although they might have been able to rent an extra field—had not the same opportunity to extend their holdings.[27]

Although many changes occurred over the years—holdings were extended, machinery of various kinds was introduced, government subsidies came in, and so on—I was told that the one absolutely crucial change was the Department of Agriculture's post-1978 policy of selling off their holdings to the tenants.[28] If I had come along before then, I would have found many of the original families still *in situ*. But with the option to purchase at 30% of the full market value, large numbers leapt at the chance to buy, and then immediately sold off the land at a tremendous profit. Some holders who had retired and had no one to leave the holding to had retained their houses but sold the land. This seemed fair enough to other holders; the only real resentment was felt about holders who had put nothing at all into their holdings—working full-time and sub-letting their land—but who had been able to purchase on the same advantageous terms as those who had worked so hard to make their holdings a success.[29]

Douglas Ritchie felt strongly that the policy was wrong because now 'there's nowhere for the young man to start.' However, both William McNay and Alfie Smith thought that since a farm under 100 acres would scarcely be viable today, the sale of smallholdings was irrelevant.[30] Another point (made by a DAFS officer to another researcher) was that the extreme security of tenure granted to the early holders caused those holdings to be locked into the original families—even if the successors had no real interest in the land—so that after the Second World War very few newcomers could get a holding for themselves.[31]

When it came to purchase the Department at least had a uniform policy. Naturally enough this was not the case with private landowners on whose estates smallholding schemes had been created. Not all such landowners have been willing to sell holdings to their tenants and, of those who have, there has been a wide disparity in the prices asked. The Ploughland holders could not buy their holdings until very recently and the prices asked made no concession to the buyers' position as sitting tenants. Holders on the adjoining estate of Harperland apparently did much better, for the landowner there was very generous to his tenants.[32]

The interviews confirmed what the Nairne Committee reported in 1928: that crofters' tenure, imported into the Lowlands as landholders' tenure, was never really understood there. For example an advantage of landholders' tenure was supposed to be that if a holder left then he could claim compensation for improvements. However, this meant keeping a record of such improvements, which no one did, and apparently most holders were not even aware of this possibility. The other advantage was the security of tenure and certainty of being able to pass the holding on to your descendants, but in fact ordinary agricultural tenants were usually permitted to do this as well. There seems no doubt that the landowners who fought the extension of this form of tenure into the Lowlands on the grounds that it was unsuitable there were absolutely right.

Landholders' tenure also caused some resentment in connection with later purchase. Under this form of tenure all repairs to buildings had to be carried out (and paid for) by the holders, whereas usually under ordinary agricultural tenure the landlord was responsible for such repairs. Yet holders in both categories ended up paying the same amount when they purchased their holdings. The original idea of landholders' tenure—long before the idea of purchasing the land was considered—had been that when the bond was paid off the house and steading belonged to the holder. Some present-day holders felt this was a swindle, since owning a house without owning the land it stood on was useless.

The final question which seemed worth exploring was whether, from the vantage point of 50 to 60 years on, the whole policy of breaking up farms to create smallholdings for ex-servicemen seemed justified to their descendants. The general consensus of opinion was that it was justified (though only if the holdings were a decent size): it had given the men a new start in life as intended.

It was anything but an easy life, but the 1920s and early 1930s were the years of dire agricultural depression, and all the families I spoke to had survived it on their holdings, undoubtedly better off than they would have been without the land to provide so many of their basic necessities. The strongest memory Mrs Gibb at Grassmillees retained of those years was one of hard work, and she remarked, 'My mum and dad always said if they had their life to live over again they would never have a holding.' However, her brother has turned the holding into a successful pig farm, and Mrs Gibb commented, 'He's sort of reaped what my dad sowed.'[33] This seems a good summary of the position of the second-generation holders whose parents gained their foothold on the land only because of the land settlement policy which followed after World War I.

The Highlands

Knowing the importance of oral history in Highland culture, I had expected to find many people with vivid memories of the post-World War I period. This did not turn out to be the case. I had to abandon more than one interview when someone old enough to have lived through that period could talk only of the Clearances (a time when they had not been alive) and recall nothing of the period I was interested in. In certain areas this continuing obsession with the Clearances may be understandable. For example, the Rev Donald Macaulay explained that the area where he lived (Great Bernera in the west of Lewis) had been very thoroughly cleared and never resettled,[34] so that the flat coastal areas, where the people had been moved to and where there is still a thriving population, received all the services. Macaulay had spent some years in local government fighting for roads, schools, public transport and the like which the more populated area got automatically.

> People away from here must wonder why people keep talking about it forever, but it grieves us here when we know that we are suffering every bit as much

today in the aftermath of the Clearances. Our roads are terrible, our schools are going down, and because of our remoteness everything is difficult. So the Highland Clearances today is as bitter here as they were, because we know that today we suffer as a result of them.[35]

However, the obsession with the Clearances goes far beyond the areas which suffer in this way.

I asked various people why they thought so little memory remained of the post-World War I period when so many crofters finally got their piece of land, and they put forward some suggestions. Everyone agreed that the younger generation did not want to know. As one woman put it, 'My family don't know a thing about all that. They're not interested. No. It's a pity. They're not interested in what was going on then.' Donald Macaulay thought 'there's more interest in a situation when it's being achieved, when it is being done. Those who inherit a croft don't always realise the value of what they get; it was just passed on to them as a gift.' As for the older generation, one suggestion was that because the immediate post-World War I period was such a difficult unsettled time, and the years which followed were such hard ones, many people preferred to forget about them.[36]

The ardent land hunger earlier in the century is interesting because there were clearly two entirely different components to it, one which might be termed the pragmatic and the other the emotional.

The liberating feeling of space and freedom experienced by people who crossed from tiny congested holdings in Lewis and Harris to decent crofts at North Talisker, Skye, has been mentioned in Chapter 8. As Liz Sutherland put it, getting that croft seemed to her father to be 'a dream come true.' Similarly, it meant a great deal to the Eriskay men who had been sharing their parents' poor crofts to get holdings of their own in Glendale, South Uist. As the daughter of one of them put it, 'it was isolated, but they got their freedom.'[37] And John MacDonald, the son of one of the two Scaristaveg raiders who got a holding when the Department purchased Luskentyre, remembered how as cottars they had not even been allowed to keep a beast.

When you have your own croft you can keep your own stock, you can plant your own potatoes, everything like that, vegetables and everything. You can keep sheep and cattle and cows, it's your land.[38]

The pragmatic reasoning was summed up as: 'the only livelihood you were assured of, however miserable, was your croft.'[39]

There is no doubt that in the above cases a genuine need existed which was satisfied by the breaking up of farms into holdings. However, as was indicated in earlier chapters, there were also cases where supposedly land-hungry men never made the slightest use of the holdings they were granted, and one must look also at the emotional drives. The author of a so-called composite portrait of a Highland community quoted a crofter as saying

In those days, among my father's generation, they still talked about the Crofters'

> Revolt of forty years before, argued about it, fought the old battles again. It's hard tae speak about all that now, all that heat, all that strong feeling, yes—even the fighting spirit—it was all real tae us! We youngsters were brought up in all that. And so we joined in the new upsurge of shouting about 'crofters rights' and so on even though we didna' understand *any* of it. All we were doing was repeating the talk we had heard ever since we were children.[40]

Although this source may be suspect, John MacInnes in South Uist said to me that at the time Lady Cathcart's farms were broken up there were still people there who recalled the original boundaries of the crofts before the people had been cleared off them. And amongst those people 'there was still a fairly smouldering remembrance about what happened to them in the Clearances.'[41]

Finlay J. Macdonald's father got one of the holdings created in South Harris after Leverhulme's death.

> For someone of his strongly romantic nature the achievement of a place of his own in South Harris represented something akin to the emotion of the Jew returning to Israel; he was one of those people whose fairly immediate ancestors had been uprooted from the south during the evictions of the previous century and his sense of history could easily be manipulated to conjure up an imagery of an Israelite far, far older than the Jew.[42]

A point made about the Balranald raid in North Uist was that the men who came back from the war had lost the deference their parents had felt toward the gentry and were therefore much readier to take militant action. As land raiding had occurred before the war, I had doubted this statement, but Neil McVicar, who was a child in North Uist at that time, had a very clear recollection of how deeply shocked the older generation had been when the ex-servicemen raided Balranald. John MacInnes in South Uist agreed that the survivors of the war were tougher and not easily intimidated. He made the interesting point that there had also been a physical change because some of the men were much better fed in the army than they had been before.[43]

Naturally the 'promise' came into it as well. Kenny Stoddart, whose father was the leader of the Kilbride raiders in Skye, said that the men 'were promised as soon as the war was over they would get the land. ... They told those who didn't have land that those who had too much, it would come off them, and it would be broken into crofts.'[44]

Finlay J. Macdonald, continuing the imagery of his father as an Israelite, added: 'He was not to know that he was not escaping from bondage but, rather, going into it.'[45] There is no question but that for those who did work their holdings in the years after the war, it was unending back-breaking labour. I saw for myself how hard it must have been when I visited Glendale in South Uist. It is a beautiful area of green braes, but when Catherine McPhee's father and the other Eriskay men came it was all heather, 'and the heather was nearly as tall as themselves, coarse, coarse heather'. They burnt the heather and then, with a spade and a wheelbarrow (the ground was too stony for a plough) they made lazy-beds and planted potatoes, brought seaweed up from the shore on their backs to use as fertiliser, and turned useless heather-covered hills into fertile ground.[46] At the same time they still carried on the fishing. And these were the men who Lady Cathcart insisted were fine as fishermen but would never be any good as crofters.[47]

Life for the women and children there was particularly hard, because when the men were away at the fishing it was they who had to do men's work like shearing, and because there was no road they had to walk everywhere, carrying everything on their backs.[48] When the men returned with their catch the children would walk for miles to Ferguson's shop to sell the flounders; if the market for the flounders was good that day they would repeat the whole journey again: 'and yet we were so happy when we got them sold.' Donald P. Morrison, a man in his eighties who lives on a croft at nearby West Kilbride, remembered how hard the women worked.

> They were weavin' and cardin' and all this and that and knittin' and guttin', guttin' herring, walking miles and miles from here to the guttin'.[49]

I was particularly interested to learn how families had survived at Shinness in Sutherland where in the 1930s, according to the M.P., they had no ancillary employment and were suffering great hardship living off their crofts alone (see Chapter 4). One man, whose father had been a labourer on the farm before it was broken up, had continued as an estate handyman, but he was the exception. Mrs Agnes Ross, the first teacher when the new Shinness school was opened in 1925, remembered that in the early years some of the men had worked on the Tongue road and that some time in the 1930s the brickworks came to the area and employed some men, but otherwise there was no paid work to be got; nor did the men leave to take season employment elsewhere. 'It was the croft that was keeping them, so that things were very hard.'[50]

May Manson's father, who got one of the first Shinness holdings, worked on the roads at first ('We were bairns, we could just remember him going off with the horse and cart and filling in holes in the road and suchlike'), but after that 'he was just crofting'. 'It was a hard life...I mean you had very little for it...they had very little but just struggling I would say.' However, there was another side to the picture, for she added, 'But they were happy as the day was long and they had their own entertainment you know, and we would have ceilidhs, one visiting the other.'[51]

This was echoed in a letter from Mrs Anne Mackinnon, whose grandfather had been the farmer on Ardroil, Lewis, and who had been given a holding there when the farm was broken up.

> The first twenty years in the new village, until the outbreak of the 2nd World War, were very happy for all the new settlers, the majority of whom were hardened veterans from the trenches of France or had been to war at sea. There was a spirit of achievement and victory, living conditions were vastly improved and they settled down in harmony, which gave rise to much spontaneous entertainment and many community activities. My father's family were delighted with

13 Cutting the peat at Talisker.

> their new neighbours and all this activity as they had been very isolated on the farm and my grandparents' declining years were much enlivened by all the activity going on around them.[52]

On the Talisker settlement Liz Sutherland noted that everyone from Lewis came from the same area (Point) and knew each other, as did the Harris people, so that 'it was very neighbourly and the community life was good'. In view of the problems highlighted in earlier chapters when crofters were absent for long periods of time and township obligations were not fulfilled, I wondered if there had been any resentment when men were away fishing at times when they were supposed to do their work with the sheep. Mrs Sutherland insisted there was none. 'If my father was away well somebody else did a few days...there was no ill feeling among them if you were away and couldn't do it.'[53] Catherine McPhee had similar remarks to make about Glendale.

> We were so happy together. One helped the other...Haymaking or gathering the corn, the whole place came together. It was happy times. We were poor, but we were clean, and clean-living, you know what I mean. Yes, we were happy.[54]

Naturally it was easier for a community spirit to be engendered if the people knew each other before they were settled on their new holdings. This was a point which Bill Lawson made about Harris. Because the people who had been cleared from the west coast had for the most part gone to Canada

> the Department's estates when they were broken up were re-settled from other

villages, and in a lot of ways those people's loyalties are still to these other villages. There's more of a community feeling in some of the older villages in the Bays than there is in some of the new villages in the machair.[55]

In Sutherland Shinness was a settlement where holders came from different parts. Mrs Ross recalled three who had come from the north coast (Bettyhill area), 14 who came from Kinlochbervie and Durness on the west coast and six who were local.[56] The Rosses had been crofting in that area for several decades, and Mrs Ross's son, Farquhar, recalled that (in the 1930s) 'we didn't integrate very well with the incomers', the main barrier being that most of the incomers were Gaelic-speaking whereas there was no Gaelic spoken locally.

Mrs Ross did not believe the new settlement achieved the same community spirit as their own, much older, settlement had, but May Manson disagreed and emphasised that 'they were very good at helping each other.' Perhaps Alastair Sutherland summed it up best when he said, 'Well, I don't know for a start would they be a community. Later on, yes.'[57]

Aside from the holders' relationship with one another they also had a relationship with the Board and then Department of Agriculture. Very few remembered the Board, but James Macaskill had a scathing opinion of the way they had divided Drynoch farm taking no account of the natural movement of sheep and the impossibility of keeping sheep confined to the holdings as laid out. He said of the Board's local officers: 'They didn't know the first thing, they didn't care, just giving a piece of land here and a piece of land there.' In Lewis Anne Mackinnon's father and grandfather felt that Ardroil farm 'had been badly divided and that the arable land had been unfairly divided.'[58]

The most vivid description of how islanders regarded the Board of Agriculture comes from Finlay J. Macdonald's *Crowdie and Cream*.

Occasionally, word would get round the community that 'men from the Board' were coming round. ... The 'men from the Board' were dapper gentlemen who travelled in pairs and wore knickerbockers and brushed their teeth.

'What is that floating in the ebb?' the old Highlander asked his crony. 'It looks like a board of wood or something.'

'If it is moving fast,' was the reply, 'it will be a plank of wood. If it's moving slowly it'll *be* the Board of Agriculture.'

He later observed

...by the time our men, at the tail end of the line, were given their bit of land, a croft had, indeed, become 'a piece of land surrounded by regulations.' It was in the supervision of these regulations that the knickerbockered twosomes always planned to arrive on us unexpectedly.

While the men from Edinburgh may not have understood the problems governing the tempo of island life, the men of the islands understood the official mentality fine. As soon as news came that an inspection was imminent all the proper seasonal work was temporarily abandoned, and work on the new houses

> was resumed with vigour even if it meant stripping off some sarking or corrugated iron that had already been laid, and going through the motions of nailing it back again. By whatever means, every man jack in the village was busy as the government's hired car jolted its way down the road, stopping here and there to justify its journey. Since a tour of the crofting communities was a coveted 'perk' for the office-bound officials, they came round in strict rotas so that, in fact, the same pair never came on successive occasions, making it extremely difficult for one delegation to decide whether or how much advance had been made on what had been seen by the previous one. The crofters, who could modulate the fluency of their English as the occasion demanded, were always cautiously reassuring.[59]

On the other hand, Finlay J. Macdonald did think that direct tenants of the Department of Agriculture, such as those at Luskentyre, had been better off than those in his own settlement were as tenants of a private landlord.[60]

Amongst those I interviewed there was nothing but praise for the Department of Agriculture as landlords. Some of this was purely pragmatic: such tenants had (or thought they had) a better chance of getting grants and loans than tenants of private landlords. The Department were seen as helpful and, if you were working your croft properly, they did not interfere. Also, their tenants felt secure. As one woman put it, 'You feel that your feet are firmly on the ground with the Department.' This was echoed when I asked a man in North Uist, tenant of a private landlord, if he recalled any of the Department's tenants telling him what they thought of their landlords. 'Yes', he replied, 'they had a good word for them. Pretty straight. You knew where you were with them. With other landlords it depended on the individual.'[61]

This universal satisfaction with the Department as landlords may be one reason why so few crofters took advantage of the Crofting Reform (Scotland) Act 1976 which offered them the chance to buy their crofts on extremely advantageous terms. However, the main reason most crofters in the Western Isles would not buy their crofts was that as owners they would lose 'the attractive grants for, for example, fencing, re-seeding—there's a kind of downward scale.'[62]

In the Crofters (Scotland) Act 1955 owner-occupiers at the same level as those on crofting tenure received the same grants for building houses, but the 1976 Act stated that after seven years an owner-occupier would no longer qualify for such a grant. Donald Macaulay feels very strongly about this.

> Why on earth should a crofter be eligible for a grant to build a house on his croft if he has got a landlord living in Switzerland dodging the British taxpayer, and if he becomes his own landlord paying tax into the country he doesn't qualify for a grant. It's the most ridiculous situation.[63]

Macaulay insists that the clause was added deliberately by landowners who did not want their tenants to buy their crofts. However, Bill Lawson presented a different point of view: 'They're buying their crofts on the east coast where there's a big demand; there's been a lot of crofts bought. ... It's a piece of legislation that's aimed at the east coast crofts.' (The difference is that many of the east coast crofts are individual holdings without common grazing shares, particularly south of the Dornoch Firth and in many Caithness parishes, and thus can be bought out as single smallholdings.)[64] Because of these circumstances the Department of Agriculture have continued to own most of the lands which they purchased decades earlier in the Western Highlands and Islands.

One major difference I discovered between Sutherland crofts and most island crofts was that on the mainland there had been a good deal of amalgamation of holdings, as in the Lowlands. Joseph Mackay told me of someone at Achnabourin who 'inherited his father's holding and then he was helpful to his neighbour and his neighbour eventually got old and she willed the farm [croft] to him...and now they're a viable unit as far as he's concerned'. Mackay knew of other such cases, and both the Shinness holders I spoke to, May Manson and Alastair Sutherland, now have joint holdings. May Manson informed me that apart from doubling one's arable acreage, acquiring a second croft also entitled one to put twice as many sheep on the common grazing. Bill Lawson pointed out that amalgamation was really a result of depopulation. In Harris, for example, there had been a good deal of amalgamation at Scarista and Borve because of the number of young people who had left. It had not occurred in communities which had retained their population.[65]

One thing I was keen to learn was the proportion of descendants of original holders who still carried on the same crofts. The only person able to quote a precise figure was Agnes Ross who calculated that out of the 29 original settlers at Shinness nine descendants remained.[66] This is a low proportion, which is likely to be greatly exceeded in most island areas. At Talisker, Skye, Danny MacLeod reckoned that nearly all the 68 crofts were still in the hands of descendants, and Dr Alastair Maclean confirmed that 'on average there will certainly be more crofts where the descendants of the original people are than not.'[67]

However, to say that the crofts are still in the hands of descendants is not to say that they are all being *worked* by those descendants, for absenteeism is as prevalent as ever. For instance, at Talisker out of 68 crofts some 16 have absentee tenants. Bill Lawson commented that the Crofters Commission were trying to edge out such tenants in order to get the land more properly used, but if there was anyone at all on the croft, even if they were not looking after it, the Commission had no powers. Dr Alastair Maclean noted that 'even in a place like Skye there are very good crops of ragwort and rushes growing in this so-called crofting area. And there's some beautiful land absolutely going to ruin, particularly because they are only grazing sheep on it and the sheep's a terrible animal to graze alone'.[68] John MacInnes remarked

> There's complaints about geese in South Uist and North Uist. Why are the geese there? Because there's such a lot of green sward now that's never ploughed, and the geese eat green grass. Nobody goes near it.[69]

No one suggested that absenteeism is higher (or lower) on settlements created by the Department of Agriculture than on other settlements. Dr

Maclean saw the present situation as a direct consequence of the land struggles in the past because the people, even if they are living in Glasgow or elsewhere, hate the idea of parting with the land. Such people perhaps come back to the croft when they retire by which time 'they're not much good for doing anything really in the way of crofting'. He added

> You can't in actual fact I suppose fault people like that. Because they probably have every bit as much right to have a croft and live in Glasgow and not work the croft than to live on the croft, work in Portree and not work the croft. It comes to about the same thing.[70]

Until comparatively recently the security of tenure that allowed descendants to hold on to their crofts without working them did not seem too great an evil (except from the point of view of land use) because in many areas there was little demand for crofts. However, it is generally agreed that this situation has changed radically over the past few years. Donald Macaulay commented that 'in the past five or ten years young people here don't want to go to Glasgow any more, they don't want to go to New York or London, they want to stay here, and this is why the demand is here for crofts now'.[71] Bill Lawson was also aware of the recent resurgence in crofting over the last few years and remarked

> I don't think it's so much young people coming back to the crofts as young people reckoning what's the point of going to the mainland to be unemployed. If you can be unemployed at home well at least there's plenty to do. Digging peats and looking after sheep and growing potatoes and stuff. It's a lot better than standing on a street corner in the city.[72]

Perhaps it is misleading to describe islanders as 'unemployed at home'. At Talisker, for example, while no one can make a full-time living from crofting, there has always been ancillary employment available. In the early years it was fishing. Then

> after the 1940s the Forestry Commission started planting trees, so a few people got work there, and then of course we have the Talisker Distillery in the area so people got work at Talisker Distillery. Then in the sixties a lot of work was available building roads in Skye...Nowadays it's more or less the same really. There's a few of them fishing, there's a few who are working at the distillery, I don't think there's anybody at all in forestry now because that has been cut back quite a bit but then there's the building trade and one thing and another, and the latest thing, the fish farm, is based at Portnalong here, and there's about twenty people working there.[73]

All of these jobs combine well with crofting. Similarly, the youngest crofter I spoke to, Ian MacDonald in North Uist, supplemented his income with part-time teaching. I asked him if he knew anyone who made a full-time living from crofting.

> Oh heavens yes, yes indeed. I don't know what the statistics are on full-time crofting in North Uist—say there's maybe between six and ten, and they do make a full-time living and can make a full-time living because they have very good crofts, in that they have ample acres of machair land and have improved hill land by re-seeding.[74]

One would assume that successful crofters descended from those who obtained holdings after World War I would agree that the breaking up of farms into crofts had been beneficial, but the 'composite' old crofter in *Scenes from a Highland Life* described it as 'a mistake, a big mistake'. The man who had farmed the land before it was broken up had been a good farmer and a good man who cared for the land and the people on it.

> For myself I canna' be sure if I gained from it. I would have worked just as hard if the break-up hadna' happened! And maybe I wouldna' have had so much sorrow as bit by bit the old life fell away leaving us only memories tae live on. That wouldna' have happened, or at least it wouldna' have happened so fast maybe. No, they shouldn't have broken up the glen into crofts.[75]

This does not accord with the opinion of any of those I spoke to. Admittedly when I asked Donald P. Morrison, a man in his eighties in South Uist, what the men had got out of their struggle for the land, he replied, 'They got nothing. Well, you got promised a lot, but you got bugger-all out of it.' When I said they had got the land he responded

> The land? Well, of course. You get the land and you get the place to build the house and you are paying your rent and they're on your backs for all your life. You need to pay up or else they'll shift you out of the place altogether.

However, when I enquired if there had been many evictions he said no, there had not been, and when I asked if many had given up he replied, 'Och well no. They were takin' all what they were needin' off the land themselves in them olden days. Ploughin' and settin' down corn and barley and oats'.[76]

Finlay J. Macdonald's books show families surviving off their crofts during the Depression years, and Neil McVicar, who lived in North Uist, brought up this theme as well.

> These were difficult times, but on the whole the island was all right. They had their own flesh, meat you know, and their own eggs and butter and that kind of thing. ... We were more or less self-sufficient in various ways and we took a great deal out of the land in the way of oats and barley and potatoes.[77]

Moving on from the early decades, when the land made an important contribution to the lives of those who had obtained crofts, to more recent times, I asked Agnes Ross if she thought the younger generation had reaped the benefits of all the hard times Shinness had been through. In her mind she went through all of the descendants of original settlers who she would consider had prospered. She was able to think of only five whom she would put in that category, although she emphasised again that Shinness had been a particularly poor farm to break up.[78]

To quantify how many people ultimately benefited was impossible, but Joseph Mackay's comments when I brought up this question echoed a point made by the Department of Agriculture themselves.

> Well, I won't say, but *some* benefited. Some didn't do so well—well of course you get good and bad farmers, good and bad holders, and although you landed on a piece of land and it's very good and everything but if you don't know much about it and have not been brought up in that environment, then it's unlikely that you'll be a successful farmer.

Mackay also made the point that if the subsidies which came in after World War II had been available after World War I then the story would have been a very different one.[79]

The effects of post-World War I land settlement policy in the Highlands and Islands are hard to gauge. In the Lowlands successful holders who are happy on the land are still working their parents' original holdings (albeit extended) while the rest have sold out. In the Highlands and Islands very few have sold out, but absenteeism is rife. The security of tenure intended to ensure that crofters could improve their holdings without fear of eviction has led to a situation where crofts are tied up by their descendants, some of whom never set foot on the land. This has had dire effects on the use of that land and has blocked young families whose ancestors did *not* get crofts from getting crofts for themselves. The situation is most unsatisfactory, but the strength of feeling about the Clearances which persists in these areas is a powerful disincentive to change.

Conclusion

The chief aims of land settlement in Scotland had been to increase, or at least retain, the rural population on the land, to meet the demand for holdings in congested districts, and to provide ex-servicemen (and later the industrial unemployed) with a fresh start. But before trying to see how far these aims were achieved in the period covered by this book, it is worth looking at the roles played by the most prominent bodies, groups and individuals as revealed in the foregoing chapters.

As the main source for the book has been material from the Board and Department of Agriculture this could have led to a bias in their favour. The Annual Reports certainly present a sanitised version of events, but because the files examined had been created for internal use only they demonstrate far more convincingly than anything produced by external critics just how dilatory, inefficient and downright incompetent the Board could be in their early years. Although ultimately the Department became respected and appreciated, the process whereby a well-organised, smoothly-running government body emerged out of the chaos was a gradual one. On the other hand, the difficulties under which they operated were graphically summarised by Sir Robert Greig.

> The provision of smallholdings by a Government Department is not a popular function. The Department is heavily handicapped from the beginning. Landlords, as a rule, do not welcome the change from a few large tenants to a large number of small ones, however liberal may be the compensation received for the change. Farmers, quite naturally, are not enamoured at the prospect of losing their farms, nor do the farm servants, in many cases, wish to look for a new job. As for the small holder and the applicant for a smallholding, the latter is disappointed when he does not get a holding, and for this he blames the Department, while the former, once installed, considers the Department responsible for everything that may go wrong except the weather. Finally, the public who are in favour of land settlement consider the rate of progress as far too slow, and those who disapprove regard any progress as much too rapid. In short, the Department is attacked on all sides.[1]

The Board/Department of Agriculture were responsible for carrying out land settlement policy, but how much effect did they actually have on that policy? In the Highlands and Islands the land raids (discussed further below) were a crucial factor, but the pro-crofter sentiments of the Board—in particular of Thomas Wilson and Colin MacDonald—undoubtedly helped to sway the views of the Scottish Office and thereby to expedite land settlement in those areas. At the same time the Board also did their best to ensure that not *all* funds and attention were diverted to the Highlands but that the Lowland land settlement programme proceeded concurrently.

Mention was made above of the Scottish Office, and the role of its chief officers is also worth considering. The pro-crofter sentiments of the first Secretary for Scotland, the Highlander Robert Munro, might have assisted land settlement on the islands,[2] but it is difficult to imagine events taking a different course had another type of man held the position. None of the subsequent holders of the office were Highlanders or held any particular brief for crofters or smallholders. The overwhelming impression is that they were all ultimately swept along by public and political pressure. When it came to approving Orders for schemes it was the Under Secretary who had the necessary facts and who advised the Secretary for Scotland accordingly. Sir John Lamb was Assistant Under Secretary from 1909 to 1921 and Permanent Under Secretary for Scotland from 1921 to 1933, so he had a depth of knowledge which none of the Scottish Secretaries (whose terms of office were of short duration) could hope to match. His advice was almost always taken, and so if anyone at the Scottish Office had any appreciable influence on land settlement policy it was Sir John. His very constancy makes it difficult to measure that influence, and his personal opinions do not emerge from the files. He was always there, in the shadows, diligent, level-headed, efficiently processing land settlement schemes without visibly influencing policy, the quintessential civil servant.

The Treasury have featured prominently in this book. Undoubtedly they slowed things down, to a far greater extent than suspected by the applicants (who blamed the Board for all delays). The bizarre thing was that while they had a knee jerk reaction in rejecting almost every proposal coming before them as too costly, the Treasury nearly always in the immediate post-war period ended up caving in to the Board's original demands. They thus impeded land settlement without appreciably cutting costs.

The individual most often quoted in the book was Sir Kenneth Mackenzie, the K & LTR in office immediately after the war. His views are important because they typify a whole section of the Scottish establishment which considered land settlement policy a terrible mistake. As a Treasury man he was naturally appalled at the amount of public money poured into the programme with little hope of return, but his attitude seems to reflect his position as a landowner more than as a public servant, a marked contrast to Sir John Lamb. Did his opposition have any effect on that policy? It clearly did not. The tide in favour of land settlement was far too strong, and although from an economic standpoint his opposition to the breaking up of well-run large farms into small units was understandable, his diatribes did not actually make an iota of difference to the situation.

With a few exceptions the landowners as a group do not appear in a favourable light in this book. Admittedly, land settlement schemes which went forward smoothly and without opposition do not provide much to write about, so this book has given more space to stories of conflict and strife. Nevertheless, the sheer *bulk* of these stories—and the various devious and nasty ways in which some landowners contrived to prevent their farms being broken up—cannot be denied. Finlay J. Macdonald wrote that the slowness of land settlement had been largely the result of 'the intransigence of landlords whose credo was 'to have and to hold', and who, in the upholding of that credo, were prepared to exploit every avenue of legality and appeal.'[3] To give credit where it is due, the insistence of Lowland landowners that a form of tenure designed for the Highlands was quite unsuitable for the Lowlands proved justified.

A question which must be asked is the effect of the land raids on Highland land settlement. It was claimed in the islands that the illegal seizure of land was the one sure way of getting it, and the chapters on the Highlands and Islands have demonstrated that this was absolutely true, no matter how often the Scottish Office denied it. But this must be seen in the light of the post-World War I situation. Although on a small scale land raids had proved an effective weapon before the war, it was the enormous public sympathy for the men who had survived the appalling carnage of the war which gave the land raids their enormous impact. The constant stress on the promise of land to men when they returned from the war made public pressure impossible for the government to withstand.

What about this promise then? The powerful land hunger in the Highlands and Islands was certainly capitalised on by recruiting agents at the outbreak of the Great War, and there is no doubt that the pledge of land for men who served their country in the war was an intrinsic part of government policy. Chapter 2 made clear that as early as 1915 legislation was being prepared to fulfil that pledge. The Coalition Government's election manifesto after the armistice reiterated this promise, and even those like the K & LTR who loathed the policy never doubted that the government was honour-bound to fulfil its pledge. The impossibility of providing a holding for every ex-serviceman who wanted one was never faced up to.

Did ex-servicemen believe the promise made when they enlisted? Certainly the memory has remained. In the 1970s a man in Tiree said: 'The land was promised to the boys when they joined the First World War. When they would come back they would get land. Anybody who had so much, the land would be taken from him and given to the ex-servicemen.'[4] However, H.M. Conacher shrewdly observed that the war had simply given Highlanders 'a new 'formula' to be used in support of their claims'.[5]

When it comes to evaluating results, the report of the Scottish Land Settlement Committee, produced during World War II, is a useful starting point. The primary reason for extending the land settlement programme to the Lowlands had been the perceived need to halt the drift from the land into towns and cities; the 1911 and 1919 statutes had been framed with that aim in mind. But although 4584 new holdings had been created under these statutes (2136 in the Highlands and 2448 in the Lowlands), the Department of

Agriculture's statistics showed a considerable fall in numbers of smallholdings during the 25 years up to the outbreak of the Second World War. Although the committee tried to sweeten the pill by insisting that it was quality rather than quantity which mattered, it was admitted that overall the land settlement programme had not had an appreciable effect on the trend of rural population.[6]

On the other hand, the demand for holdings was still very much in evidence. The committee found that in the Lowlands applications for holdings were constant and 'competition considerable for tenancies as they arise'. The only vacant holdings on Departmental properties which had been unlet for a considerable time were in the Highlands and Islands. They numbered 49, of which 39 were in Skye. It was understood that the failure to attract suitable applicants arose from 'lack of housing as well as the high cost of ingoing and the uncertainty of the future.'[7] They might also have added the change in expectations, for a new generation were no longer willing to live in remote areas up dead-end roads (see Chapter 8), nor to build their own houses, just for the sake of having a croft of their own. Demand in other parts of the Highlands continued to exceed supply.

The committee compared the number of smallholdings created with the number of outstanding applications. Although they did not believe that the demand on paper was necessarily the true demand, and emphasised that many of the applicants were not properly qualified and that the Department were being much more selective in who they gave holdings to, the statistics still appear fairly damning. From 1912 to 1943 the Department had received 33,196 applications for new holdings or enlargements; of these, 12,916 had been withdrawn and 8207 satisfied, leaving 12,073 outstanding.[8]

A fairly obvious question which the committee ignored was whether more of the rural population might have been retained had the supply of smallholdings come anywhere near matching demand. How many of those who had withdrawn their applications were qualified but had become too discouraged to wait any longer? And how many more might have applied if they thought they had any real chance of getting a holding? The Lands Officer at Dumfries recalled that in the 1950s they had sent a standard letter to all the applicants on file asking if a holding was still desired. A reply from the descendant of one applicant stated 'He was no longer interested as he had got his own bit of land eventually. It measures 6 ft × 3 ft.'[9]

The committee did not know how many farm workers had taken up smallholdings as a means of advancing themselves but believed that a significant number had done so successfully. They were less enthusiastic about the thousand or so small-type holdings (mentioned in Chapter 3) created in the industrial belt during the 1930s: 'The great difficulty about settling people used to urban industrial conditions and a weekly wage is that they cannot easily change their outlook and habits to take a view that encompasses the whole of a year, with preparations for the following year. Following on disappointments that season and market bring, they are inclined to neglect the land and rely on full-time work outside their holdings for a livelihood.'[10]

The committee did not therefore consider land settlement an appropriate way of dealing with industrial unemployment. Nor did they consider it an appropriate way of dealing with demobilised men: 'Statistics show that failures among holders settled by the Department occurred chiefly among ex-Service men settled under Government pledge in the last post-war period.' They did think that land settlement had relieved congestion in the Highlands, but the price paid was too many uneconomically small holdings.[11]

The committee distinguished two types of holdings created by the Department: the small family farm bordering on the statutory limit for acreage and the 5-10 acre holdings designed for specialised, intensive production (clearly they looked only at the Lowlands in this connection). The committee had no doubt at all that the most successful holdings had been the large ones, devoted to milk production. Although they had found a number of successful men on the small intensively worked holdings, overall they felt that such holdings had not achieved anything like the success of the larger type.[12]

The Scottish land settlement programme of the first half of the twentieth century has nowadays been largely forgotten. James Hunter discussed it in one chapter of *The Making of the Crofting Community*, but his book was specifically about the Highland land question. In a book on Scottish farming written in the 1950s, J.A. Symon devoted several pages to land settlement, but he extracted all his information from Board and Department of Agriculture Annual Reports, and his analysis did not extend beyond that provided by the Department's 1938 Review.[13] The only general history of Scotland in which I found the subject mentioned was R.H. Campbell's *Scotland Since 1707*. He wrote: 'Two cases of aid in 1919 were peripheral to the mainstream of Scottish agriculture: smallholding and afforestation.' He described Highland land settlement as a 'minor, and largely ineffective, attempt to deal with the situation.'[14] This book has demonstrated that land settlement in the Highlands after World War I was far more important—and effective—than has hitherto been appreciated (other than by Hunter[15]). A.S. Mather, in his monograph on Scottish land settlement wrote

> Land settlement policies, particularly those of the interwar years, have left their mark in many parts of the country, both in the Highlands and Islands where numerous crofting townships have been constituted in place of sheep farms, and in the Lowlands where the distinctive bungalows of interwar holdings are familiar features of many rural landscapes.[16]

Studies could usefully be carried out comparing areas with and without settlements with regard to population levels, size of holdings, prosperity and so on. Until someone attempts such a comparison, there is no way of knowing how much local impact the land settlement programme still has at present.

Another question—hypothetical in nature— is what might have happened in Scotland if by some miracle all the land demanded by ex-servicemen had been made available to them. This did occur in Australia, and in her study of soldier settlement in Victoria, Marilyn Lake found that over 60% of the settlers had turned their backs on the land before the outbreak of World War II: 'The magnitude of soldier settlement failure, especially its cost, and the inordinate publicity it attracted—a result of the peculiar status of the settlers—spelt the end of the eighty-year project of land settlement.'[17] Might Scottish ex-servicemen have become similarly disillusioned? Since for every holding vacated there were usually numerous applicants, the emphasis in Scottish land settlement was always on unsatisfied demand rather than on failure. However, if disillusionment had been the norm demand would have withered.

Twenty years ago one might have predicted that crofting as a way of life was doomed when that generation died out, but its current resurgence shows how false such a prophecy would have been. As for the Lowlands, if the attempt to re-establish people on the land in smallholdings was indeed 'peripheral' to the mainstream of Scottish agriculture then that for me is a matter for regret. Perhaps agribusiness is a trend that can never be reversed and this book is a historical record of a way of thinking that cannot be recaptured. But perhaps not. I came across a book which began

> A nation's survival as a free, independent, and self-respecting entity hangs on the ability of its people to nourish and protect themselves; to provide the means of building and maintaining healthy minds in healthy bodies, and to develop the enterprise, resilience, and determination to surmount natural disasters and adapt to ever-changing conditions.

These introductory sentences to a practical manual for the would-be smallholder were not written in 1905 but in 1985.[18] Although this sounds more like a bugle call to bygone values than the genuine reveille of a new generation of smallholders, that author is not alone in his belief that in years to come more and more people will again wish to return to the land. Disenchantment with cities, urban overcrowding and unemployment, and a simple wish to breathe fresh country air are leading many to try their luck at small scale agriculture, and indeed there is now a helpful journal called *The Smallholder*. If this trend continues then there are many lessons to be learned from the land settlement experience of the first half of the century.

NOTES

INTRODUCTION pp. 1 to 4

1 See E.J. Jacoby and C.F. Jacoby, *Man and Land* (London 1971). They define land settlement as 'an agrarian reform programme particularly designed to relieve the pressure in overpopulated rural areas and promote a more homogeneous distribution of land and labour', p.275. This definition might apply to Highland Scotland, although not to the Lowlands.
2 Marilyn Lake, *The Limits of Hope: Soldier Settlement in Victoria, 1915-1938* (Oxford 1987), p.xviii. Alexander S. Mather, *State-Aided Land Settlement in Scotland* (O'dell Memorial Monograph No.6, University of Aberdeen 1978), p.1.
3 E.H. Whetham, *The Agrarian History of England and Wales Volume VIII 1914-39* (Cambridge 1978), p.137. Because of their proximity to villages up to half of these holdings did not require to be equipped with buildings, an option rarely available in Scotland. On the other hand, the figure quoted is only for the post-World War I period; there were thousands of holdings created before the war as well.
4 James Hunter, *The Making of the Crofting Community* (Edinburgh 1976), p.90.
5 It is worth emphasising that, unlike the Irish, the Highlanders had no interest whatsoever in owning their holdings. Hunter, *Crofting Community*, 185.
6 Hunter, *Crofting Community*, 159. Jacoby and Jacoby in *Man and Land*, 88-9, also noted the Old Testament as the first expression of the Agrarian Creed. Donald E. Meek has discussed this in depth in 'The Land Question Answered from the Bible; The Land Issue and the Development of a Highland Theology of Liberation', *Scottish Geographical Magazine* (Vol.103, No.2, 1987), pp.84-9.
7 The Act was operational only in the crofting counties: Argyll, Inverness, Ross & Cromarty, Sutherland, Caithness, Orkney and Shetland.
8 I owe this last point to T.C. Smout.
9 The Crofters Commission created 2051 enlargements of existing holdings.
10 The CDB also had various functions other than land settlement. See A.S. Mather, 'The Congested Districts Board for Scotland', in W. Ritchie, J.C. Stone, and A.S. Mather, *Essays for Professor R.E.H. Mellor* (Aberdeen 1986).
11 H.A. Moisley, *UIG A Hebridean Parish Part 1 & 2* (Nottingham & Glasgow 1961), p.18.
12 This was before the creation of a specifically Scottish Board of Agriculture.
13 *Report on the Decline of the Agricultural Population of Great Britain, 1881-1906* (P.P.1906, XCVI), p.5.
14 Ibid., 16.
15 Ibid., 82.
16 Ibid., 16-17.
17 The effects of ancillary occupations on crofting are discussed in Moisley, *UIG*

and in J.B. Caird, *PARK A Geographical Study of a Lewis Crofting Township* (Nottingham & Glasgow 1959). One author has recently noted that the definition of 'crofter' in the 1886 Act had been construed to mean that a crofter was bound to reside on his croft, but that after the passage of the 1911 Act the Court of Session decided in 1917 that continuing residence was not required: 'This important decision gave legal cover to the rise of the class of absentee crofters.' D.J. MacCuish, 'Crofting Legislation since 1886', *Scottish Geographical Magazine* (Vol.103, No.2, 1987), p.91.

18 Cf. 'The greater number of small holdings within the limits of rent and area prescribed by the Act of 1911 are not self-sustaining. The tenants, in order to live, must have some auxiliary or subsidiary occupation, employment, or business. Their holdings neither occupy their whole time nor yield the means of bare subsistence, after payment of rent, to the tenant and his household.' Scottish Land Court *Report for the Year 1914*, p.xxxviii.

19 *Land Settlement in Scotland: Report of the Scottish Land Settlement Committee* (P.P. 1944-5, V). The Committee saw 'no objection to a holder engaging in outside employment, so long as he makes proper use of the holding as an agricultural subject.', pp.33-4.

20 Ibid., 17.

CHAPTER 1 pp. 5 to 19

1 H.V. Emy, *Liberals, Radicals and Social Politics 1892-1914* (Cambridge 1973), pp.204-5 & 207-8.

2 See J. Brown, 'Scottish and English Land Legislation 1905-1911', *Scottish Historical Review XLVII* (1968); Lady Pentland, *The Right Honourable John Sinclair, Lord Pentland: A Memoir* (London 1928), pp.86-98; J. Gibson, *The Thistle and the Crown: A History of the Scottish Office* (Edinburgh 1985), pp.39-42; I.G.C. Hutchison, *A Political History of Scotland 1832-1924* (Edinburgh 1986), p.243.

3 SRO.AF43/6.

4 Ibid.

5 SRO.GD325/1/13. Extract from Memorandum by the North-East of Scotland Land Defence Association.

6 *H of C*, 18 Feb 1908, Cols. 666, 683 & 686.

7 Ibid., 668-9, 715.

8 Pentland, *Memoir*, 95.

9 See Scottish Land and Property Federation correspondence in SRO.GD325/1/12, 13, 22, 23, 24 and 247.

10 Pentland, *Memoir*, 96.

11 Education, research, and other functions of the Board, which also drew on the Fund, are not discussed in this book.

12 For potted biographies of these men see AF68/18. For K & LTR's personal views of them see E824/469.

13 SRO.E824/469.

14 SRO.AF68/95.

15 SRO.E824/469.

16 SRO.AF83/153.

17 'The present provisions imposing so much work as regards new small holdings on the Commissioner for Small Holdings should be modified so as to make other officials of the Board of Agriculture available (if necessary) for this work. It is

clearly impossible to avoid delay unless alteration is made in this respect.' *Scottish Land Rural and Urban: The Report of the Scottish Land Enquiry Committee* (London 1914), p. 121. *The Glasgow Herald* commented on 14 March 1914 that it was not really surprising that so few holders had been settled when the business had been in the hands of only one official of the Board 'and a Land Court which has been perambulating Scotland in order to cut down rents.'

18 J.P. Day, *Public Administration in the Highlands and Islands of Scotland* (London 1918), p.229.

19 B.O.A.S. *Second Report*, pp.viii-ix. Cf. Letter from the Duke of Argyll's Chamberlain to the Board of Agriculture 13 Dec. 1912. 'Writing without prejudice I admit that it was never intended to do anything else but agree to your scheme, but, unfortunately, I never fully realised until now that, under section 17, if no objection is taken, future claims for loss are barred, and, as there is certain to be a loss when in due course the holdings are thrown back on the Landlord's hands, it is wished, naturally enough, to preserve this right. You will readily understand my difficulty. It can be said that the landlord has not refused to negotiate but...that no agreement can be reached.' SRO.AF83/153.

20 Day, *Public Administration*, 229.

21 SRO.E824/469. The K & LTR insisted, from his own 'personal knowledge', that the majority of landowners would otherwise have been happy to further the object of the Act; one cannot avoid feeling somewhat sceptical about this.

22 SRO.GD325/1/14.

23 B.O.A.S. *Second Report*, xiv-xv. *Third Report*, viii-ix.

24 SRO.GD325/148. This 'Memorandum relative to the administration of the Small Landholders (Scotland) Act', printed in March 1914, presented the Board's actions as unfavourably as the Board had presented landowners' actions in their own Annual Reports.

25 B.O.A.S. *Third Report*, xii.

26 SRO.E824/469.

27 Scottish Land Court's *Report* for 1916. 'It is with great regret that we have to report that the compulsory provisions of the Small Landholders Acts have been rendered practically unworkable by judicial interpretation of the clause in Section 7 (11), which deals with compensation to the landlord.' p.xxv.

28 SRO.AF83/899 & 906.

29 The Board's opinion 'was based on the ground that a hypothetical loss in selling value founded upon the supposed sentiments of possible purchasers and applied to lands which the proprietor had no intention to sell was not a loss due to the constitution of small holdings in the sense contemplated by Section 7 (11) (proviso) of the Statute.' *Fourth Report*, ix.

30 SRO.AF83/907.

31 The Secretary for Scotland (McKinnon Wood) expressed himself with some bitterness on the subject in the Commons ('the landlord went for his pound of flesh and got a hundredweight') but still thought the Board's action had been justifiable: 'The advantage is that we now know exactly what the law is, and that has always been a very expensive proceeding.' *H of C* 9 March 1916, Col.1782.

32 SRO.AF83/920 & 923. The amount which the proprietrix actually claimed was £19,420, of which £9180 was for general depreciation in the value of the estate.

33 SRO.AF83/885.

34 SRO.AF83/886. 'The Proprietrix's Factor and Agent...said that, if Small Holdings with security of tenure would tend to arrest the depopulation of rural districts, the Proprietrix and Captain Palmer Douglas were in favour of their

constitution, as they recognised that the strength of the country lay in its rural population.'

35 SRO.AF83/890.
36 SRO.AF83/891.
37 B.O.A.S. *Seventh Report*, xiv-xv.
38 SRO.AF83/1270. However, the claimant had asked for a sum of £5904.14*s*.2*d*., of which £2098.9*s*.2*d*. was for buildings, £1806.5*s*. for damage to letting value, £500 for depreciation of shootings, and £1500 for general depreciation of the estate. The arbiter found no sum payable for damage to letting value or for depreciation of shootings. He awarded £1330.10*s*. for buildings and £384.17*s*.11*d*. for depreciation of the value of the estate, making a total of £1715.7*s*.11*d*. plus interest and expenses. (For material on Borrowston Mains prior to the hearing see SRO.AF83/99-101.)
39 SRO.AF83/111.
40 SRO.AF83/157-159.
41 SRO.AF83/153.
42 SRO.AF83/433.
43 SRO.AF83/272-276.
44 *Scottish Land Rural and Urban*, 54 & 63. (N.B. I found no contemporary allusions to this Report, the tone of which is strongly anti-landlord.)
45 Ibid., 115-122.
46 Ibid., xxx. Various precedents were quoted, such as the Crofters Act of 1886 (which had led to the reduction of many rents and cancellation of a large amount of arrears of rents without any compensation being paid to landlords), the Ground Game Acts, under which landowners lost valuable sporting rights, the Agricultural Holdings Acts, and the Housing & Town Planning Act of 1909.
47 B.O.A.S. *Fourth Report*, vii. Scottish Land Court's *Report* for 1916, ix: 'Numerous Schemes passed in 1915 and previous years have been abandoned during 1915, mainly, it is believed, in consequence of the serious liabilities in connection with arbitration.'
48 SRO.AF43/34. See also GD325/148.
49 H.M. Conacher & W.R. Scott, *Interim Report to the Board of Agriculture for Scotland on the Economics of Small Farms and Small Holdings in Scotland* (HMSO Edinburgh, 1919), pp.35-6.
50 SRO.AF83/558-560.

CHAPTER 2 pp. 20 to 38

1 This is mentioned again and again after the war, both in letters by men clamouring for land and in government documents: for example, one report commented that the Small Holdings Colonies Act had been passed in 1916 'as a step towards fulfilment of the pledge given to men who had volunteered for naval or military service during the War that they would be settled on the land on their return'. *Report of the Committee on Land Settlement* (P.P.1928, xi), p.10.
2 W.R. Scott, 'Scottish Land Settlement' in *Rural Scotland During the War* (London 1926), p.247.
3 James Hunter, *The Making of the Crofting Community* (Edinburgh 1976), p.195.
4 *Departmental Committee on Land Settlement for Sailors and Soldiers* (P.P.1916, xii), p.6.
5 The Agricultural Policy Sub-Committee of the Reconstruction Committee,

whose report appeared in 1918, declined to express an opinion on the comparative productivity of large farms and small holdings ('We do not think it necessary to take either side in this controversy, because we believe that no generalisation on the subject can be safely or usefully made.'). Although the committee wholeheartedly approved the policy of creating smallholdings for a number of reasons, the Board of Agriculture for Scotland were very annoyed at the committee's failure to agree with their own strong convictions that the formation of small holdings led to greater food production. SRO.AF43/94.

6 The Board discussed the difficulties of utilising these Acts for Scotland in their *Seventh Report*, p.xvii.

7 *H of C* 9 August 1916, Cols.1100-1104. An author writing in the early 1920s thought that it would 'have been wise if steps had been taken to have a certain number of holdings ready as soon as possible after demobilization'. He admitted the uncertainties of 1917 and 1918 and granted 'the unfortunate slowness of the normal action of a public department', but nevertheless found it a matter of regret that more forward planning had not been undertaken. Scott, 'Scottish Land Settlement', 244.

8 *H of C* 9 August 1916, 1130-1131.

9 See L. Leneman, 'Borgie: A Debatable Gift to the Nation?', *Northern Scotland* (forthcoming 1989).

10 SRO.AF83/613 & 614. The Duke of Sutherland actually sold this farm before the holders were settled on it, but with the understanding that the new proprietor would be bound by his arrangements with the Board.

11 Hunter, *Crofting Community*, 195; *Glasgow Herald*, 5 October & 6 December 1917.

12 Material in this and subsequent paragraphs on behind-the-scenes political machinations during the war years comes from The Scottish Land & Property Federation file SRO.GD325/1/147.

13 Lord Lovat thought the demand for smallholdings after the war would be 'not very extensive', a good indication of how far out of touch some Scottish landowners were with public sentiment.

14 SRO.AF83/57. There were in fact two separate booklets issued under this title, one of them being addressed to officers.

15 *The Times* 22 Nov 1918.

16 SRO.AF66/114/2.

17 SRO.GD325/1/147. Lord Lovat concluded one diatribe (letter to Col. Gilmour M.P., 3 May 1919), by stating his belief that Munro represented 'the Extreme doctrinaire Radical side, that is to say, the side which wishes first to injure Landlords and secondly, but only secondly, to benefit the people.'

18 SRO.GD325/1/21. (Much of the material in this file is duplicated in GD325/1/26.)

19 SRO.GD325/1/147.

20 The Land Settlement (Facilities) Act, 1919 is 9 & 10 Geo.5. Ch.59; the Land Settlement (Scotland) Act, 1919 is 9 & 10 Geo.5 Ch.97.

21 The need for this had been made manifest in the years immediately following the passage of the 1911 Act: 'There is a strong feeling that no Small Landholders Act will be satisfactory which does not provide for the case of the man of experience and character but insufficient means.' *Scottish Land Rural and Urban: The Report of the Scottish Land Enquiry Committee* (London 1914), p.113. This had been reiterated in a 1919 report: 'It seems to us that...a well-qualified candidate for a small farm constituted by the Board of Agriculture should be in a position to obtain assistance from public funds to supplement his own working capital, rather than that the size of holdings should be kept down to a level at

which the majority of applicants could stock and equip them from their own resources.' H.M. Conacher & W.R. Scott, *Interim Report to the Board of Agriculture for Scotland on the Economics of Small Farms and Small Holdings in Scotland* (HMSO Edinburgh, 1919), p.39.

22 SRO.GD325/1/21.

23 The Secretary for Scotland explained all this to the House of Commons. *H of C* 4 Aug 1920, Cols.2464-2467.

24 The Secretary for Scotland considered the fact that the Board had so rapidly 'exhausted the possibilities of the Act in the direction of acquiring land' commendable, though he went on to admit that 'the position with regard to funds is serious when viewed in the light of the present unsatisfied demand'. Ibid., 2474.

25 See *Report of the Royal Commission on Scottish Affairs* (1953), vol.ii, p.112, and also *Scotch Offices Inquiry Commission Report* (1870), pp.39 & 45. I am grateful to Dr. Athol Murray for these references.

26 SRO.AF66/25.

27 Scott, 'Scottish Land Settlement', 245.

28 B.O.A.S. *Eighth Report*, p.xiv.

29 *The Times* 3 Aug 1920. The piece concluded, 'The agrarian trouble in the Highlands would never have reached its present intensity if the Board had acted with greater readiness and efficiency. They are now regarded with hostility and mistrust.'

30 Land settlement in England was also encountering problems at this time—albeit not on the same scale and without the raiding and press coverage—as can be seen from a document in SRO.E824/469.

31 Sir Arthur Rose D.S.O. was Chairman of the Edinburgh Education Authority and President of the Association of Education Authorities of Scotland. During the war he commanded a battalion of the Royal Scots at the front, and afterwards he acted as Food Controller for Scotland. His appointment was made possible by the transfer of John Sutherland, the former Small Holdings Commissioner, to the Department of Forestry. SRO.AF66/24.

32 Indeed, everyone seemed to bend over backwards to exonerate him from any of the blame. See *H of C* 28 July 1921 and *The Scotsman* 30 July 1921.

33 SRO.E824/469. All Treasury material on this subject discussed in subsequent paragraphs is in this file.

34 SRO.AF66/27.

35 SRO.E824/472.

36 For background on the drafting of the Bill see SRO.AF66/33.

37 Borrowing actually ceased at a total of £2,158,185 on 31 March 1926, when land settlement again came to be financed out of the Agriculture (Scotland) Fund. *Report of the Committee on Land Settlement* (1928), 12.

38 SRO.E824/482.

39 See SRO.E824/473 & 475.

40 *The Scottish Farmer*, 1921, pp.364, 392, 417, 451, 480, 945.

41 SRO.GD325/1/149.

42 *H of C* 28 July 1921, Cols.755-792. For Notes for the Secretary for Scotland in connection with this debate, see SRO.AF66/34.

43 SRO.GD325/1/149. Without knowing more of the inner workings of the political parties of the time it is difficult to judge how much reliability to place on this version of events.

44 *The Scotsman* 30 July 1921. The journal's hostility was not directed only at the Board but also at the whole policy of land settlement.

45 This letter appears in a file on Raasay still retained by the Department of

Agriculture & Fisheries for Scotland and available for consultation only by prior application.

46 *The Scottish Farmer*, 1921, 915.

47 SRO.GD325/1/149. One of the more rabidly right-wing members of the Federation, James Scott, wrote, 'So long as Connacher and Sir Robert Greig are on the Board of Agriculture they will simply be under the paw of the Secretary for Scotland. In the Northern Counties, advise [sic] would never be taken from a landlord or his agents, while 95% of the population are agitators.'

48 SRO.AF67/153. The announcement appeared in *The Scotsman* on 13 Dec 1921.

49 SRO.GD325/1/33.

50 The K & LTR (Sir James Adam) wrote to the Treasury on 15 November 1922: 'I notice that in White Hart Parks...you came down heavily in favour of Part II schemes. ... There is no doubt, however, that purchase outright solves many difficulties. The Board are, I think, coming to the conclusion that a system of dual ownership or divided control should not have been introduced into the Lowlands and I feel inclined to agree.' SRO.E824/519.

51 SRO.AF66/55. Example of opposition to the Board and land settlement policy may be found in Minutes of the Central Executive Committee of the NFU 28 October 1919 and 6 May 1920. A letter quoted in the minutes of 11 June 1920 referred to the Board as 'a miserably effete Institution whose leanings are for the most part Socialistic.' I am grateful to the National Farmers' Union of Scotland for allowing me access to this material.

52 SRO.AF83/54/1.

53 SRO.E824/483.

54 SRO.AF66/44.

55 SRO.AF83/52.

56 SRO.E824/469. All of the Treasury material in subsequent paragraphs, unless otherwise footnoted, is also in this file.

57 SRO.AF83/52.

58 On settlements which were not situated on the Board's estates the revaluation was to apply to buildings only; on the Board's estates revision of fair rents was to be carried out in connection with any revaluation of the buildings.

59 SRO.AF83/52. For complications in the years following the announcement, see SRO.AF83/53.

60 Scott, 'Scottish Land Settlement', 260-1. For details of this emigration see J. Wilkie, *Metagama: A Journey from Lewis to the New World* (Edinburgh 1987).

61 SRO.AF67/376. This was reported in *The Glasgow Herald* 23 May 1923.

62 SRO.AF67/377.

63 The Board in that year produced a survey of land raids since January 1923, with the reasons for the forcible seizures and the action taken in each case. SRO.AF67/159.

64 *H of C* 26 June 1923, 2169-2263.

65 All of the material on this subject, unless otherwise footnoted, is in SRO.E824/489.

66 SRO.AF66/54.

67 SRO.AF67/387.

68 B.O.A.S. *Fourteenth Report*, pp.10-11.

69 SRO.AF66/57.

70 SRO.AF43/240.

71 Ibid. (This appeared in *The Scotsman* 9 May 1928.)

72 D.O.A.S. *Twenty-Seventh Report*, p.42. In 1935 Sir Robert Greig had written of the immediate post-war period: 'No time could have been more disadvantageous

for land settlement from the economic point of view. The price of land, of sheep stocks, of building materials, and of every kind of equipment was at the peak.' 'Agricultural Administration During the Present Reign', *Scottish Journal of Agriculture* (April 1935), p.109.

CHAPTER 3 pp. 39 to 52

1 *Report of the Committee on Land Settlement* (P.P.1928, xi), p.4.
2 Ibid., 25.
3 Ibid., 29.
4 Ibid., 31.
5 They did not think that devolving any of the powers and duties connected with land settlement onto local authorities was feasible. Their recommendation regarding changes in rating proved irrelevant, as the government announced new proposals for the rating of agricultural subjects while the report was being printed.
6 Alexander S. Mather, *State-Aided Land Settlement in Scotland* (O'dell Memorial Monograph No.6, University of Aberdeen 1978), p.14.
7 James Scott had been concerned with land reform for a long time. Some of the clauses in his Bill had been suggested as amendments to the 1911 Act in his pamphlet, *Land Reform in Scotland* (Edinburgh 1913).
8 In 1926 the Secretary for Scotland had become Secretary of State for Scotland. The Board of Agriculture for Scotland became the Department of Agriculture for Scotland in 1928.
9 SRO.AF66/62.
10 It is worth noting that one member of the Nairne Committee, Norman Reid, emphatically disagreed with the majority report's recommendation that landholders' tenure be discontinued in the Lowlands. *Report of the Committee on Land Settlement*, 57.
11 Letter from J. Rowley Orr (solicitor and landowner) 21 March 1930. SRO.GD325/1/144. Further Scottish Land and Property Federation material on this Bill and on the Small Landholders & Agricultural Holders (Scotland) Bill, 1930 is in SRO.GD325/1/122, 126, 128, and 145.
12 A fourth—the right to kill game which was destroying crops—falls into rather a different category and was (as the Department said at the outset) something which really belonged to game laws.
13 'The main object of the compromise in 1911 as regards the statutory small tenant was to prevent the setting up of a separate class of tenants on landed estates and to avoid judicial interference with ordinary estate management.' SRO.GD325/1/145.
14 SRO.AF66/49.
15 SRO.GD325/1/128.
16 SRO.GD325/1/144.
17 *H of C* 13 Dec 1929, Cols.855-934.
18 *H of C* 23 May 1930, Cols.730-778.
19 *H of C* 10 Nov 1930, Cols.1385-1435.
20 SRO.AF66/69 & 70.
21 *H of C* 20 March 1931, Cols.2290-2374.
22 *H of L* 12 May 1931, Cols.1119-1176.
23 I owe this point to Dr. Roger Davidson.

24 SRO.DD10/254. See also DD10,255/1.
25 Mather, *State-Aided Land Settlement*, 19.
26 SRO.AF66/84. Only £100,000 had been provided the previous year and £175,000 was the maximum available for land settlement under existing legislation.
27 SRO.AF66/85. With the emphasis on Lowland Scotland, it had been hoped by the Department and Secretary of State that less could be spent on Highland land settlement, but pressure from Highland M.P.s meant an assurance had to be added that land settlement in the Highlands would not be prejudiced by the provision of extra money for the industrial belt.
28 *Land Settlement in Scotland: Report of the Scottish Land Settlement Committee* (P.P. 1944-5, v.), pp.12-13. It was claimed this was a result of the Nairne Committee's recommendation in 1928, but something which occurs six years after being recommended is difficult to accept as a 'result'.
29 D.O.A.S. *Twenty-Second Report*, p.15; *Twenty-Third Report*, 11; *Twenty-Sixth Report*, 80.
30 *H of C* 4 July 1935, Cols.2067-2069 & 2098. The Department subsequently provided training schemes for men who wanted to graduate from plots to holdings but lacked the necessary experience. D.O.A.S. *Twenty-Seventh Report*, 36-7.
31 D.O.A.S. *Twenty-Fourth Report*, 13-14. According to the Department's 25th & 26th Reports, demand remained high in 1936 but fell off in 1937.
32 SRO.AF43/290. The report was published in July 1936 as *Economic Survey of Small Holdings Outside the Crofting Counties*. The version I used was the first draft of the report (before it had been tidied up for public consumption).
33 Small fruit growers were the other group to complain most about the size of their holding, and the authors of the report commented, 'While it is impossible to state dogmatically what is the most economic size of holding for different forms of production, it might be suggested that any tendency to make holdings of as small an area as possible can easily be carried too far.'
34 SRO.AF43/372. The report—dated 13/4/37—is marked 'Confidential'.
35 Ibid. The resulting report is not dated, but it received an acknowledgement in April 1937.
36 SRO.AF66/59.
37 This information comes from the memorandum in the above file; I have not discovered any files presenting the Department's side to this story.
38 *H of C* 28 June 1935, Cols.1489-1498.
39 *Land Settlement in Scotland*, 11.
40 D.O.A.S. *Twenty-Seventh Report*, 35-46.
41 Mather, *State-Aided Land Settlement*, 25-6.
42 See A.S. Mather, 'The rise and fall of government-assisted land settlement in Scotland', *Land Use Policy* (July 1985), pp.217-24.

CHAPTER 4 pp. 53 to 70

1 James Hunter, *The Making of the Crofting Community* (Edinburgh 1976), p.27. For a detailed modern description of the Sutherland Clearances see Eric Richards, *A History of the Highland Clearances* (London 1982), pp.288-360.
2 SRO.AF83/801.
3 A.S. Mather, 'The Congested Districts Board for Scotland' in W. Ritchie, J.C.

Stone and A.S. Mather, *Essays for Professor R.E.H. Mellor* (Aberdeen 1986), p.198.

4 SRO.AF83/54/1 and AF83/595.

5 SRO.AF83/1274 & 1275. These files deal with the pre-war period. Apart from an isolated file headed Miscellaneous Applications and containing a few letters of 1920—listed as AF83/1276—none of the post-war files appear to have survived. The account of events during that period relies, therefore, on other sources.

6 SRO.GD325/1/249 and *Glasgow Herald* 23 June, 3 July, 18 August, and 11 October, 1920.

7 SRO.E824/599.

8 *Caithness Courier*, 26 May 1922. I owe this reference to Jim A. Johnston.

9 SRO.AF83/591 & 592.

10 SRO.AF83/391-395.

11 The differences between the leases and the agreement were primarily concerned with valuation of stock as against fixed prices at the outgoing of the tenant. Too much verbiage would be required to explain this more fully, but the explanation can be found in an internal memo in SRO.AF83/393. It is made clear that when the leases were entered into there must already have been a verbal agreement to amend them quite radically, with the object of penalising the Department if they proceeded with a scheme before the termination of the lease in 1940.

12 SRO.AF83/806.

13 At least Scibercross was eventually settled. For an example of how much time and energy could be expended on a farm where a scheme was never even drawn up, let alone implemented, see the files on Forsinain, SRO.AF83/328-330.

14 SRO.AF83/595-597 and AF66/25.

15 The proprietor also made the farm of Achnabourin available for smallholdings and enlargements, and it was settled without any difficulty at Whitsunday 1923. SRO.AF83/681.

16 The proprietor's agents refused to accept the offer of £300 compensation, and the case went before the Land Court in August 1929. The Court ordered the Department to pay £530. SRO.AF83/599.

17 Armadale files are still held by DAFS and are open to inspection only by prior application. (Such files are hereafter cited as DAFS files.) The farm is now once again in the possession of a single man. One might have expected some feeling of bitterness to have accompanied this revelation, but not a bit of it. The man is considered to be a good worker who has got the farm 'on its feet'. Interview with Joseph Mackay, Melness, 5 August 1988 (hereafter Mackay).

18 DAFS have retained the files relating to this estate because in 1922 the Board provided enlargements from the estate of 5500 acres to neighbouring crofters, who remained tenants of the Department.

19 SRO.E824/567.

20 Interview with Mackay.

21 DAFS files. Negotiations were carried on simultaneously with the owners of this farm and the neighbouring estate of Balnakeil. However, in 1921 the Board dropped Balnakeil.

22 SRO.E824/523.

23 SRO.E824/592.

24 SRO.AF66/59.

25 P.T. Wheeler, 'The Sutherland Crofting System', *Scottish Studies* Vol.8 (1964), p.177. Interview with Mackay and with Bernard Haynes, Durness, 4 August 1988. Haynes' father had been secretary of the club.

26 SRO.AF83/801 & 802.
27 The various files have different headings, e.g. Scheme, General Works, Sheep Stock Club, which are not consecutive (even the material in some individual files occasionally jumps backwards and forwards in time), and which overlap. The material can all be found somewhere within the following: SRO.AF83/614, 615, 624, 625, 626, 633.
28 At this time the sheep stock club was dissolved; thereafter the holders had equal numbers of sheep on the common grazing, an arrangement which they much preferred. Interview with Alastair Sutherland (son of one of the original holders), Shinness, 5 August 1988.
29 For the dreadful state of the houses on two of the holdings in the early 1930s and later, see SRO.AF83/1640 & 1641. The latter contains a letter dated 8 August 1933 from the Medical Officer of Health concerning Holding No.12: 'This house has fallen into such a state of disrepair and is so devoid of sanitary facilities that, in my opinion, it is not in its present state fit for habitation.'
30 Interview with Mrs Agnes Ross, Shinness, 4 August 1988.

CHAPTER 5 pp. 71 to 91

1 SRO.AF83/514-517.
2 *Scottish Land Court Report for 1915*, p.viii. The Report continued, 'In consequence of this decision [to abandon the scheme] Mr. Rudd will not get his compensation, and the expenses of arbitration have been avoided; but fruitless expense has been incurred and the time of the Board and the Land Court in connection with the Scheme has been wasted, while the proceedings have not resulted in the relief of congestion in Ardnamurchan.'
3 SRO.E824/631.
4 SRO.AF83/705-707 and E824/496.
5 SRO.AF83/249-251.
6 James Hunter, *The Making of the Crofting Community* (Edinburgh 1976), p.196.
7 Hugh MacEachern interviewed by Margaret Mackay, School of Scottish Studies, SA1974/130.B.
8 John MacLean interviewed by Eric Cregeen, School of Scottish Studies, SA1974/117.A.
9 The files are still in the possession of DAFS and are available for inspection only by prior application. (All subsequent files of this nature in the chapter will be cited as DAFS files.)
10 E824/658. He added, 'The Scottish Office is, I believe, fully aware of the danger of the present position in the West, but in this case, where I understand the property is practically bankrupt, I think the Board are offering far more than the place is worth, and they ought to have made a better bargain.'
11 In the period in question the islands of Skye, Harris and Uist were part of Inverness-shire, but they are dealt with separately in later chapters.
12 SRO.AF83/729-731.
13 SRO.AF83/714-717 and E824/519.
14 SRO.AF83/610-612.
15 The file was not, however, closed immediately, for the estate procrastinated over signing the order to be lodged with the Land Court for the registration of Donald Mackintosh as a new holder, and this was not completed until August 1924.
16 DAFS files.

17 SRO.E824/671.
18 DAFS files.
19 SRO.E824/503.
20 Although the isle of Lewis was part of the county of Ross & Cromarty, it is covered in a later chapter.
21 Hunter, *Crofting Community*, 206.
22 SRO.AF83/755-757 and E824/636.
23 DAFS files.
24 SRO.E824/501.
25 DAFS files.
26 SRO.E824/671.
27 H.M. Conacher, 'Land Settlement in Scotland', *Scottish Journal of Agriculture*, IV (1921), p.178.
28 Ibid., 176. See also *Interim Report on the Economics of Small Farms and Small Holdings in Scotland* (HMSO, Edinburgh 1919), P.26.
29 SRO.AF83/463-468 and E824/543.
30 There were various points of disagreement, but in the end the chief one was that the Board were attempting to settle the compensation claim under the 1919 Act whereas the agents claimed they had obtained entry by notices served under the 1911 Act; ultimately the Board conceded the justice of this.
31 SRO.AF83/693.
32 In January 1922 the M.P. represented that there were still ex-service men without land, and that more of Quendale farm could be used for this purpose. Sir Arthur Rose explained that because it was a home farm the Board could not use compulsory powers. At the Board's Departmental Committee meeting on 6 March 1922 it was made clear that even if all the schemes which the Board had under consideration were carried out, there would still be an unsatisfied demand in Shetland of over a hundred ex-servicemen. AF83/54/1.
33 SRO.AF83/694.

CHAPTER 6 pp. 93 to 115

1 James Hunter, *The Making of the Crofting Community* (Edinburgh 1976), p.82.
2 Ibid., 148, 190-1.
3 Although this firm of solicitors is still in existence, they share none of the anti-crofting sentiments of their predecessors, in fact at time of writing the senior partner is a crofter's son (letter from Skene, Edwards & Garson, 30 May 1988).
4 SRO.AF83/74-78.
5 SRO.AF83/144-148 (also AF67/146).
6 They also forwarded to the Board a copy of a letter from the local minister pleading the crofters' desperate need for peat. 'Coals are and will be out of question for the people of Eriskay; it is impossible were it within their means to make use of coals; having open fires on their floors, and home made fireplaces.' To which the agents had replied, '...if the existing fire places in the houses are not suitable for coal fires, they should be adapted for that purpose'—which almost falls into the 'let them eat cake' category.
7 He continued, 'I know it is hopeless to expect even the site of fishermen's houses from her [Lady Cathcart]. The fact that many of her people fought—some giving up their lives—and kept for her her Estate, does not seem to have opened her

mind or that of her advisers, to the necessity of making available the lands she holds for these men to obtain homes upon and earn a livelihood from.'

8 Unlike the Askernish raid, which is well remembered by the islanders, the fact that two men had been interdicted for taking possession of land at Glendale appears to have been entirely forgotten. In the course of interviews in South Uist I was categorically assured that no raid had ever taken place at Glendale.

9 SRO.AF83/190-192 (also AF67/147).

10 As will be seen later in the chapter, the fact that Lady Cathcart had refused to become involved in the selection of tenants for the new holdings never for a moment inhibited her from complaining about those whom the Board chose.

11 Interview with John MacInnes, 15 July 1988.

12 Drimore files are SRO.AF83/206-208; Drimsdale files are AF83/210-214. The two cases became so intertwined that the later stages of the Drimore case are to be found in Drimsdale files. Treasury material is in E824/569. Material specifically on land raids is in AF67/152.

13 In March 1920 the agents wrote to the Board, 'The impression formed by the Factor is that there is no great enthusiasm for holdings on Drimore, and not much likelihood of any determined effort to get the place broken up for holdings.' In April, concerning Drimsdale, they reported him as stating, 'there had been no recent demonstrations and he scarcely thought a serious effort would be made to get this farm as the people realised that it was quite unsuitable for small holdings.'

14 On being advised of the Secretary for Scotland's terms, the proprietrix's agents replied, 'The difficulty in these Islands in adopting legal proceedings is, as you know, the circumstances that, in effect, the King's Writ does not run there. Moreover, as I think you are aware, Lady Cathcart, after the Glendale experience when, after she had, in accordance with a suggestion from the Scottish Office, adopted her civil remedies by obtaining interdicts against the Glendale raiders, she was approached almost hysterically by the Government with a request that she should refrain from following out her remedy to its logical conclusion, is most unwilling to run the risk of a repetition of that incident.'

15 NRA(S) 1883, Box A6 Bundle 5. I am very grateful to Skene, Edwards & Garson for allowing me access to this material.

16 SRO.AF83/230 & 238 (also AF67/154).

17 SRO.AF83/192, 194, 198, 199, 200, 204.

18 Hunter, *Crofting Community*, 187-92. For a Gaelic account of the Vatersay raid by Lisa Storey, see D. MacAhmlaidh et.al., *Oighreachd agus Gabhaltas* (Aberdeen 1980), pp.49-56.

19 The Eoligarry files are still in the possession of DAFS and are not open to the public except by arrangement with the Department (such files are hereafter termed DAFS files).

20 In June 1917, when the Small Holdings Commissioner reviewed the situation for the Scottish Office, he wrote that he suspected the proprietors 'were at one time apprehensive that they would be put to the trouble and expense of resisting forcible measures on the part of the cottars, and were therefore not unwilling to sell, even at a figure which would have given them no profit. But they may have been advised that the Board would be forced to take the property bit by bit and every step would be accompanied by heavy compensation payments, hence the withdrawal of the offer of May 1914.'

21 Material specifically on the raids can also be found in SRO.AF67/143 & 148.

22 In July 1921 the Board asked the Treasury for sanction to utilise lands which formed part of the common grazing on Vatersay, because the demand on Barra

was so great and there was no other land available. The K & LTR wrote that although this meant 'putting more people on an already congested area, it is the only way out of the difficulty of meeting the demand in Barra where there are many ex-service men clamouring for settlement.' SRO.E824/669.

23 SRO.AF83/385-389.

24 DAFS files.

25 Material on land raids at Newton can also be found in SRO.AF67/151. No memory of these raids appears to have survived in North Uist.

26 I was told that a number of the holdings were given to the older, crofter-fishermen applicants. Interview with Mrs. Chrissie MacLeod, Newton, 16 July 1988.

27 Unless otherwise stated, what follows is based on material in DAFS files.

28 The first of these accounts is Uilleam MacDhomhnaill, 'Toirt a-mach Bhaile Raghnaill, 1919-1921' in MacAmhlaidh et.al., *Oighreachd agus Gabhaltas*, 57-62, translated from the Gaelic by myself. The author was not one of the raiders, but he clearly did get a first-hand account for it differs only in a few minor details from that of Angus MacAulay (still alive at time of writing, aged 92), who took part. A translation of the latter's story, related in Gaelic in 1975, appears in *Comunn Eachdraidh Uibhist a Tuath*, *Croft Histories No.1—Balranald and Paiblesgarry* (Lochmaddy, forthcoming), pp.6-9. The third account was by the piper who led the raid. Donald Ewan MacDonald interviewed by Eric Cregeen, School of Scottish Studies, SA73.38.A.

29 MacDhomhnaill, 'Toirt a-mach', 4-5, MacAulay, *Croft Histories*, 7.

30 SRO.AF67/152. Captain MacDonald corresponded with the Scottish Land and Property Federation at this time, complaining in particular about the uselessness of taking legal action when he had to pay all the expenses himself, including the cost of extra policemen to enforce arrests. SRO.GD325/1/249 & 252. Surprisingly, none of the accounts from the raiders' side mentions this incident.

31 See *Croft Histories*, 12-28.

32 Ibid., 8.

CHAPTER 7 pp. 117 to 131

1 James Hunter, *The Making of the Crofting Community* (Edinburgh 1978), pp. 171-7.

2 As mentioned in the previous chapter, the present senior partner of the firm is the son of a crofter, and no vestige of the anti-crofter sentiments of the earlier period remains.

3 The pre-war files for Galson are SRO.AF83/71-73; for Orinsay & Stimervay AF83/352-354; Carnish & Ardroil AF83/355-357; Gress AF83/360-362. The correspondence is virtually duplicated in the files for each farm.

4 Skene, Edwards & Garson opposed any postponement because, said the Board, it denied the agents their 'further opportunities of vexations, opposition and litigation'.

5 Nigel Nicolson, *Lord of the Isles* (London 1960) is still the best all-round account of Lord Leverhulme and the Hebrides. Hunter discusses the Leverhulme period in *Crofting Community*, 196-204.

6 SRO.AF83/354.

7 He concluded: 'That Lord Leverhulme is convinced the solution of the Lewis problem lies in the development of industrialism seems to me clear, and that he is honestly bent on taking such measures as will in his opinion solve that problem

I have no doubt. But the mass of the people of Lewis are quite convinced and determined that the land must be given them, and I do not think any solution will be final which does not give them the land.'

8 Nicolson, *Lord*, 135.

9 SRO.AF83/363. Subsequent material discussed or quoted, covering the years 1919 and 1920, is in this Gress file unless otherwise footnoted.

10 Colin MacDonald described this meeting very vividly in his book of reminiscences, *Highland Journey* (Edinburgh & London 1943), pp.143-4. Parts of his narrative have been quoted in every subsequent description of Lord Leverhulme in Lewis.

11 *Glasgow Herald* 16 February 1920; Nicolson, *Lord*, 152.

12 According to Nicolson Leverhulme was advised that while he had the power to get the raiders imprisoned for breach of interdict, the Secretary for Scotland could order their release. Nicolson, *Lord*, 153-4.

13 Ibid. 155-64.

14 The scheme file for these farms is SRO.AF83/718. Treasury material is in E824/642. Croir farm was also made available by Leverhulme slightly later. AF83/751 and AF66/106.

15 Nicolson, *Lord*, 165-7.

16 Letter of 11 March 1921, NRA(S) 188, Box A 6 Bundle 5. (I am very grateful to Skene, Edwards & Garson for allowing me access to this material).

17 Nicolson was convinced that Thomas Wilson's sympathy for the crofters had a significant effect on Scottish Office policy. Nicolson, *Lord*, 170.

18 Nicolson, *Lord*, 168-71. Hunter, *Crofting Community*, 204.

19 SRO.AF83/760. He begged that Thomas Wilson be sent out to Lewis, because several crofters had asked for him, 'and to me he seemed to have their confidence in a way no other person had.' This reinforces Nicolson's view of Wilson as a forceful personality.

20 AF83/763.

21 SRO.AF83/767-769. Treasury material is in E824/572. Correspondence between Lord Leverhulme and the Secretary for Scotland (some, but not all, of the letters are duplicates of those in the AF83 files) and Scottish Office internal discussions are in AF67/391 & 392.

22 In the months before the confirming of the final Order various measures were taken to ensure the men did not lose patience and spoil everything by raiding—everything short of actually promising them holdings in fact.

23 The bulk of them remained in his hands until his death. For his 'grand gesture' in offering Lewis to the Lewis people, and its unsatisfactory results, see Nicolson, *Lord*, 193-203. One person I spoke to in Lewis insisted that a reason why so few crofters took advantage of the opportunity of buying their crofts at that time was because Leverhulme's employees dissuaded them from doing so. Interview with Rev. Donald Macaulay, 9 September 1988 (hereafter Macaulay).

24 SRO.AF83/382. The K & LTR advised the Treasury that this scheme 'promises to be an economic success owing to the provision for occupation of the men as ghillies.' E824/606.

25 Aline, AF83/378-380; Barvas Glebe, AF83/748; Bosta, AF83/805; Maryhill & Marybank, AF83/807-808. The Laxdale farm raid, which brought about the last of these schemes, in also in AF67/156. See L. Leneman 'The Last Successful Scottish Land Raid', *Northern Scotland* (forthcoming).

26 SRO.AF83/816.

27 Interview with Bill Lawson 10 September 1988 (hereafter Lawson).

28 Interview with Donald Smith 9 September 1988.

29 Interview with Macaulay.
30 For specialised studies of crofting in Lewis in more recent times see H.A. Moisley, *Uig: a Hebridean parish* (Nottingham & Glasgow 1961 and 1962); Iain Macleod, 'Crofting and Weaving in the Isle of Lewis' (unpublished MA thesis, University of Aberdeen 1972); and Peter G. Mewett, 'Social change and migration from Lewis' (unpublished PhD thesis, University of Aberdeen 1980).
31 SRO.AF83/644-645.
32 Nicolson, *Lord*, 209-212. The Board had effected a scheme of 15 new holdings on part of Rodel farm in 1914. SRO.AF83/162-165.
33 Some of the people were moved to the Bays area on the east coast, but the 1820s clearance was to a large extent a transatlantic one to Cape Breton in Canada. Interview with Lawson.
34 SRO.AF83/787.
35 SRO.AF83/790.
36 SRO.E824/645.
37 Although initially a Part II scheme, the Department of Agriculture many years later purchased the farm and therefore the files are still with DAFS and may be consulted only be prior application (such files are hereafter termed DAFS files).
38 SRO.AF83/795-799.
39 Thomas Wilson, who was by this time retired, offered to mediate, as he knew both the proprietor and raiders well. However, no solution offered by Wilson was going to adhere to the Secretary for Scotland's insistence on standing firm against the raiders, so his offer was declined.
40 The Secretary of the Board considered the report rather incoherent and wired Stewart to redraft it, remarking internally, 'Probably when he has had time to cool down, we shall get a report in a shape which we can properly send to S.O.'. Stewart was more than a little irritated by the telegram and replied that he thought his report 'conveys to the ordinary being clearly what there was to report'. It is obvious that Stewart, like Wilson before him, was not a detached civil servant but had become emotionally committed to the crofters and cottars.
41 The son of one of the two raiders (called the Black Shepherd by Finlay J. MacDonald) advised me that Stewart had got it wrong, and that the policeman had *accidentally* hit one of the women with his elbow when he turned; it had not been intentional. (Interview with John MacDonald, 7 September 1988—hereafter MacDonald) Finlay J. gave a very different account of the incident, in which he had the landlord amongst those being deluged with pails of urine by the women, but he was writing fifty-odd years after the event. Finlay J. MacDonald, *Crowdie and Cream* (London pbk edition 1983), p.25.
42 DAFS file. Finlay J's version is very different: 'The Department of Agriculture made every effort to get the Leverhulme trustees to subdivide the land and rent it out as crofts in the same way as our landlord had been compelled to do, but trustees and tenant alike remained obdurate. At last the Department invoked its powers of compulsory purchase and threw Venables out lock, stock and barrel, refusing to leave him any land whatsoever.' MacDonald, *Crowdie and Cream*, 137-8. This is an interesting example of the way folk memory can distort facts.
43 Interview with MacDonald.
44 DAFS files.
45 An interesting comment which they made to the Secretary of State at that time was that 'the purchase of Borve will meet any criticism of the Highland area that we are doing most of our settlement in the South and little in the North.'
46 SRO.E824/537.

CHAPTER 8 pp. 133 to 148

1 The bulk of material in this section comes from files still in the possession of the Department of Agriculture & Fisheries for Scotland which are available for consultation only by prior application (hereafter DAFS files). There is some additional material in SRO.AF67/149. The Treasury file is SRO.E324/149. A few paragraphs appear in James Hunter, *The Making of the Crofting Community* (Edinburgh 1976), pp.202-3.

2 The Board advised the Secretary for Scotland in 1916, 'It was suggested to the Estate that the new holders would be valuable to them as labourers, but they say that they have been unable to get Raasay or Rona men to work in the mines although there are vacancies for a large number of workmen, and many cottages are empty.'

3 Shaw (who acted for the defendants in all the Hebridean raiding cases) wrote to the Secretary for Scotland on 25 October 1921: 'With the possible exception of one or two townships in Lewis, I know of no place in Scotland where the assistance of the Board was more needed than in Rona and I am amazed at the Board's indifference to the awful conditions under which the people of that islet existed.'

4 The quotation comes from a radio interview conducted by Cailean Maclean with Donald MacLeod, the last surviving Raasay raider (who died the week before I visited Skye). I am very grateful to Cailean Maclean for the tape and to Joan MacDonald who translated it from the Gaelic for me. However, when I met the daughter of one of the raiders she told me she had vowed never to talk to anyone about that time and asked me how I would feel if my father had been in prison; clearly for her there was some stigma attached.

5 As noted in the previous chapter, Nicolson was convinced that Thomas Wilson's sympathy for the Lewis crofters greatly influenced everyone at the Scottish Office, thereby affecting government policy. It is clear that Wilson's eloquent report on the Raasay raiders had much the same effect.

6 Interview with Dr. Alastair Maclean, 11 September 1988.

7 SRO.AF83/457-460.

8 SRO.AF83/341-344. Calum Robertson, whose father got a croft on Drinan in 1926, insisted that Glasnakille had been broken up into crofts long before the war, and that it was only Drinan that was settled after the war. However, he also said that eight of the Drinan crofts were given to land raiders, which does not tally at all with the facts as they appear in the files, so clearly there has been some confusion in his mind over what happened where and when. (Interview with Calum Robertson, 11 September 1988—hereafter Robertson)

9 Kingsburgh and Bracadale material is in DAFS files.

10 SRO.E824/538.

11 DAFS files and SRO.E824/647. The Board wrote to the Treasury again two months later stating that their original intention had been to form 33 large holdings and two enlargements, but they now thought they could provide an additional fifteen to twenty small village holdings for Portree residents who already had allotments on the farm. The Treasury were unhappy about the estimated cost of fencing, but the K & LTR advised that prices of fencing material had recently fallen sharply so it ought to work out much less. 'I think you should agree to the scheme, as it will keep a lot of people quiet, and is not more expensive than others you have sanctioned.'

12 SRO.AF67/158. All the material on the Strathaird raiders prior to the offer to them of land on Kilbride is in this file.

13 *H of C* 26 Feb 1923, 1698-1704.
14 SRO.GD325/1/292.
15 *H of C* 30 May 1923, 1394-1431.
16 *H of C* 1 June 1923, 1710-1720. The announcement was by no means universally acclaimed. On 4 June *The Scotsman* wrote of the 'lack of steady purpose in the policy of the Government in regard to land raiding in the Highlands' and thought the public would quite rightly infer that raiding was the best way of getting land.
17 Most of the material in this next section comes from DAFS files; however, material specifically on the raids is in SRO.AF67/151 & 157.
18 Kerr subsequently wrote, 'I gather that the Board intend to take no steps to remove the impression created by the issue of the order, which, I understand, *is the first order which has ever been issued* under the Act. Why, under all the circumstances, the Macdonald Estate should have been selected for this honour seems to require some explanation!' But he never did get any satisfaction from the Board.
19 Interview with Robertson.
20 SRO.AF83/548-549.
21 Files raised in connection with threats to raid Claigan in 1919, 1920 and 1924 can be found in SRO.AF67/146, 148, 156, & 168.
22 SRO.AF67/148 & 149 and AF83/664-670.
23 The local sub-commissioner was nevertheless asked to double-check on this. He reported back in June 1923, 'Those applicants I met were emphatic in their demand for land. They stated that their applications have been lodged for over five years now, and bitterly complained of the treatment meted out to them by the Board, in ignoring their needs hitherto.'
24 The agent wrote a separate, confidential letter to the Secretary of the Board, stating that he had always believed there was another year to go and this had come as a complete surprise to him; he had never deliberately misled the Board. He was clearly deeply embarrassed, and the truth of what he said seems borne out by the fact that the young man who had inherited the estate switched agents—to the arch-opponents of the crofters, Skene, Edwards and Garson.
25 A thorny question which arose at about this time was who the rightful owner of the property actually was. Gossip apparently had it that the lands embraced in the scheme were never part of the property put into trust by Captain Macdonald for his grand nephew, and in fact the young man disappeared while all this was going on, leaving his father to deal with it. The Land Court report also noted the question mark hanging over the ownership of the estate. However, according to a letter in the file answering a query of 1944, the grand nephew had in fact been the legitimate proprietor under the trust; he conveyed the property to his father, 'Waternish', in 1929.
26 SRO.E824/670.
27 SRO.AF83/30. (Colin MacDonald's report is in this file and is not footnoted again.)
28 SRO.E824/660.
29 Interview with Mrs L. Sutherland, 3 August 1988 (hereafter Sutherland). There is contradictory evidence on this matter in the files: according to the Treasury file in 1929 there were still 15 cases where permanent dwellings had not been built, while according to a DAFS file at 31 December 1929 there were only seven houses not yet built.
30 DAFS file.
31 Interview with Danny MacLeod, 11 September 1988 (hereafter MacLeod).
32 Interview with Sutherland.

33 A.T.A. Learmonth, 'The Population of Skye', *Scottish Geographical Magazine* LXVI (1950), p.95.
34 Interview with MacLeod. He added: 'If you were back in the same circumstances today...you wouldn't get fish off the lochs or in a boat; there's nothing left. It's all been trawled away and there's nothing left.'
35 SRO.AF83/1550-1553.

CHAPTER 9 pp. 149 to 164

1 H.M. Conacher, 'Land Settlement in Scotland', *Scottish Journal of Agriculture* (April 1921), p.183.
2 Alexander Mather, *State-Aided Land Settlement in Scotland* (O'dell Memorial Monograph No.6, University of Aberdeen 1978), p.17. H.M. Conacher & W.R. Scott, *Interim Report to the Board of Agriculture for Scotland on the Economics of Small Farms and Small Holdings in Scotland* (HMSO Edinburgh, 1919), p.4. According to the latter, Aberdeenshire had about 7000 holdings rented not higher than £50.
3 These files are still held by DAFS and are available for consultation only by prior application (hereafter DAFS files).
4 SRO.E824/558.
5 DAFS files and SRO.E824/628.
6 Mather has pointed out to me that the Whitemyres scheme was a kind of forerunner of many 1930s-type schemes.
7 SRO.AF83/59.
8 SRO.AF83/1095-1098.
9 The surveyor who reported in March 1918 thought the farm was freely offered to the Board 'on account of the existing poor state of the buildings.'
10 SRO.E824/553.
11 DAFS files.
12 DAFS files.
13 He continued, 'Moreover, the preparation of such estimates would entail much time and labour on the part of the Board's present staff, which is already inadequate for the purpose of discovering and reporting upon suitable properties and also for the management of lands acquired, and the preparation of schemes in regard thereto, not only under the Small Holding Colonies Acts but under the Landholders Acts and otherwise. Meantime the Board have only purchased 4500 acres of the total acres of 20000 acres authorised by the Small Holding Colonies Act. It appears urgent to them that the limit of purchase be soon attained in order to satisfy public opinion and Parliament.'
14 SRO.E824/570.
15 DAFS files.
16 SRO.E824/566.
17 DAFS files.
18 SRO.E824/514.
19 Conacher & Scott, *Interim Report*, 3.
20 DAFS files.
21 The K & LTR had been unusually positive in his letter to the Treasury in May 1920. 'This is a good place, and though it may have been unorthodox I think they were wise to take it on lease pending the Land Settlement Act. ... Had they

not acted as they did, the opportunity of acquisition might have been lost altogether.' SRO.E824/665.
22 SRO.AF83/1142-1144.
23 The tenant's agents did the same. An internal Board memo stated, 'It was understood that the tenant was prepared to facilitate a scheme, and on that understanding it was proposed to allocate to him and his son Holdings 1 and 2, with the existing dwelling house and steading. If he does not facilitate the scheme, there will be no question of assigning holdings to him or his son.'
24 DAFS files and SRO.E824/634.
25 Interview with Mrs J. Waugh, 17 May 1988.
26 Conacher & Scott, *Interim Report*, 3. Conacher, 'Land Settlement in Scotland', 186.
27 DAFS files and SRO.E824/563.
28 SRO.AF83/59.
29 DAFS files.
30 SRO.E824/663.
31 SRO.AF83/59.
32 SRO.AF83/1149 and SRO.E824/597.
33 SRO.AF83/59.
34 SRO.AF83/1235 and SRO.E824/648.

CHAPTER 10 pp. 165 to 183

1 Cf. 'Land settlement in Scotland is best dealt with by treating separately the crofting counties (with which should be reckoned the island of Arran and parts of Perthshire) and the rest of Scotland.' H.M. Conacher, 'Land Settlement in Scotland', *Scottish Journal of Agriculture* (IV, 1921), p.175.
2 SRO.AF83/881-884.
3 R.H. Campbell has pointed out to me that it was actually the Marchioness, his wife, who was the proprietor; however the Board's dealings were all with the Marquis.
4 SRO.AF83/1265.
5 SRO.AF83/940 & 1132-1133.
6 SRO.AF83/1189.
7 SRO.E824/653.
8 These files are still held by DAFS and are available for consultation only by prior application (hereafter DAFS files). The Treasury file is SRO.E824/607.
9 DAFS files.
10 The resolutions can be found in the relevant files; mention is also made in the minutes of the Central Executive Committee of the NFU (hereafter NFU minutes) 28 October and 2 December 1919. These volumes are still held at the National Farmers' Union of Scotland headquarters and I am grateful to the Union for allowing me access to them.
11 According to NFU minutes of 5 October 1921 a delegation waited on the Board and 'stated the case on behalf of several of the tenants who were to be dispossessed.' The deputation reported that 'in some cases the Board had agreed to allow the tenants to remain on for another year.'
12 SRO.E824/577.
13 SRO.AF83/59.
14 DAFS files.

15 'At Terregles, one of the largest post-war settlements carried out by the Board in the South, several holders are adopting methods of intensive cultivation with marked success, particularly in growing forage crops for consumption by dairy stock. Others have been very successful in glass-house work and in the cultivation of small fruit.' B.O.A.S., *Thirteenth Annual Report*, p.18.
16 *Scotsman* 17 Jan, *Dumfries & Galloway Standard* 24 Jan, *Glasgow Herald* 24 Jan, *Farming News* 31 Jan, *Scottish Farmer* 3 Feb. The *Herald* claimed that half the Terregles holders were facing failure; Manson wrote that this was untrue, 'though some certainly are.'
17 Another local officer added that he had never understood why in the south-east £1200-£1500 was allowed for buildings, while in the south-west only £700-£900 was allowed. 'Buildings for which money is so whittled down are bound to be of inferior quality.'
18 SRO.AF83/59.
19 Manson's comment is borne out by earlier material in the relevant DAFS file.
20 Interviews with Mr A. Smith and Miss M. Brunton, 7 July and 15 June 1988.
21 SRO.AF83/1108 & 1109.
22 DAFS files.
23 It is not clear from the files what the thinking was behind this offer. R.H. Campbell has advised me that the apparently odd proposal needs to be seen in the context of the Duke's large-scale estate reorganisation at that time.
24 SRO.E824/511.
25 SRO.AF83/1174-1178.
26 The Board asked the Solicitor General whether this claim was competent; if it was, then they wanted to know whether the claim would be obviated by the Board taking all risks of damage from this cause. The Solicitor General did not think the claim competent, and added that if his opinion were proved incorrect, the answer to the Board's second question was yes.
27 In April 1922 the Land Court assessed the compensation due by the Board to the landlord as £2200 in respect of buildings only. Various other matters still had to be adjusted, and at a further Land Court hearing in November the Board were found liable for an additional £147 for increased cost of management. At that time the Board tried to evade their promise to pay full legal costs, on the grounds that it was the landlord's fault negotiations had been broken off. Having perused all the correspondence, the Court considered the blame for the non-resumption of negotiations lay with the Board and found them liable for expenses.
28 The relevant files for Harperland are SRO.AF83/1245 & 1248, and for Ploughland AF83/1257 & 1259.
29 According to the sons of two of the original Plougland holders, in recent years the landlord of Harperland was more generous in his dealings with smallholding tenants who wished to purchase than was the landlord of Ploughland. (Interview with Robert Kirk and Bob Fraser, 22 June 1988)
30 SRO.AF83/1200-1202 and E824/618.
31 SRO.AF83/1236.
32 Conacher, 'Land Settlement in Scotland', 186.

CHAPTER 11 pp. 184 to 202

1 I am grateful to William Gillies in the Department of Celtic and Donald Archie MacDonald in the School of Scottish Studies, Edinburgh University, for pro-

viding me with some initial contacts. In Skye Dr. Alastair Maclean gave me useful information himself and the names of others to talk to; Mrs. Dorothy Green not only runs a splendid guest house, she also helpfully provided me with more contacts.

2 Interview with Mrs J. Waugh, 17 May 1988 (hereafter Waugh).
3 Interviews with Mrs Isobel Gibb, 22 June 1988 (hereafter Gibb), with Daniel Mackay, 24 May 1988 (hereafter Mackay), and with Waugh.
4 Interview with Robert Kirk and Bob Fraser, 22 June 1988 (hereafter Kirk & Fraser).
5 Interview with Alfie Smith, 7 July 1988 (hereafter A. Smith). He added, 'the likes of my father, he wouldnae have went into a holding of that size'.
6 Interview with Waugh.
7 Interview with Miss Mary Brunton, 15 June 1988.
8 Interview with Gibb.
9 Interview with David Martin, 15 June 1988 (hereafter Martin). Another holder there told me that they were very aware of the difference between Locharwoods, where all the holdings (even one of ten acres) were self-supporting and where the holders kept going until they died and Terregles, where most either had other jobs or gave up. Interview with Janet Tarbin, 15 June 1988 (hereafter Tarbin).
10 Interview with Mrs A. Mason, 13 June 1988 (hereafter Mason).
11 Interview with Gibb.
12 Interview with William McNay, 7 July 1988 (hereafter McNay).
13 Interview with A. Smith.
14 Interview with Douglas Ritchie, 16 June 1988. When I remarked to 87-year-old Daniel Mackay (who had worked a 10-acre holding at the same time as full-time employment on the railways) that his wife must have had to work very hard, he replied 'Oh, she was a guid yin'.
15 Interview with McNay. He added, 'That's all gone now. You've got to be independent.' Mrs Waugh also remembered, 'when you got the threshing mill in to harvest, the rest of the holders came to help you and when they had it you went to help them. It was done like that.'
16 Interview with Gibb. She reckoned it was only with the influx of miners at the time of World War II that Mauchline became less insular.
17 Interview with Kirk & Fraser.
18 Letters from Mr R. McClumpha, 8 June and 6 July 1988 (hereafter McClumpha letters).
19 Interview with Mason.
20 Interview with Tarbin. When I told her of the idea that smallholders would require village entertainment in order to be happy, she said, 'This is the difference between that class of people and the ordinary working people. They don't know how the other half lives. And they're sure they know what the other half want, but they don't.'
21 Interview with A. Smith.
22 McClumpha letters.
23 When I put this allegation to the DAFS officer in charge of smallholdings he did not deny it but pointed out that holders complained to their M.P.s if they felt the Department was not looking after them properly.
24 Interview with Tarbin. She added, 'The Department of Agriculture were actually here, in our field, at the time, so that's how we knew because they had to leave us to go down to Gretna to sort it out and let the man get his bullock. ... Stories like that are rife. Absolutely rife.'
25 Interviews with McNay and Ritchie.

26 Interviews with A. Smith, McNay, Ritchie, and Martin.
27 Interviews with Gibb and with Fraser & Kirk. Robert Kirk noted that difference between the Ayrshire estate of Collenan, which was government-owned and where successful holders obtained additional land, and Ploughland and Harperland where this had not been possible.
28 See A.S. Mather, 'The rise and fall of government-created land settlement in Scotland', *Land Use Policy* (July 1985), pp.217-224. The reason for the policy was the realisation that the cost of administering land settlement schemes was so much greater than the rental income from them. Mather points out that no criteria other than the purely economic were used in deciding on the new policy. It is noteworthy that this 'right-to-buy' policy preceded the election of a Conservative government in 1979.
29 Admittedly, even now not all the holders have taken advantage of the chance to purchase; William McNay at Terregles and the two Gretna holders I spoke to, Douglas Ritchie and John Smith, were still tenants, though McNay and Ritchie were considering purchasing their holdings in the near future.
30 Interviews with Ritchie, McNay and A. Smith.
31 Letter from Irene Evans, 26 October 1988.
32 Interview with Fraser & Kirk.
33 Interview with Gibb.
34 J.B. Caird disputed this: 'Kirkibost was cleared circa 1822 and Croir and Little Bernera before 1845. This left Tobson, Bosta and Breaclete still in small tenant/crofter occupancy: Hacklete was apparently occupied by the Ground Officer along with cottars and subtenants. The Bernera tenants also lost most of their shieling grounds. Kirkibost was re-settled in 1878 by crofters from Bosta which was let as a grazing enlargement to Tobson. Twenty new crofts were formed in Hacklete in 1880; Little Bernera and Eilean Kearstay were detached from Linshader Farm...and became grazings for the Bernera crofters. Croir was resettled in 1921 by 8 crofters'. Letter from J.B. Caird (hereafter Caird letter), 25 November 1988. I am very grateful to Professor Caird for his helpful comments on an earlier draft of this half-chapter.
35 Interview with Rev Donald Macaulay, 9 September 1988 (hereafter Macaulay).
36 Interviews with Macaulay, with Mrs Chrissie MacLeod, 16 July 1988, and with Neil McVicar, 18 July 1988 (hereafter McVicar).
37 Interviews with Mrs Liz Sutherland, 3 August 1988 (hereafter L. Sutherland) and with Mrs Catherine McPhee, 17 July 1988 (hereafter McPhee).
38 Interview with John MacDonald, 7 September 1988 (hereafter J. MacDonald).
39 Interview with Joseph Mackay, 5 August 1988 (hereafter Mackay).
40 Ralph Glasser, *Scenes from a Highland Life* (London 1981), p.84.
41 Interview with John MacInnes, 15 July 1988 (hereafter MacInnes).
42 Finlay J. Macdonald, *Crowdie and Cream* (London, pbk edition 1983), pp.9-10. I was advised that this was actually much more common in Lewis than in Harris because so many of the Harris people had been shipped across to Canada whereas in Lewis the people had been shuffled around the island and were continually casting their eyes back to where their fathers had lived. Interview with Bill Lawson, 10 September 1988 (hereafter Lawson).
43 Uilleam MacDhomhnaill, 'Toirt a-mach Bhaile Raghnaill, 1919-1921' in D. MacAmhlaidh et.al., *Oighreachd agus Gabhaltas* (Aberdeen 1980), pp.57-62. Interviews with McVicar and MacInnes.
44 Interview with Kenny Stoddart, 12 September 1988 (hereafter Stoddart). One of the other remaining Kilbride holders, a cousin of Stoddart's, is the son of a man who did not raid. He is apparently as proud of the fact that his father did *not*

break the law as Kenny Stoddart is of the fact that his father *did* (information supplied by Dorothy Green).

45 MacDonald, *Crowdie and Cream*, 10.

46 For a description of how this was done see Margaret Fay Shaw, *Folksongs and Folklore of South Uist* (Aberdeen 1986), p.3. The author lived on a croft in North Glendale from 1929 to 1935.

47 Interview with McPhee. When I told her what Lady Cathcart had thought of the Eriskay men she said, 'They proved her wrong.'

48 Glendale did not get a road until the 1950s. Catherine McPhee told me it was Dr. Alastair Maclean who had spurred them on to keep after the local authority until the road was built. It was generally agreed by those I spoke to that the settlement could not have survived much longer without a road to it, and Dr. Maclean remarked that it was one of the few cases where a road had not come too late to save a community.

49 Interview with Donald P. Morrison, 17 July 1988 (hereafter Morrison).

50 Interviews with Alastair Sutherland, 5 August 1988 (hereafter A. Sutherland) and with Mrs Agnes Ross, 4 August 1988 (hereafter Ross).

51 Interview with May Manson (Mrs Sinclair), 5 August 1988 (hereafter Manson). She added, 'och there's no ceilidhs now, too much of that blooming box.'

52 Letter from Mrs A. Mackinnon, 7 October 1988 (hereafter Mackinnon letter).

53 In view of by Mrs Sutherland's description I was surprised when Bill Lawson said the Talisker settlement was one which hadn't really 'gelled' as a community. I asked Danny MacLeod, a second-generation crofter, about this, and he told me that in the early sixties there had been a nasty conflict over sheep grazing regulations. Mrs Sutherland herself said that the settlement had changed greatly since she left in the early sixties, but if the community spirit did not survive into later decades that is no reason to doubt its strength during the inter-war period. Interviews with L. Sutherland, Lawson, and with Danny MacLeod, 11 September 1988 (hereafter MacLeod).

54 Interview with McPhee. She went on to say that at school they had both Protestants and Catholics who got on very well together: 'we were just like one big family.'

55 Interview with Lawson.

56 Interview with Ross.

57 Interviews with Manson and A. Sutherland.

58 Interview with James Macaskill, 12 September 1988. Mackinnon letter.

59 Finlay J. Macdonald, *Crowdie and Cream* (London, pbk edition 1983), pp.26-30.

60 Ibid., 138.

61 Interview with Mrs MacDonald-Valliquie, 16 July 1988. Interviews with MacLeod, Macaskill, J. MacDonald, Stoddart, and McVicar.

62 Interview with Ian MacDonald, 16 July 1988 (hereafter I. MacDonald).

63 Interview with Macaulay.

64 Interview with Lawson and Caird letter. It was Lawson who made me realise just how marked the differences were between the north-west Highlands and Islands and the rest of the crofting counties like Orkney, Shetland, Caithness, Inverness-shire and even Argyllshire, the scale of which he had not appreciated himself until he became a member of the Crofters Commission.

65 Interviews with Manson, Sutherland, and Lawson.

66 Interview with Ross. She said that most of those who had moved away had done so within the last decade or two.

67 Interviews with MacLeod and with Dr. Alastair Maclean, 11 September 1988 (hereafter Maclean).
68 Interviews with Lawson and Maclean.
69 Interview with MacInnes.
70 Interview with Maclean. Young people who got crofts and then did not work them were understandably much resented by the islanders.
71 Interview with Macaulay.
72 Interview with Lawson.
73 Interview with MacLeod. He could not think of anyone in the area who was unemployed.
74 Interview with I. MacDonald. In Skye Kenny Stoddart has made a full-time living out of crofting at Kilbride since the 1960s, but I was told he had a particularly fine reputation as a crofter whose stock was always of the highest standard (information supplied by Dorothy Green).
75 Glasser, *Scenes*, 86.
76 Interview with Morrison.
77 Interview with McVicar.
78 Interview with Ross.
79 Interview with Mackay.

CONCLUSION pp. 203 to 208

1 R. Greig, 'Agricultural Administrative in the Present Reign', *Scottish Journal of Agriculture* (April 1935), pp.108-9.
2 Nigel Nicolson in *Lord of the Isles: Lord Leverhulme in the Hebrides*, (London 1960) rated Munro's importance very much higher than I do.
3 Finlay J. Macdonald, *Crowdie and Cream* (London, pbk edition 1983), p.28.
4 Donald Ewan MacDonald interviewed by Eric Cregeen, School of Scottish Studies, SA73.38.A.
5 H.M. Conacher, 'Land Settlement in Scotland', *Scottish Journal of Agriculture* (April 1921), p.176.
6 *Land Settlement in Scotland: Report of the Scottish Land Settlement Committee* (P.P. 144-4, v.), p.18.
7 Ibid., 14.
8 Ibid., 18-19.
9 The wording may not be exact as Colin Currie was quoting from memory. (Mr. Currie wrote in response to my letter in the *Dumfries and Galloway Standard* and gave me the names of some older tenants who he thought might be willing to talk to me, for which I am very grateful to him.)
10 *Land Settlement in Scotland*, 19.
11 Ibid., 20.
12 Ibid., 21.
13 J.A. Symon, *Scottish Farming Past and Present* (Edinburgh & London 1959), pp.292-8.
14 R.H. Campbell, *Scotland Since 1707* (2nd edition, Edinburgh 1985), pp.216 & 223.
15 See *The Making of the Crofting Community* (Edinburgh 1976), p.206.
16 Alexander S. Mather, *State-Aided Land Settlement in Scotland* (O'dell Memorial Monograph No.6, University of Aberdeen 1978), p.27. In a private com-

munication to me he wrote, 'The landscape and social environment of parts of Skye, Lewis and Harris, Tiree and other areas were transformed.' Donald Meek told me that he did not believe this was true of Tiree.

17 Marilyn Lake, *The Limits of Hope: Soldier Settlement in Victoria 1915-1938* (Oxford 1987), pp.xviii & 238.

18 Sedley Sweeny, *The Challenge of Smallholding* (Oxford 1985).

APPENDIX

pp 236–7	Small Holdings Scheme, Askernish, South Uist
238	Small Holdings Scheme, Grassmillees, Ayrshire

both scheme plans reproduced courtesy of the Keeper of the Records of Scotland

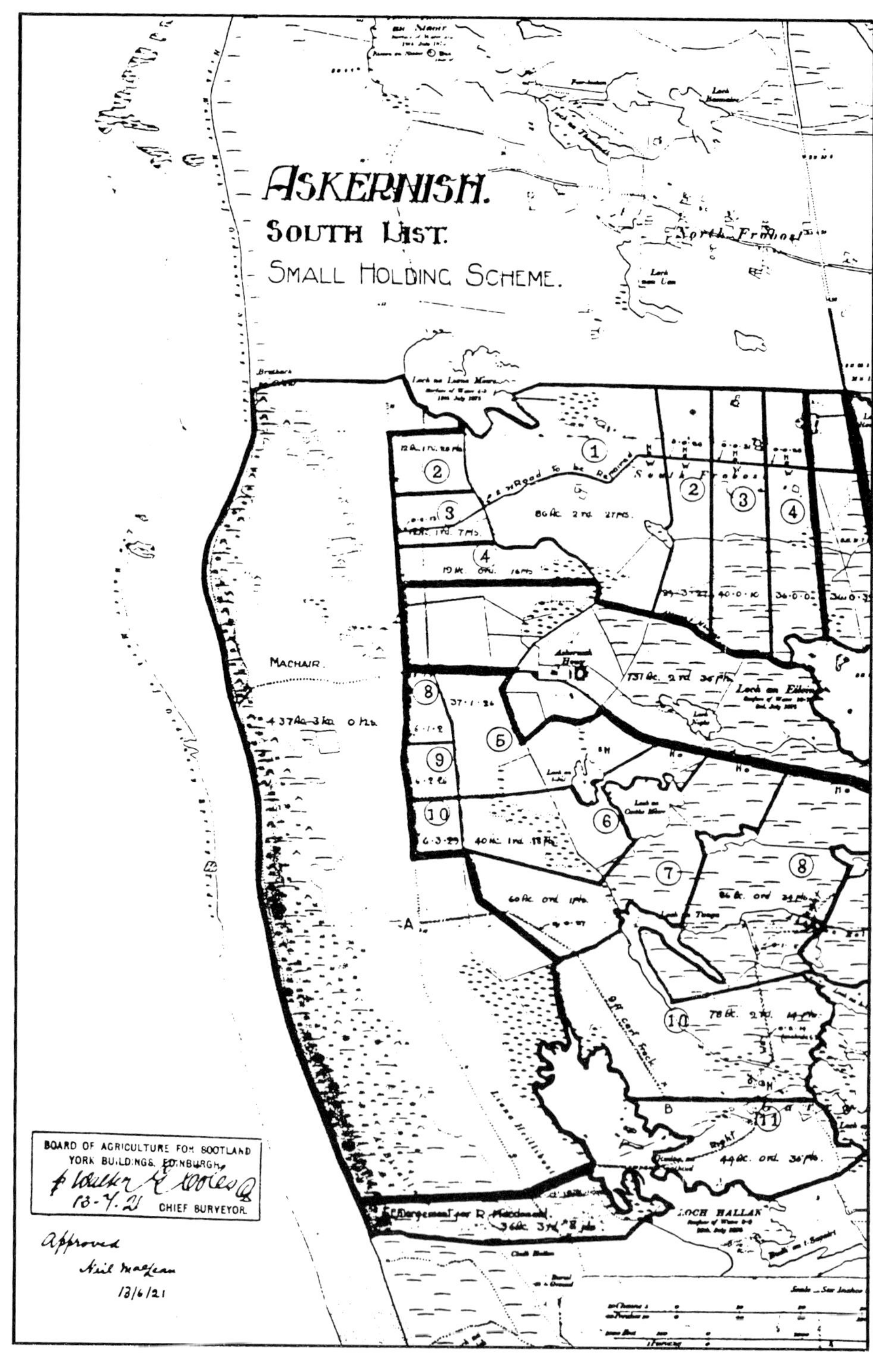
ASKERNISH.
SOUTH LIST.
SMALL HOLDING SCHEME.
MACHAIR.
437 Ac. 3 Ro. 0 Pls.
LOCH HALLAN
BOARD OF AGRICULTURE FOR SCOTLAND
YORK BUILDINGS, EDINBURGH.
CHIEF SURVEYOR.
13-7-21
Approved
Neil MacLean
13/6/21

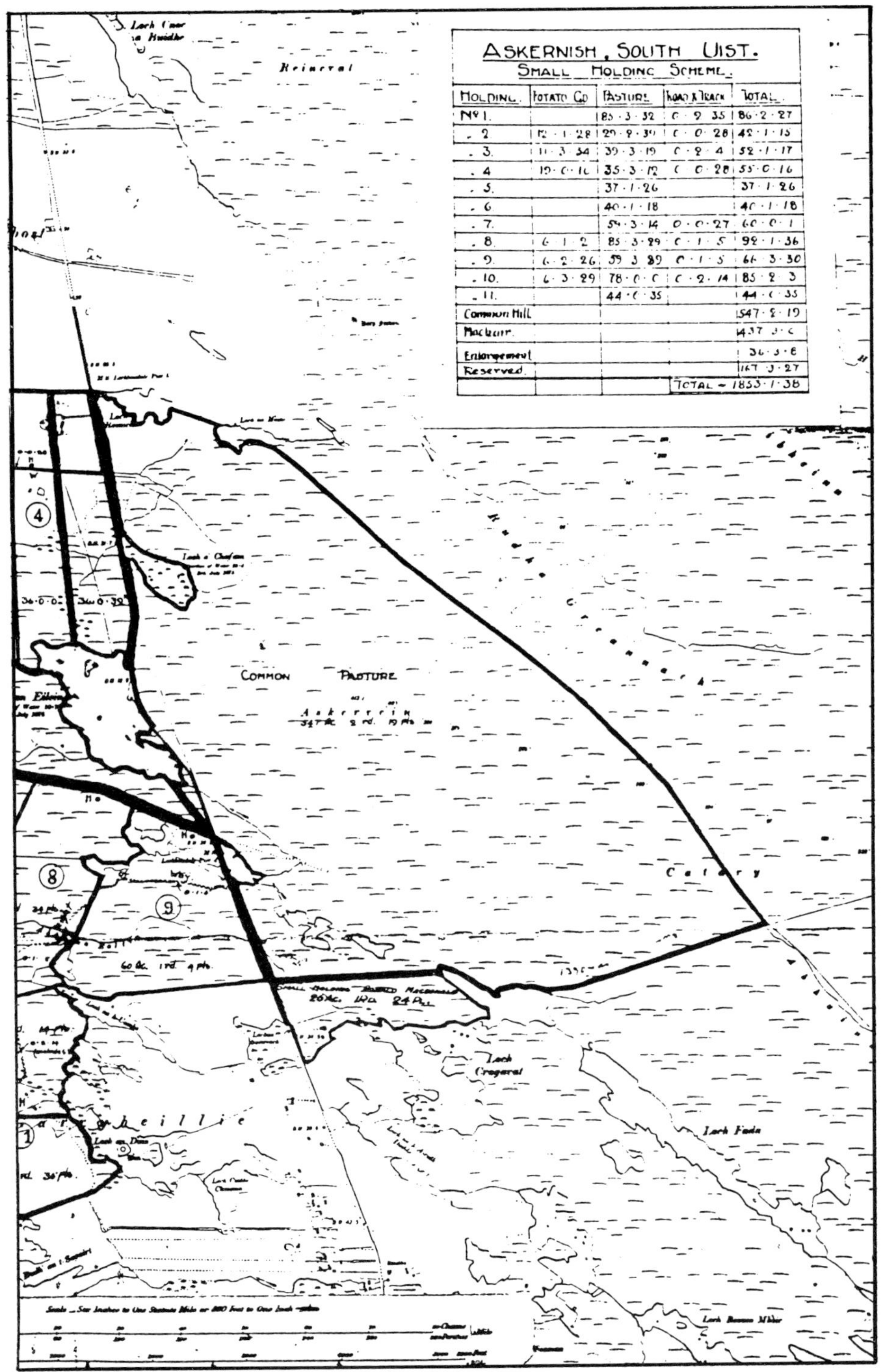

Askernish, South Uist.
Small Holding Scheme.

Holding.	Potato Gd.	Pasture.	Road & Track.	Total.
No. 1.		85 · 3 · 32	0 · 2 · 35	86 · 2 · 27
" 2.	12 · 1 · 28	29 · 2 · 39	0 · 0 · 28	42 · 1 · 15
" 3.	11 · 3 · 34	39 · 3 · 19	0 · 2 · 4	52 · 1 · 17
" 4.	19 · 0 · 16	35 · 3 · 12	0 · 0 · 28	55 · 0 · 16
" 5.		37 · 1 · 26		37 · 1 · 26
" 6.		40 · 1 · 18		40 · 1 · 18
" 7.		59 · 3 · 14	0 · 0 · 27	60 · 0 · 1
" 8.	6 · 1 · 2	85 · 3 · 29	0 · 1 · 5	92 · 1 · 36
" 9.	6 · 2 · 26	59 · 3 · 39	0 · 1 · 5	66 · 3 · 30
" 10.	6 · 3 · 29	78 · 0 · 0	0 · 2 · 14	85 · 2 · 3
" 11.		44 · 0 · 35		44 · 0 · 35
Common Hill				547 · 2 · 19
Machair.				1437 · 3 · 0
Enlargement				36 · 3 · 8
Reserved.				167 · 3 · 27
			TOTAL –	1853 · 1 · 38

Reineval
4
COMMON PASTURE
Askernish
8
9
Loch Fada

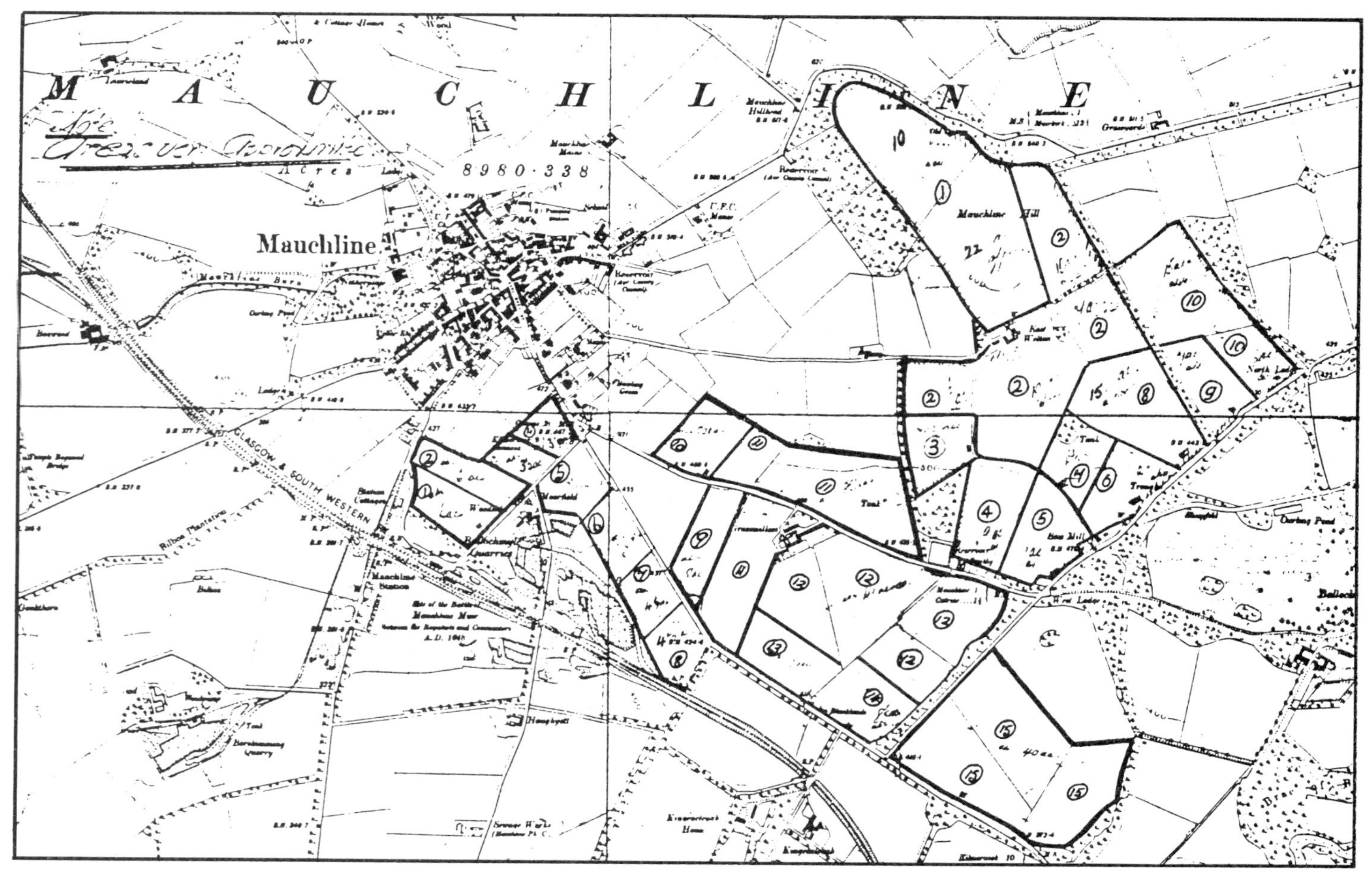
MAUCHLINE
8980·338
Acres
Mauchline
Mauchline Hill
GLASGOW & SOUTH WESTERN
Mauchline Station
Station Cottages
Flowering Green
Curling Pond
Kingencleugh
Site of the Battle of Mauchline Muir between the Royalists and Covenanters A.D. 1648

INDEX